Peeling Design Patterns

-To All Our Readers

Designed by *Narasimha Karumanchi*

Acknowledgements

First and foremost, we would like to thank our *families*, and dear *friends* whose support and encouragement throughout our lives have made it possible for us to build the skill set necessary to succeed.

We would like to express our gratitude to many people who saw us through this book, to all those who provided support, talked things over, read, wrote, offered comments, allowed us to quote their remarks and assisted in the editing, proofreading and design. In particular, we would like to thank the following individuals.

- *Kalyani Tummala*, IIT Kharagpur, Xilinx Pvt. Ltd.
- *Prof. Girish P. Saraph*, Founder, Vegayan Systems Pvt. Ltd.
- *Manoj Patra*, Senior Manager, Microsoft India Pvt. Ltd.
- *A. Vamshi Krishna*, IIT Kanpur, Mentor Graphics Pvt. Ltd.
- *Rambabu Dubbukuri*, IIT Kanpur, Microsoft India Pvt. Ltd.
- *Venkata Ramana Sanaka*, Nokia Pvt. Ltd.
- *Kishore Jinka*, IIT Bombay
- *Vikas Kedia*, IIT Bombay, Google India Pvt. Ltd.
- *Suman Somavarapu*, IIT Bombay, De-Shaw India Pvt. Ltd.
- *Anil Bhat*, IIT Roorkee, Microsoft India Pvt. Ltd.
- *Chaganti Siva Rama Krishna Prasad*, Founder, StockMonks Pvt. Ltd.
- *Kumar and Jagan*, Founders, Impression Design Studio Pvt. Ltd.

-Prof. Sreenivasa Rao Meda
Ph. D., Director, School of IT,
JNTU, Hyderabad

-Narasimha Karumanchi
M. Tech, *IIT Bombay*
Founder of *CareerMonk.com*

Preface

Dear Reader,

Please Hold on! We know many people do not read preface. But we would like to strongly recommend reading preface of this book at least. This preface has something *different* from regular prefaces.

This book assumes you have basic knowledge about computer science. Main objective of the book is *not* to provide you the *catalog* of design patterns and *design interview* questions. Before writing the book, we set the following *goals*:

- The book be written in *such a way* that readers without any background in software design should be able to understand it *easily* and *completely*.
- The book should present the concepts of design patterns in *simple* and straightforward manner with a *clear – cut* explanation.
- After reading the book, they should be in a position to come up with *better* designs than before and participate in design discussions which happen in their *daily* office work.
- The book should provide enough *realtime* examples so that readers get better understanding of the design patterns and also useful for the interviews. We mean, the book should cover *design interview* questions.
- After reading the book, the programmers should be in a position to try for software architect positions.

Design patterns were introduced to programming practices at the end of 1980*s* as a result of dissatisfaction with software's state of affairs. In those days, few means of abstraction (algorithms and data structures) suited well for procedural/functional programming. They were *not* well connected with object-oriented programming.

The introduction of design patterns marks a turning point in the history of software design. In 1995 we have seen the publication of a catalogue (*Gamma*, *Helm*, *Johnson* & *Vlissides*, 1995) with *twenty-three* design patterns written by four experienced object-oriented designers. The catalogue, which came to be known as the *Gang of Four* (*GoF*) catalogue, was a super success.

Design patterns *help* novices (and *beginners*) to avoid common *mistakes* and encourage experienced programmers to build better software.

This book is an enthusiastic celebration of design patterns, especially those which are given by *GoF*. In the recept past, most of the object-oriented architectures are built with *full* of design patterns.

In this book, *we* explained the design patterns with simple examples which helps *students* and *instructors* in understanding them easily. At the end of book, he gave common *design interview questions* which helps job seekers to perform better in their interviews.

A thorough understanding of the design patterns, processes, and methods in this book will likewise help you develop better software applications and infrastructure. If you want thorough coverage of the key patterns then read this book. We have learned much from it and I am confident that you will too.

As a job seeker if you read complete book with good understanding, we are sure you will challenge the interviewers and that is the objective of this book.

This book is very much useful for the students of engineering degree and masters during their academic preparations. All the chapters of this book contain theory and their related problems. If you read as a student preparing for competition exams, content of this book covers all the required topics in full details.

It is *recommended* that, at least *one complete* reading of this book is required to get full understanding of all the topics. In the *subsequent* readings, you can directly go to any chapter and refer. Even though, enough readings were given for correcting the errors, due to human tendency there could be some minor typos in the book. If any such typos found, they will be updated at www.*CareerMonk*.com. We request you to constantly monitor this site for any corrections, new problems and solutions. Also, please provide your valuable suggestions at: *Info@CareerMonk.com*.

Wish you all the best. Have a nice reading.

-Prof. Sreenivasa Rao Meda
Ph. D., Director, School of IT,
JNTU, Hyderabad

-Narasimha Karumanchi
M. Tech, *IIT Bombay*
Founder of *CareerMonk.com*

Table of Contents

PEELING DESIGN PATTERNS

(FOR BEGINNERS AND INTERVIEWS)

Other Titles by *Narasimha Karumanchi*

Success keys for Big Job Hunters

- Data Structures and Algorithms Made Easy (C/C++)
- Data Structures and Algorithms Made Easy in Java
- Data Structures and Algorithms for GATE
- Coding Interview Questions

Chapter-1

INTRODUCTION

1.1 What Is This Book About?

A *design* pattern is a documented solution that has been applied successfully in multiple environments to solve a problem that repeatedly occurs in a specific set of situations. A design pattern is *not* an *invention*.

A design pattern is a documented best way of solving a problem that is observed during the study of many software systems.

Design patterns capture the experience of expert software developers, and present common recurring problems, their solutions, and the consequences of those solutions in systematic way.

This book explains:

- *Why* patterns are useful and important for object-oriented design and development?
- How patterns are *documented*, *categorized*, and *cataloged*?
- *When* patterns should be used?
- *How* patterns are implemented?
- Common *design* interview questions

Design patterns provide a structure in which problems can be solved. When solving a real problem, we have to consider many small variations of a solution to that problem to see whether any fits a design pattern.

To understand and get used to design patterns is really difficult. It can be done by studying applications of design patterns, not just the patterns.

This book is not just about design patterns. This book is *different* from *other* design pattern books because it is not about catalog of patterns, but presents a way of decomposing a problem space that maps easily to patterns.

It also gives great introduction to object-oriented programming, *UML* notations and design *patterns* interview questions.

1.2 Brief History Of Design Patterns

Patterns originated as an *architectural* concept by *Christopher Alexander* who is a *civil* engineer. In 1987, *Kent Beck* and *Ward Cunningham* began experimenting with the idea of applying patterns to *programming* and presented their results at a conference that year. In the following years, *Beck*, *Cunningham* and others followed up on this work.

Design patterns gained popularity in computer science after the book Design Patterns: Elements of Reusable Object-Oriented Software was published in 1994 by the so-called Gang of Four (*GoF*).

1.3 Should I Take This Book?

This book is for programmers who *want* to learn design patterns to improve their object-oriented design, development skills and also for those who want to apply for companies which need these skills.

After reading this tutorial you will:

- Understand what design patterns are and how they are described and categorized.
- Be able to use design patterns as a vocabulary for understanding and discussing object-oriented software design.
- Understand a few of the most common design patterns and know when and how they should be used.
- Understand the commonly asked design questions in technical interviews.

This book assumes that you are familiar with *Java* language and with basic object-oriented concepts such as *polymorphism*, *inheritance*, and *encapsulation*.

Some understanding of the Unified Modeling Language (*UML*) is helpful, but not required; this book will provide an introduction to the basics of UML.

1.4 Is It Useful For Interviews?

Peeling Design Patterns (*PDP*) is a book that aims to help software engineers interviewing for software development positions as well as their interviewers. It consists of concepts and solved design problems as well.

It covers basic required concepts, for example, UML notations, and covers all fundamental design patterns in detail.

It also gives tips which help readers as a quick reference. *PDP's* team is with extensive academic and industrial experience. They have published many articles on algorithms, applied their skills at *Google*, *Microsoft*, *Amazon*, and a number of smaller software startups, and conducted many job interviews for various computer science jobs.

1.5 How To Use this book?

We would like to recommend at least two readings of this book. Upon first reading, you will start to recognize these patterns in the frameworks you see.

In the second reading, you'll begin to see how these patterns can help you in your own designs, and may also start to see new patterns not listed in the book.

Once you become familiar with the pattern concept, you will be able to originate your own patterns, which will serve you well in the future.

One of the most valuable contributions of this book is that it is designed not merely to help you identify patterns, but to give you a sense of which patterns are appropriate in which contexts.

In the subsequent readings, you can directly go to any chapter and refer.

1.6 Organization Of Chapters

The main objective of writing this book is to present design patterns in an easy to understand manner with simple examples. This book discusses all the design patterns given by *GoF*.

In addition, it also covers few *miscellaneous* concepts (Design Interview Questions, Java Interview Questions, MVC pattern etc..).

The chapters are arranged in the following way:

2. *All about UML*: Gives introduction and necessary concepts of UML which are used in all the remaining chapters.
3. *Design Patterns Introduction*: Provides introduction to design patterns, categories of patterns etc..
4. *Creational Patterns*: Discusses creational patterns (Abstract Factory, Factory Method, Builder, Prototype and Singleton patterns).
5. *Structural Patterns*: Discusses structural patterns (Adapter Design, Bridge, Composite, Decorator, Facade, Flyweight and Proxy patterns).
6. *Behavioral Patterns*: Discusses behavioral patterns (Chain of Responsibility, Command, Interpreter, Iterator, Mediator, Memento, Observer, State, Strategy, Template Method, and Visitor patterns).
7. *Glossary and Tips*: Provides summary of all design patterns and gives few tips for beginners.
8. *Design Interview Questions*: Covers common interview questions with real-time examples.
9. *Miscellaneous Concepts*: Covers Java interview questions and few other concepts like MVC pattern etc..

Each design pattern discussion starts with an explanation of the pattern followed by an example implemented in Java programming language. How a given pattern is applied in the example is discussed in detail along with code segments and UML diagrams.

At the end of each pattern discussion, a few questions are provided for you to improve your understanding of the pattern. Wherever applicable, patterns are compared with other similar patterns.

The examples in this book are kept simple for easy understanding. The objective is to enhance the explanation of each pattern with examples for a better understanding.

The *UML* chapter provides an overview of the Unified Modeling Language (UML) and discusses various elements of class and sequence diagrams.

In *Design Interview Questions* chapter, few real time problems were discussed which uses different design patterns. This chapter discusses how various patterns can be used in designing and also covers common interview questions as well.

1.7 Source Code Disclaimer

Both the author and the publisher make no representations or warranties about the suitability of the software, either expressed or implied, including but not limited to the implied warranties of merchantability, fitness for a particular purpose or non-infringement.

Both the author and the publisher shall not be liable for any damages suffered as a result of using, modifying or distributing the software or its derivatives.

1.8 Tools Used For Book

The examples in this book are all written in the *Java* language. It is possible and sufficient to read the code as a mental exercise, but to try out the code requires a minimal Java development environment.

A simple text editor (such as *notepad* in Windows or *vi* in a UNIX environment) and the Java Development Kit (version 1.2 or later) are all you need. A number of tools are also available for creating UML diagrams (say, Start UML).

Chapter-2

UML BASICS

2.1 What Is UML?

UML stands for *Unified Modeling Language*. It was initially started to capture the behavior of complex software and non-software system and now it has become a standard. UML follows the object oriented concepts and methodology. So object oriented systems are generally modeled using the pictorial language.

UML diagrams are drawn from different perspectives like design, implementation, deployment etc. UML can be *defined* as a modeling language to capture the architectural, behavioral and structural aspects of a system.

UML is a standard modeling language, not a software development process. UML is different from the other common programming languages like C++ and Java, and COBOL etc... UML is not a programming language but tools can be used to generate code in various languages using UML diagrams.

UML can be described as a visual modeling language to visualize, specify, construct and document software system. Although UML is generally used to model software systems but it is also used to model non software systems as well like process flow in a manufacturing unit etc...

2.2 Why UML?

Objects are the key to object oriented world. The basic requirement of object oriented analysis and design is to identify the objects efficiently. After that responsibilities are assigned to them. Once this task is complete the design is done using the input from analysis.

A *picture* is worth a thousand words, this absolutely fits while discussing about UML. Object oriented concepts were introduced much earlier than UML. So at that time there was no standard method to organize and consolidate the object oriented development. At that point of time UML came into picture. The UML has an important role in this object oriented analysis and design. The UML diagrams are used to model the design. So the UML has an important role to play.

2.3 UML Notations

UML notations are the most important elements in modeling. Efficient and appropriate use of notations is very important for making a meaningful model. The model is useless unless its purpose is depicted properly.

So learning UML notations should be done at very beginning. Different notations are available for things and relationships. And the UML diagrams are made using the notations of things and relationships.

2.4 Object Oriented Concepts

Since UML has an important role in object oriented analysis and design, let us review the object oriented concepts. An object contains both data and methods (also called *functions*) that control the data. The data represents the state of the object. A *class* describes an object and they also form hierarchy to model real world system.

The hierarchy is represented as *inheritance* and the classes can also be associated in different manners as per the requirement.

Note: Refer *Miscellaneous* chapter to understand the *Java* concepts and frequent interview questions.

The objects are the real world entities that exist around us and the basic concepts like abstraction, encapsulation, inheritance, polymorphism all can be represented using UML.

UML is powerful enough to represent all the concepts exists in object oriented analysis and design. UML diagrams are representation of object oriented concepts. So before learning UML, it is important to understand object oriented concepts in details. Following are some fundamental concepts of object oriented world.

- *Objects*: Objects are key to understanding object-oriented technology. Look around right now and you'll find many examples of real-world objects: dog, desk, television, bicycle, .

  Real-world objects share *two* characteristics: They all have state and behavior. Dogs have state (name, color, hungry) and behavior (barking, fetching, wagging tail). Bikes also have state (current gear, current speed) and behavior (changing gear, applying brakes). Identifying the state and behavior for real-world objects is a great way to begin thinking in terms of object-oriented programming.

- *Class*: In real world, we often find many individual objects which are of same kind. There may be thousands of other bikes in existence, all of them have same making style and model. Each bike was built from the same set of blueprints and therefore contains the same components. In object-oriented terms, we say that our bike is an instance of the class of objects known as bike. A class is the blueprint from which individual objects are created.

A class is a pattern, template, or blueprint for a category of structurally identical items (*objects*). The items created using the class are called *instances* (also called *objects*). A *class* is a thing that consists of both a pattern and a mechanism for creating items (*objects*) based on that pattern. A *class* is the set of all *objects* created using a specific pattern.

- *Abstraction*: We usually think of classes as being complete definitions. However, there are situations where incomplete definitions are useful. For example, in everyday conversation, we might talk about such items as bank accounts, insurance policies, and houses. In object-oriented programming, we call this concept with special name, *abstraction*. For example, consider the concept of an *automobile* which is not a complete definition for any vehicle.
- *Encapsulation*: Encapsulation is the mechanism of binding the *data* and *operations* together and hiding them from outside world. It is the process of binding the data and code to access that data (*operations*). Encapsulation refers to a container which has a data and its related functions in it. When an objects state and behavior are kept together they are encapsulated.
- *Specialization and Inheritance*: Different kinds of objects often have a certain amount in common with each other. *Mountain bikes* and *road bikes*, for example, all share the characteristics of bikes (current speed, current gear). Yet each also defines additional features that make them different: road bikes have two seats; some mountain bikes have one seat, an additional chain ring.

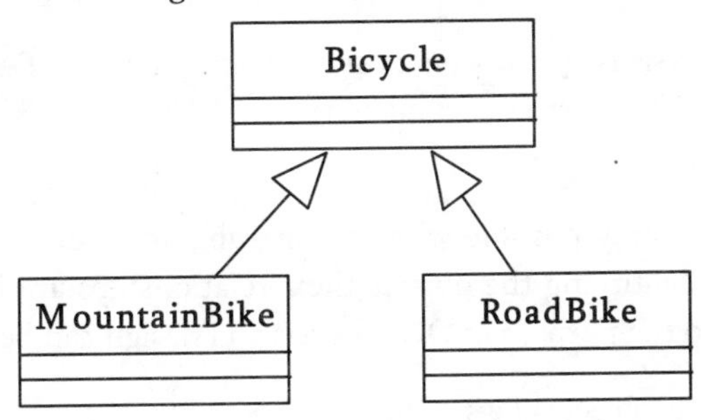

Object-oriented programming allows classes to inherit commonly used state and behavior from other classes. In this example, *Bicycle* now becomes the superclass of *MountainBike* and *RoadBike*. In the Java programming language, each class is allowed to have one direct superclass, and each superclass has the potential for an unlimited number of subclasses.

In an object-oriented context, we speak of specializations as *inheriting* characteristics from their corresponding generalizations. *Inheritance* can be defined as the process whereby one object acquires (gets, receives) characteristics from one or more other objects. Some object-oriented systems permit only *single inheritance*, a situation in which a specialization may only acquire characteristics from a single generalization. Many object-oriented systems, however, allow for *multiple inheritance*, a situation in which a specialization may acquire characteristics from two or more corresponding generalizations.

- *Polymorphism*: It defines the mechanism to exist in different forms. There are basically two types of polymorphism. *Compile time* (also knows as *Early binding*) and *Run time* (also knows as *Late binding*) Polymorphism.

  In compile time polymorphism object knows about itself at compile time. *Overloading* is a compile time polymorphism. In overloading method should have same name with different arguments. Simple example of overloading is if you have scenarios in which you want do *sum* of two or three number whatever user will pass. So you can create two methods with same name *sum* and assign 2 and 3 arguments into it.

  In run time polymorphism, object does not know about itself at compile time it assigns all the properties and methods at runtime. *Overriding* or *inheritance*-based polymorphism are kind of polymorphism. Simple and very common example is if you have a class *Shape* which is inherited to *Triangle*, *Square* and *Circle* classes. Shape class has a method name as *Draw* which will definitely inherit to all inherited classes. Now, if we declare a variable of *Shape* class and initialize it with any of the inherited class it will call the method of inherited class.

2.5 OO Analysis and Design (OOAD)

Object Oriented Analysis is the process of investigating objects. Design means collaboration of identified objects. The most important purpose of OO analysis is to identify objects of a system to be designed.

An efficient analysis is only possible when we are able to think in a way where objects can be identified. After identifying the objects their relationships are identified and finally the design is produced. So the purpose of OO analysis and design can be described as:

- Identifying the objects of a system.
- Identify their relationships.
- Make a design which can be converted to executable using OO languages.

There are three basic steps where the OO concepts are applied and implemented. The steps can be defined as

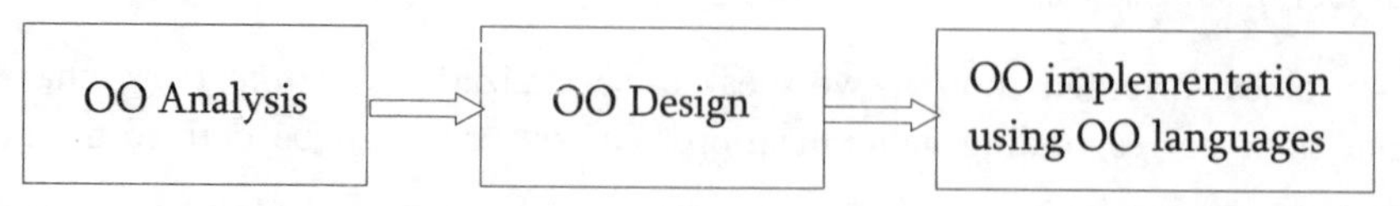

Now the above three points can be described in details:

- During object oriented analysis the most important purpose is to identify objects and describing them in a proper way. If these objects are identified efficiently then the next job of design is easy. The objects should be identified with responsibilities. Responsibilities are the functions performed by the object. Each and every object has some type of responsibilities to be performed. When these responsibilities are collaborated the purpose of the system is fulfilled.
- The second phase is object oriented design. During this phase emphasis is given upon the requirements and their fulfillment. In this stage the objects are collaborated according to their intended association. After the association is complete the design is also complete.
- The third phase is object oriented implementation. In this phase the design is implemented using object oriented languages like $Java$, $C++$ etc.

2.6 UML Building Blocks and Notations

UML is popular for its diagrammatic notations. We all know that UML is for visualizing, specifying, constructing and documenting the components of software and non-software systems. Here the $visualization$ is the most important part which needs to be understood and remembered by heart.

UML notations are the most important elements in modeling. Efficient and appropriate use of notations is very important for making a meaningful model. The model is useless unless its purpose is depicted properly.

So learning notations should be emphasized from the very beginning. Different notations are available for things and relationships. And the UML diagrams are made using the notations of things and relationships. Extensibility is another important feature which makes UML more powerful and flexible.

As UML describes the real time systems it is very important to make a conceptual model and then proceed gradually. Conceptual model of UML can be mastered by learning the following three major elements (building blocks):

- UML building blocks (Things are Objects)
- Rules to connect the building blocks (Relationships)
- Common mechanisms of UML (Diagrams)

2.7 Things

Things are the most important building blocks of UML. Things can be:

- Structural

- Behavioral
- Grouping
- Annotational

2.7.1 Structural Things

The *Structural things* define the static part of the model. They represent physical and conceptual elements. Graphical notations used in structural things are the most widely used in UML. Following are the list of structural things.

- Classes
- Interface
- Collaboration
- Use case
- Active classes
- Components
- Nodes

2.7.1.1 Class Notation

UML *class* is represented by the diagram shown below. The diagram is divided into four parts.

- The top section is used to *name* the class.
- The second one is used to show the *attributes* of the class.
- The third section is used to describe the *operations* performed by the class.
- The fourth section is *optional* to show any *additional* components.

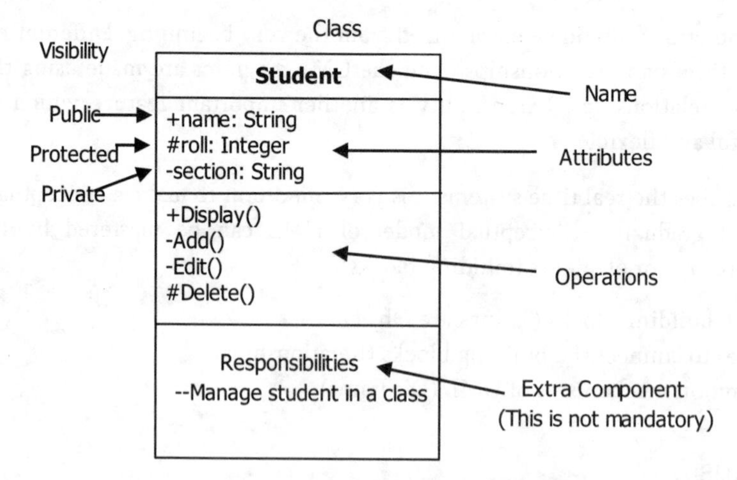

Symbols used for access specifiers (for more details refer *Miscellaneous* chapter):

Access Specifier	Symbol
private	-

protected	#
public	+
No specifier	No Symbol

2.7.1.2 Object Notation

Student

+name: String
#roll: Integer
-section: String

+Display()
-Add()
-Edit()
#Delete()

The *object* is represented in the same way as the class. The only difference is the *name* which is *underlined* as shown above. Since object is the actual implementation of a class which is known as the *instance* of a class, it has the same usage as the class.

2.7.1.3 Interface Notation

Interface is represented by a circle as shown below. It has a name which is generally written below the circle. Interface is used to describe functionality without implementation.

Interface is like a template where we define different functions but not the implementation. When a class implements the interface it also implements the functionality as per the requirement.

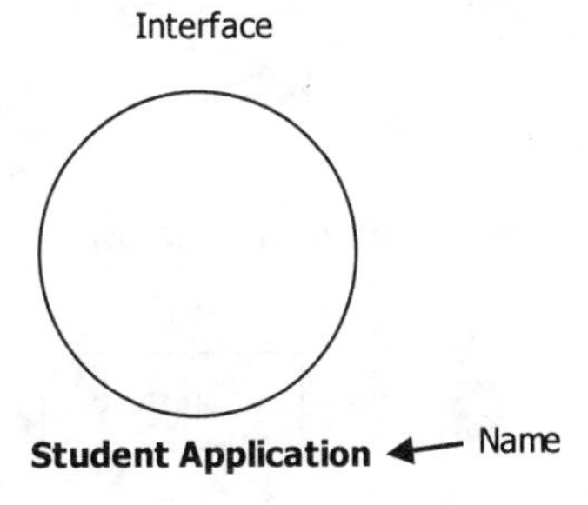

2.7.1.4 Collaboration Notation

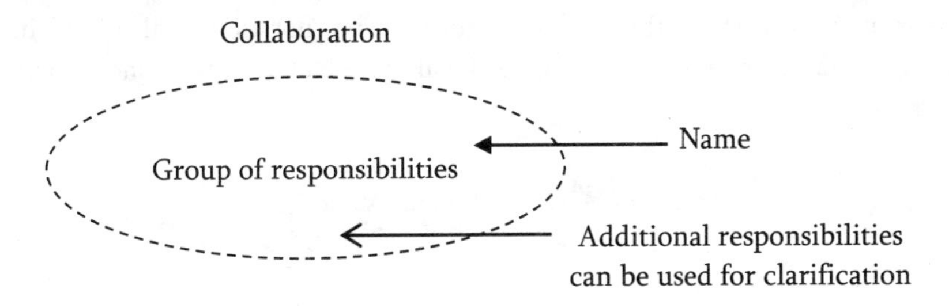

Collaboration is represented by a dotted ellipse as shown below. It has a name written inside the ellipse. Collaboration represents responsibilities. Generally responsibilities are in a group.

2.7.1.5 Use case Notation

Use case is represented as an ellipse with a name inside it. It may contain additional responsibilities. Use case is used to capture high level functionalities of a system.

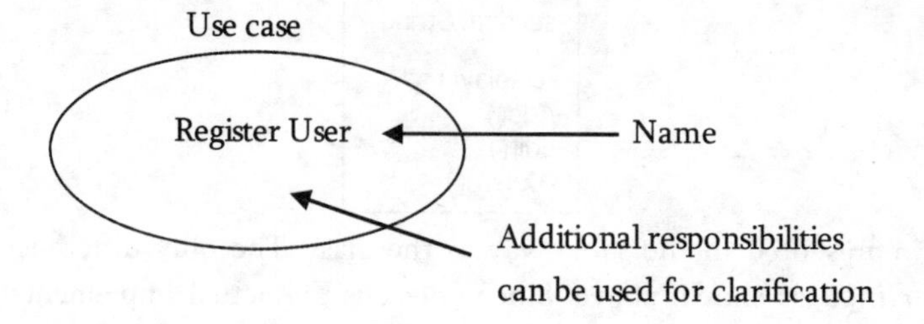

2.7.1.6 Actor Notation

An *actor* can be defined as some internal or external entity that interacts with the system. Actor is used in use case diagrams to describe the internal or external entities.

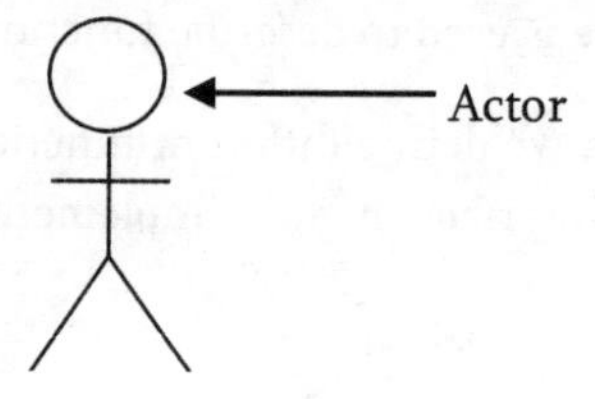

2.7.1.7 Initial State Notation

Initial state is defined to show the start of a process. This notation is used in almost all diagrams.

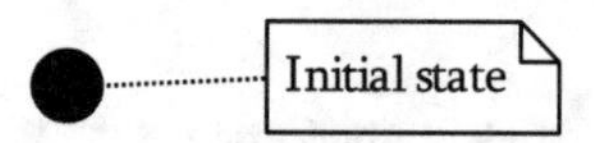

2.7.1.8 Final State Notation

Final state is used to show the end of a process. This notation is also used in almost all diagrams to describe the end. The usage of Final State Notation is to show the termination point of a process.

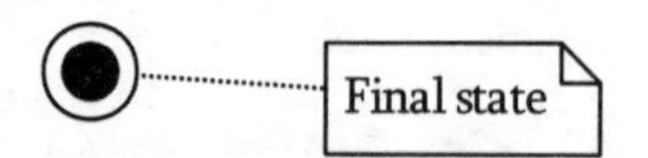

2.7.1.9 Active Class Notation

Active class looks similar to a class with a solid border. Active class is generally used to describe concurrent behavior of a system.

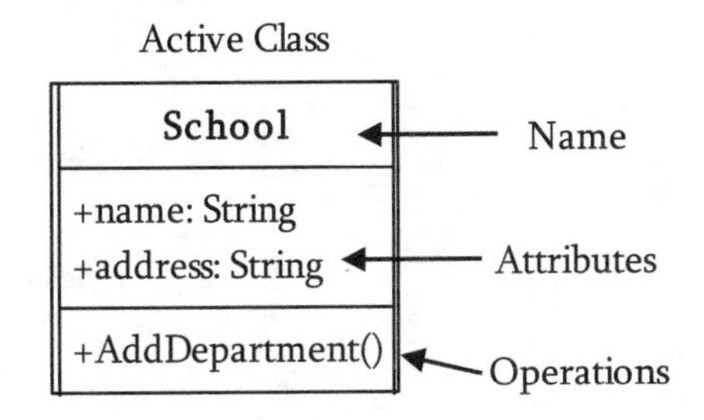

2.7.1.10 Component Notation

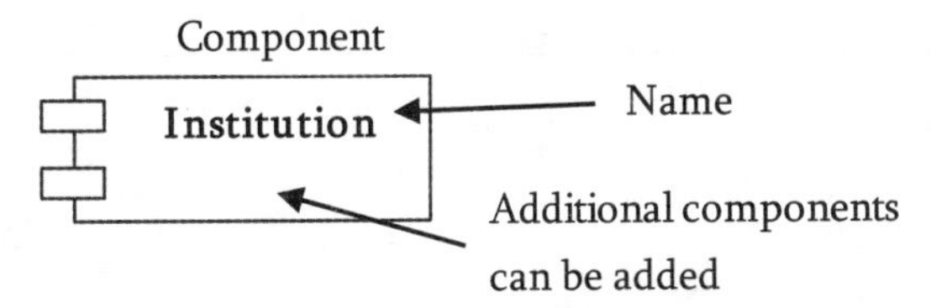

A *component* in UML is shown as below with a name inside. Additional elements can be added wherever required. Component is used to represent any part of a system for which UML diagrams are made.

2.7.1.11 Node Notation

A *node* in UML is represented by a square box as shown below with a name. A node represents a physical component of the system. Node is used to represent physical part of a system like server, network etc...

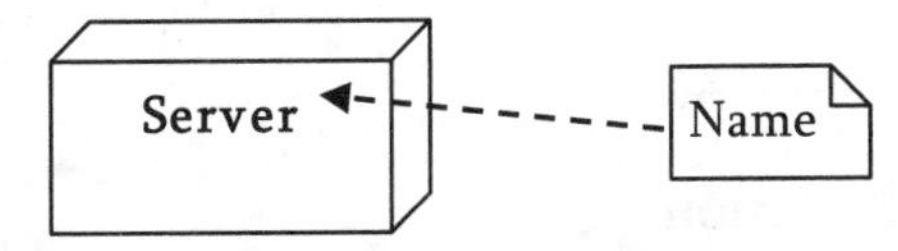

2.7.2 Behavioral Things

Dynamic parts are one of the most important elements in UML. UML has a set of powerful features to represent the dynamic part of software and non-software systems. These features include *interactions* and *state machines*.

2.7.2.1 Interaction Notation

Interaction is basically message exchange between two UML components. Interaction is defined as a behavior that consists of a group of messages exchanged among elements to accomplish a specific task. The following diagram represents different notations used in an interaction.

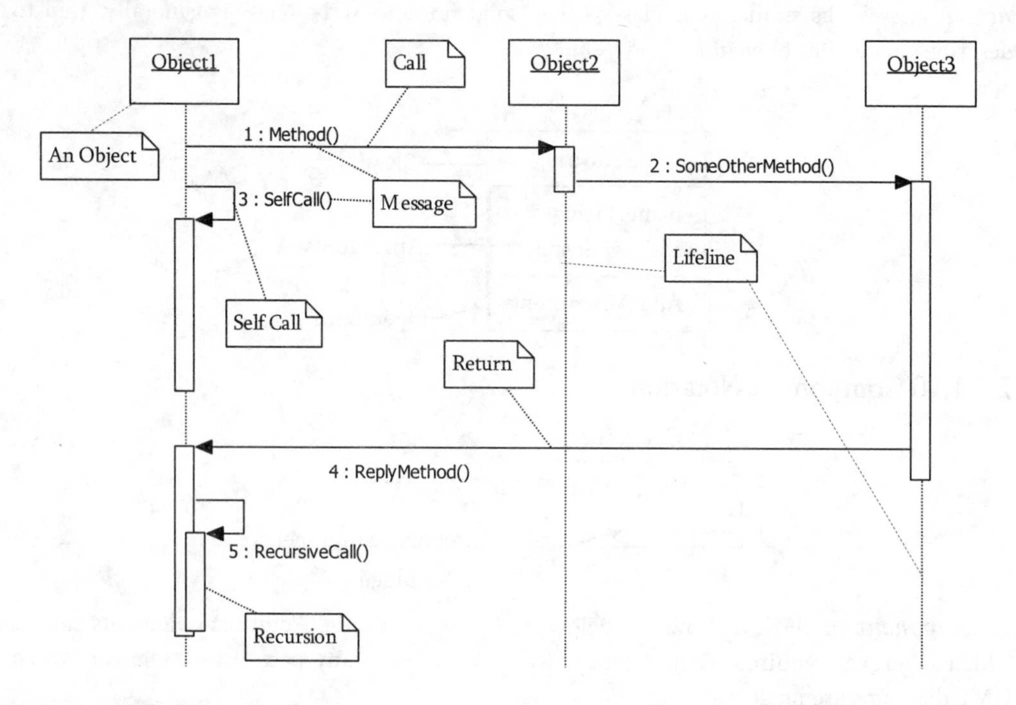

Basic Sequence Diagram Notation

- *Message*: Messages are arrows that represent communication between objects. Represented with a message expression on an arrowed line between objects.
- *Object Lifeline*: The *vertical dashed* line underneath an object. Objects do not have a lifeline until they are created.
- *Destroying Objects*: Objects can be terminated early using an arrow labeled "<< destroy >>" that points to an *X*.

2.7.2.2 State Machine Notation

State machine describes different states of a component in its life cycle. The notations are described in the following diagram. State machine is useful when the state of an object in its life cycle is important.

It defines the sequence of states an object goes through in response to events. Events are external factors responsible for state change. The state can be active, idle or any other depending upon the situation.

A *state machine* is a behavior which specifies the sequence of states an object visits during its lifetime in response to events, together with its responses to those events. A *state* is a condition during the life of an object during which it satisfies some condition, performs some activity, or waits for some external event.

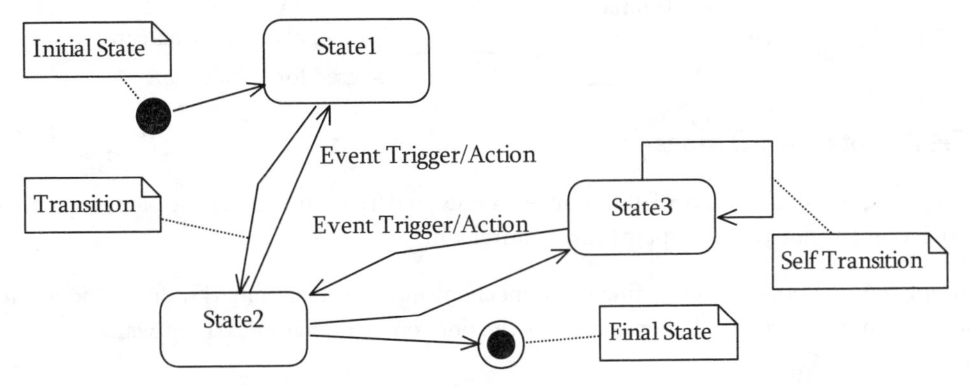

An *event* is the specification of a significant occurrence. For a state machine, an event is the occurrence of a stimulus that can trigger a state transition.

A *transition* is a relationship between two states indicating that an object in the first state will, when a specified set of events and conditions are satisfied, perform certain actions and enter the second state. A *transition* has transition components:

- A source state
- An event trigger
- An action
- A target state

A *self – transition* is a transition whose source and target states are the same. An *action* is an executable, atomic (with reference to the state machine) computation. *Actions* may include operations, the creation or destruction of other objects, or the sending of signals to other objects (events).
A *substate* is a state that is nested in another state. A state that has substates is called a *composite* state. A state that has no substates is called a *simple* state. Substates may be nested to any level.

2.7.3 Grouping Things

Organizing the UML models are one of the most important aspects of the design. In UML there is only one element available for grouping and that is package. *Grouping things* can be defined as a mechanism to group elements of a UML model together.

2.7.3.1 Package Notation

Package is the only one grouping thing available for gathering structural and behavioral things. Package notation is shown below and this is used to wrap the components of a system.

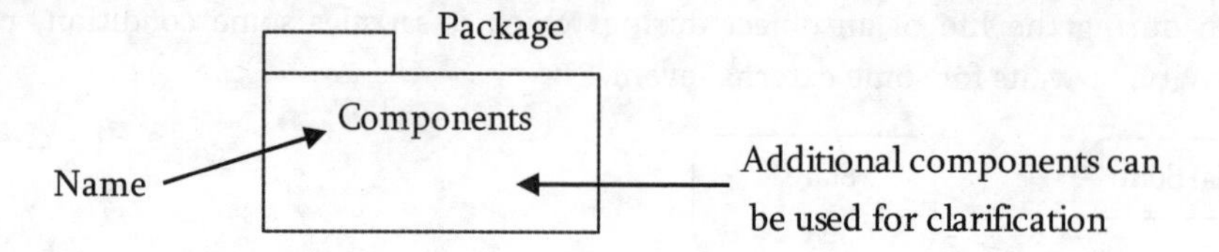

2.7.4 Annotational Things

In any diagram explanation of different elements and their functionalities are important. UML has *notes* notation to support this requirement.

Annotational things can be defined as a mechanism to capture remarks, descriptions, and comments of UML model elements. *Note* is the only one Annotational thing available.

2.7.4.1 Note Notation

This notation is shown below and they are used to provide necessary information of a system. A *note* is attached to a UML diagram to provide additional information for a symbol such as comments, constraints or code.

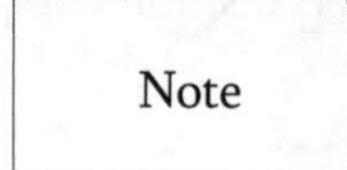

2.8 Relationship

Relationship is another most important building block of UML. It shows how elements are associated with each other and this association describes the functionality of an application.

A model is not complete unless the relationships between elements are described properly.

The *Relationship* gives a proper meaning to an UML model. Following are the different types of relationships available in UML.

- Dependency
- Association
- Generalization
- Extensibility

2.8.1 Dependency Notation

Dependency defines a relationship in which changes to one package will affect another package. Dependency is an important aspect in UML elements. It describes the dependent elements and the direction of dependency.

Dependency is a relationship between two things in which change in one element also affects the other one. Dependency is represented by a *dotted arrow* as shown below.

The arrow head represents the independent element and the other end the dependent element. Dependency is used to represent dependency between *two* elements of a system.

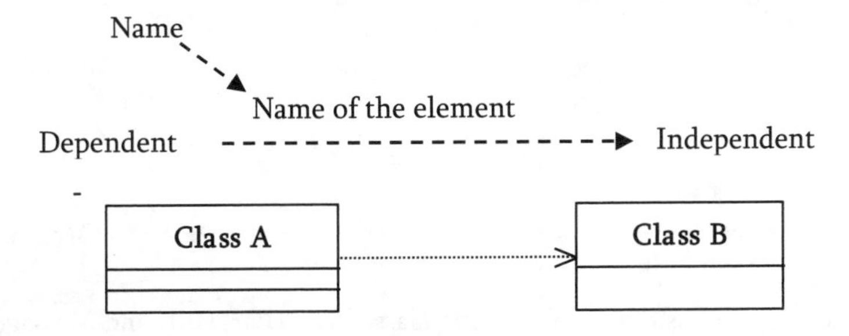

2.8.2 Generalization Notation

Generalization describes the inheritance relationship of the object oriented world. It is parent and child relationship. Generalization is represented by an arrow with hollow arrow head as shown below. One end represents the parent element and the other end child element.

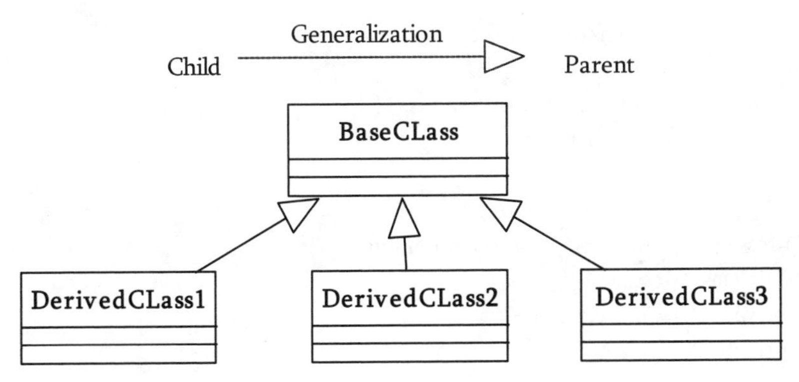

2.8.3 Association Notation

Association describes how the elements in an UML diagram are associated. In simple word it describes how many elements are taking part in an interaction.

The most abstract way to describe relationship between classes is using the *association* link, which simply states that there is some kind of a link or a dependency between two classes or more.

Association represents the ability of one instance to send a message to another instance. This is typically implemented with a pointer or reference instance variable, although it might also be implemented as a method argument, or the creation of a local variable. Association can be represented by a line between classes with an arrow indicating the navigation direction. In case arrow is on the both sides, association has *bidirectional* navigation.

Association is represented by a dotted line with (without) arrows on both sides. The two ends represent two associated elements as shown below. The multiplicity is also mentioned at the ends (1, * etc.) to show *how many* objects are associated.

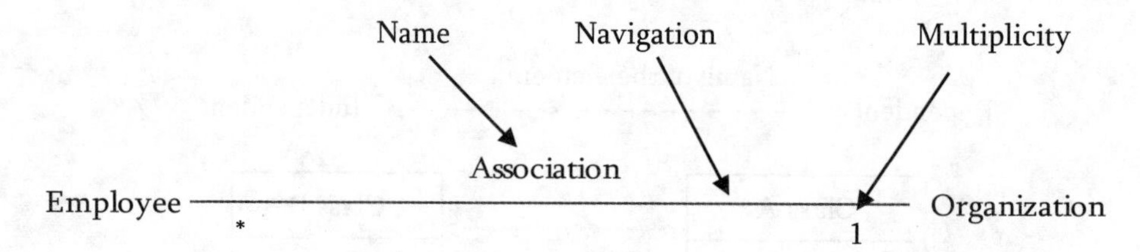

Example: As an example consider the following classes Test, Bar, Utils and Message.

```
// Test has an association with Bar
public class Test {
   public void doSomething() {
      System.out.println(Bar.doSomethingElse());
   }
}
// Utils has an association with Message
public class Utils {
   public static void print(Message msg) {
      System.out.println(msg.toString());
   }
}
// Message has an association with Person
public class Message {
   private Person recipient;
   private Person sender;
   private String text;

   public Message(Person recipient, Person sender, String text) {
      this.recipient = recipient;
      this.sender = sender;
      this.text = text;
   }
}
```

Question: What is the difference between dependency and association?

Answer: Dependency is often confused as Association. Dependency is normally created when we receive a reference to a class as part of a particular operation / method. Dependency indicates that we may invoke one of the APIs of the received class reference and any modification to that class may break current class as well. Dependency is represented by a dashed arrow starting from the dependent class to its dependency. Multiplicity normally doesn't make sense on a Dependency.

Association represents the ability of one instance to send a message to another instance. This is typically implemented with a pointer or reference instance variable, although it might also be implemented as a method argument, or the creation of a local variable. In simple word it describes how many elements are taking part in an interaction.

2.8.4 Composition and Aggregation

Composition is a special type of aggregation that denotes a strong ownership between classes *Class A* (the whole) and *Class B* (its part). Filled diamond is used for representing a composite. Composition depicts *contains* relationship.

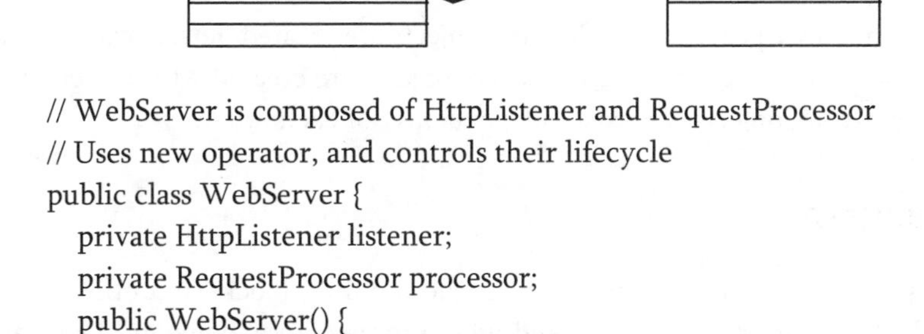


```
// WebServer is composed of HttpListener and RequestProcessor
// Uses new operator, and controls their lifecycle
public class WebServer {
   private HttpListener listener;
   private RequestProcessor processor;
   public WebServer() {
      this.listener = new HttpListener(80);
      this.processor = new RequestProcessor("/test/abcd");
   }
}
```

In the above example, if we delete WebServer then *HttpListener* and *RequestProcessor* will also get deleted.

Use a hollow diamond to represent a simple aggregation relationship, in which the *whole* class plays a more important role than the *part* class, but the two classes are not dependent on each other. Composition depicts *has − a* relationship.

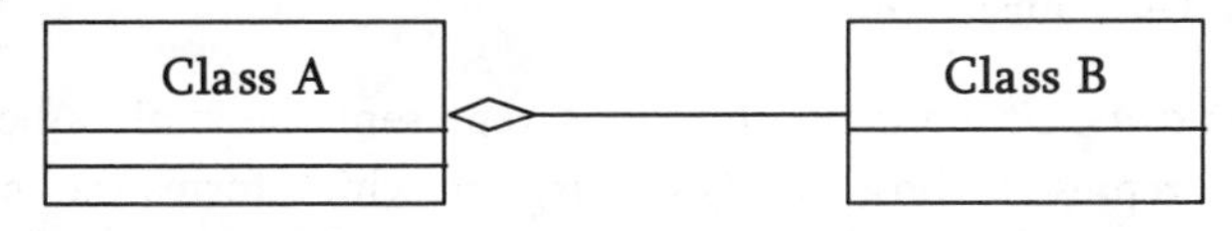

The diamond end in both a composition and aggregation relationship points toward the *whole* class *or* the *aggregate*.

```
// WebServer is an aggregation of a HttpListener and a RequestProcessor
// Uses arguments for setting objects
public class WebServer {
```

```
        private HttpListener listener;
        private RequestProcessor processor;
        public WebServer(HttpListener listener, RequestProcessor processor) {
            this.listener = listener;
            this.processor = processor;
        }
    }
```

In the above example if we deletion of WebServer object does not need deletion of HttpListener and RequestProcessor.

As an another example, A *person* needs to have a heart, a liver, a head. We would model this as *composition*. A *person* may have a car, a house, a sun-workstation. This would be an *aggregation*. The conclusion which we can derive from this is *Aggregation* and *Composition* are two types of association.

- Aggregation is a weak sort of bond where objects are created outside each other.
- Composition is a strong kind of bond where objects are created within each other.
- In an aggregation, objects can exist independently of each other.

2.9 UML Diagrams

In the previous sections we have discussed about the building blocks and other necessary elements of UML. Now we need to understand where to use those elements. The elements are like components which can be associated in different ways to make a complete UML diagram.

Any complex system can be easily understood by making some kind of diagrams. These diagrams have a better impact on our understanding. A *single* diagram is *not* enough to cover all aspects of the system. UML defines various kinds of diagrams to cover most of the aspects of a system.

There are two broad categories of diagrams and then are again divided into sub-categories:

- Structural Diagrams
- Behavioral Diagrams

Structural Diagrams: *Structural diagrams* represent the static aspect of the system. These static aspects represent those parts of a diagram which forms the main structure and therefore stable. These static parts are represented by classes, interfaces, objects, components and nodes.

The four structural diagrams are:

- Class diagram
- Object diagram

- Component diagram
- Deployment diagram

Behavioral Diagrams: Any system can have two aspects, static and dynamic. So a model is considered as complete when both the aspects are covered fully.

Behavioral diagrams basically capture the dynamic aspect of a system. Dynamic aspect can be further described as the changing/moving parts of a system.

UML has the following five types of behavioral diagrams:

- Use case diagram
- Sequence diagram
- Collaboration diagram
- State Machine diagram
- Activity diagram

Note: Among many UML diagrams, we will be using only few of them in our book (say, *Class* diagrams, *Sequence* diagrams and *State* diagrams). For remaining diagrams we will just understand what they represent.

2.9.1 Class Diagrams

Class diagrams are the most common diagrams used in UML. Class diagrams basically represent the object oriented view of a system which is *static* in nature.

The class diagram shows a collection of classes, interfaces, associations, collaborations and constraints. It is also known as *structural diagram*.

The class diagrams are widely used in the modeling of object oriented systems because they are the only UML diagrams which can be mapped directly with object oriented languages.

Purpose: The purpose of the class diagram is to model the *static* view of an application.

How to draw Class Diagram?

Class diagrams are the most popular UML diagrams used for construction of software applications. So it is important to understand the drawing procedure of class diagram.

Class diagram is basically a graphical representation of static view of the system and represents different aspects of the application. So a collection of class diagrams represent the whole system.

The following points should be remembered while drawing a class diagram:

- The name of class diagram should be meaningful to describe aspect of the system.
- Each element and their relationships should be identified in advance.
- Responsibility (attributes and methods) of each class should be clearly identified.

- For each class minimum number of properties should be specified. Because unnecessary properties will make the diagram complicated.
- Use notes whenever required to describe some aspect of the diagram. Because at the end of the drawing it should be understandable to the developer/coder.
- Finally, before making the final version, the diagram should be drawn on plain paper and rework as many times as possible to make it correct.

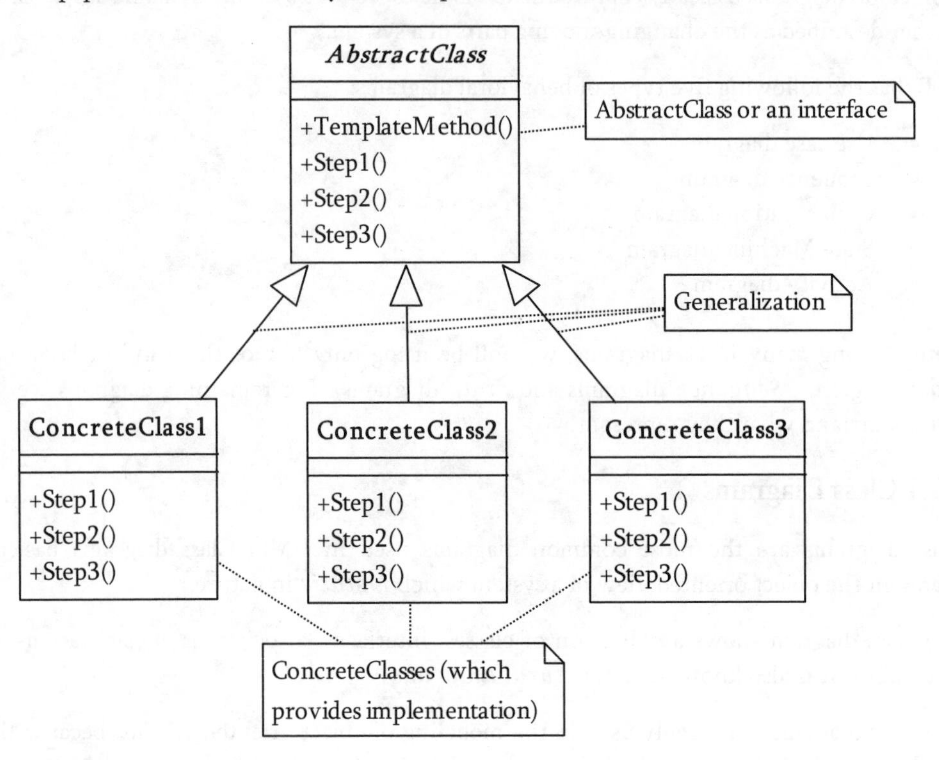

2.9.2 Object Diagrams

UML object diagrams use a notation similar to class diagrams and are used to illustrate an instance of a class at a particular point in time. Object diagrams represent an instance of a class diagram. The basic concepts are similar for class diagrams and object diagrams.

The *difference* is that a *class* diagram represents an abstract model consisting of classes and their relationships. But an *object* diagram represents an instance at a particular moment which is concrete in nature.

***How to draw Object Diagram*?**

We have already discussed that an object diagram is an instance of a class diagram. It implies that an object diagram consists of instances of things used in a class diagram. Both diagrams are made of same basic elements but in different form.

To capture a particular system, numbers of class diagrams are limited. But in object diagrams we can have unlimited number of instances which are unique in nature. So only those instances are considered which are having impact on the system.

The following things are to be decided before starting the construction of the diagram:

- The object diagram should have a meaningful name to indicate its purpose.
- The most important elements are to be identified.
- The association among objects should be clarified.
- Values of different elements need to be captured to include in the object diagram.
- Add proper notes at points where more clarity is required.

2.9.3 Component Diagrams

Component diagrams represent a set of components and their relationships. These components consist of classes, interfaces or collaborations. A component diagram describes the organization of the physical components in a system.

2.9.4 Deployment Diagrams

Deployment diagrams represent the physical resources in a system including *nodes*, *components*, and *connections*.

Deployment diagrams are a set of nodes and their relationships. These nodes are physical entities where the components are deployed. Deployment diagrams are used for visualizing deployment view of a system. This is generally used by the deployment team.

Deployment diagrams are used to visualize the topology of the physical components of a system where the software components are deployed.

2.9.5 Use case Diagrams

Use case diagrams model the functionality of a system using actors and use cases. Use cases are services or functions provided by the system to its users. Use case diagrams are a set of use cases, actors and their relationships. They represent the use case view of a system.

A use case represents a particular functionality of a system. So use case diagram is used to describe the relationships among the functionalities and their internal/external controllers. These controllers are known as *actors*.

2.9.6 UML Interaction Diagrams

From the name *Interaction* it is clear that the diagram is used to describe some type of interactions among the different elements in the model. So this interaction is a part of dynamic behavior of the system.

This interactive behavior is represented in UML by two diagrams known as *Sequence diagram* and *Collaboration diagram*. The basic purposes of both the diagrams are similar. Sequence diagram emphasizes on time sequence of messages and collaboration diagram emphasizes on the structural organization of the objects that send and receive messages.

Purpose: The purposes of interaction diagrams are to visualize the interactive behavior of the system. Now visualizing interaction is a difficult task. So the solution is to use different types of models to capture the different aspects of the interaction.

That is why sequence and collaboration diagrams are used to capture dynamic nature but from a different angle.

Interaction is used to represent communication among the components of a system.

2.9.6.1 Sequence Diagrams

Sequence diagram is the most commonly used interaction diagram, which focuses on the message interchange between a number of components. Sequence diagram describes an interaction by focusing on the sequence of messages that are exchanged, along with their corresponding occurrence specifications on the lifelines.

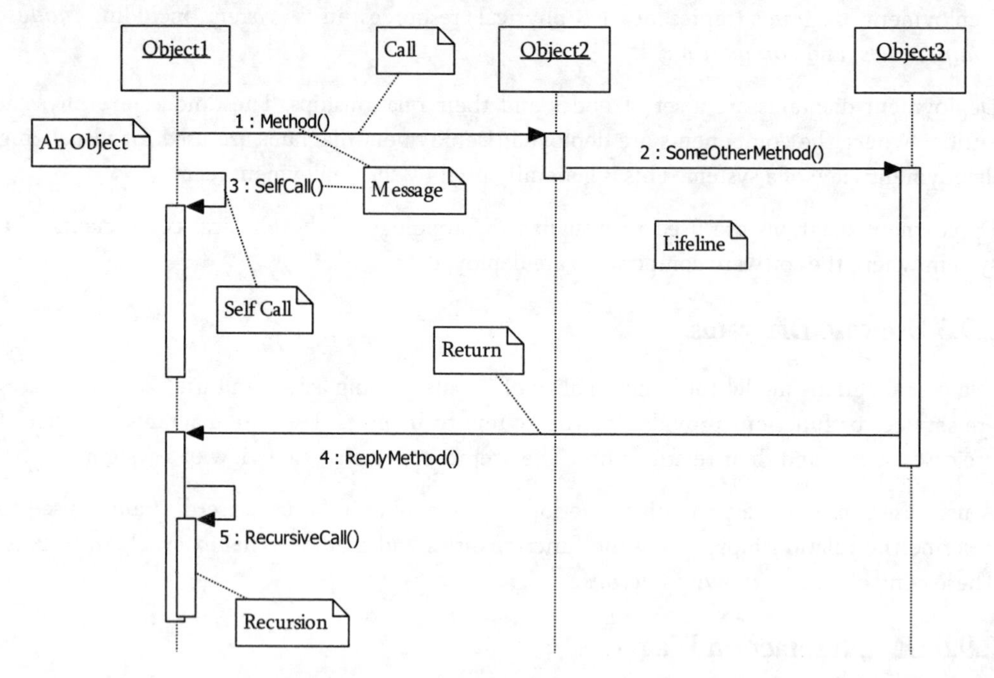

A sequence diagram is an interaction diagram. From the name it is clear that the diagram deals with some sequences, which are the sequence of messages flowing from one object to another.

Sequence diagrams describe interactions among classes in terms of an exchange of messages over time.

2.9.6.2 Collaboration Diagrams

Collaboration diagram is another form of interaction diagram. It represents the structural organization of a system and the messages sent/received. Structural organization consists of objects and links.

The purpose of a collaboration diagram is similar to sequence diagram. But the specific purpose of collaboration diagram is to visualize the organization of objects and their interaction.

A collaboration diagram describes interactions among objects in terms of sequenced messages. Collaboration diagrams represent a combination of information taken from class, sequence, and use case diagrams describing both the static structure and dynamic behavior of a system.

2.9.7 Statechart Diagrams

State machine (also called *Statechart*) describes the different states of a component in its life cycle. The notations are described in the following diagram. State machine is useful when the state of an object in its life cycle is important. It defines the sequence of states an object goes through in response to events. Events are external factors responsible for state change. The state can be active, idle or any other depending upon the situation.

A *state machine* is a behavior which specifies the sequence of states an object visits during its lifetime in response to events, together with its responses to those events. A *state* is a condition during the life of an object during which it satisfies some condition, performs some activity, or waits for some external event.

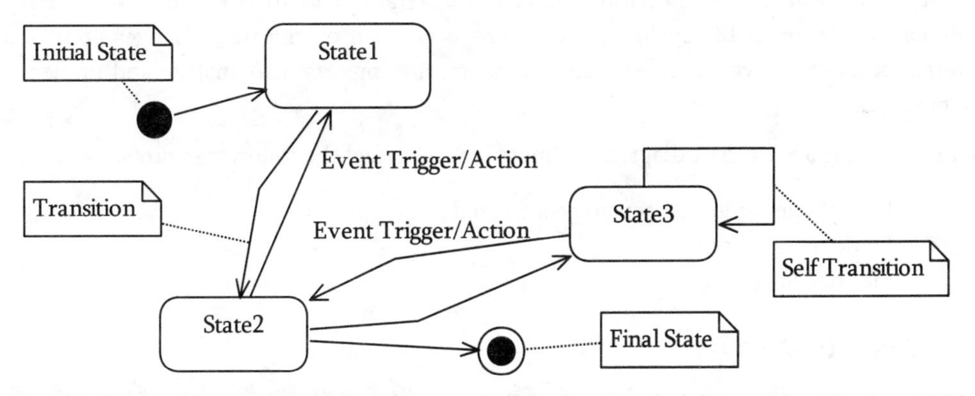

An *event* is the specification of a significant occurrence. For a state machine, an event is the occurrence of a stimulus that can trigger a state transition.

A *transition* is a relationship between two states indicating that an object in the first state will, when a specified set of events and conditions are satisfied, perform certain actions and enter the second state. A *transition* has transition components:

- A source state
- An event trigger
- An action
- A target state

A *self – transition* is a transition whose source and target states are the same. An *action* is an executable, atomic (with reference to the state machine) computation. *Actions* may include operations, the creation or destruction of other objects, or the sending of signals to other objects (events).

A *substate* is a state that is nested in another state. A state that has substates is called a *composite* state. A state that has no substates is called a *simple* state. Substates may be nested to any level.

Statechart diagram is used to represent the event driven state change of a system. It basically describes the state change of a class, interface etc..

Statechart diagram is used to visualize the reaction of a system by internal/external factors. The name of the diagram itself clarifies the purpose of the diagram and other details. It describes different states of a component in a system. The states are specific to a component/object of a system.

Purpose: Statechart diagram is one of the five UML diagrams used to model dynamic nature of a system. They define different states of an object during its lifetime. And these states are changed by events. So, Statechart diagrams are useful to model reactive systems. Reactive systems can be defined as a system that responds to external or internal events.

How to draw Statechart Diagram? Statechart diagram is used to describe the states of different objects in its life cycle. So the emphasis is given on the state changes upon some internal or external events. These states of objects are important to analyze and implement them accurately.

Before drawing a Statechart diagram we must have clarified the following points:

- Identify important objects to be analyzed.
- Identify the states.
- Identify the events.

2.9.8 Activity Diagrams

Activity diagram describes the flow of control in a system. So it consists of activities and links. The flow can be sequential, concurrent or branched.

An activity diagram illustrates the dynamic nature of a system by modeling the flow of control from activity to activity. An activity represents an operation on some class in the system that results in a change in the state of the system.

Typically, activity diagrams are used to model workflow or business processes and internal operation. Because an activity diagram is a special kind of statechart diagram, it uses some of the same modeling conventions.

Question: What is the difference between Association, Composition and Aggregation?

Answer: An association implies dependency. At the code level a reference to another class or instance usually is at least an association. An association allows one object instance to allow another to act on its behalf (by sending a message from one to the other).

Aggregation and *Composition* are two types of association. Aggregation differs from ordinary composition in that it does not imply ownership. In composition, when the owning object is destroyed, so are the contained objects. In aggregation, this is not necessarily true.

Aggregation: Car is aggregation of StereoSystem (it creates StereoSystem with *argument*).

```
class StereoSystem {
    private boolean state ;
    StereoSystem() {}
    StereoSystem(boolean state) {
        this.state = state ;
        System.out.println("Stereo System State: " + (state == true ? "On!" : "Off!")) ;
    }
}
// Car composed of StereoSystem
class Car {
        private StereoSystem s ;
        Car() {}
        Car(String name, StereoSystem s) {
                this.s = s ;
        }
        public static void main(String[] args) {
                StereoSystem s = new StereoSystem(true) ;
                Car c = new Car("BMW", s) ;
        }
}
```

Composition: Engine composed of components (it creates Component *new* operator).

```
class Component {
        private Date componentDate ;
```

```
        Piston() {
                componentDate = new Date() ;
                System.out.println("Manufactured Date :: " + componentDate) ;
        }
}
class Engine {
        private Component c ;
        Engine() {
                c = new Component() ;
        }
        public static void main(String[] args) {
                Engine engine = new Engine() ;
        }
}
```

Composition depicts *contains* relationship and aggregation depicts *has − a* relationship.

Question: Can you come-up with relationship between a university, its departments and professors?

Answer: University owns various departments (e.g., computer science), and each department might have a number of professors. If the university closes, the departments will no longer exist, but the professors in those departments will continue to exist. Therefore, a University can be seen as a composition of departments, whereas departments have an aggregation of professors. In addition, a Professor could work in more than one department, but a department could not be part of more than one university.

Question: Can you come-up with relationship between a team, its players and their organs?

Answer: A Team is an aggregate of its players and a Player is composed of organs line limbs, heart, brain, and so forth.

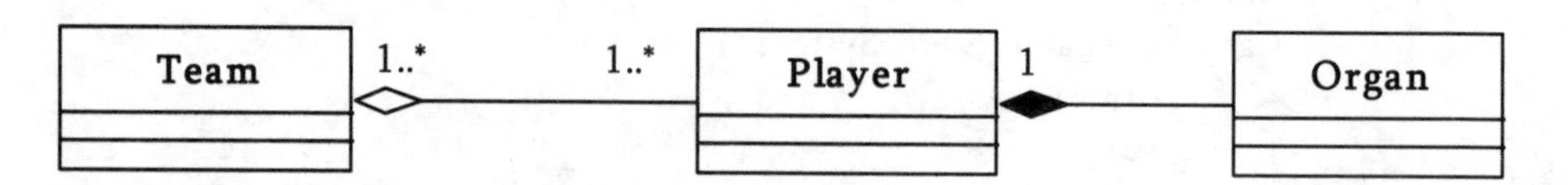

Question: What are *n*-ary associations?

Answer: An n-ary association relates three or more classes. For example, in the project management system, the use of a worker involves the worker, units of work, and associated work products.

In a UML class diagram, an n-ary association is shown as a large diamond with solid-line paths from the diamond to each class. An n-ary association may be labeled with a name. The name is read in the same manner as for binary associations.

Below figure shows an n-ary association associated with the project management system using the most basic notation for n-ary associations. This association states that utilization involves workers, units of work, and work products. As with a binary association, an n-ary association is also commonly named using a verb phrase.

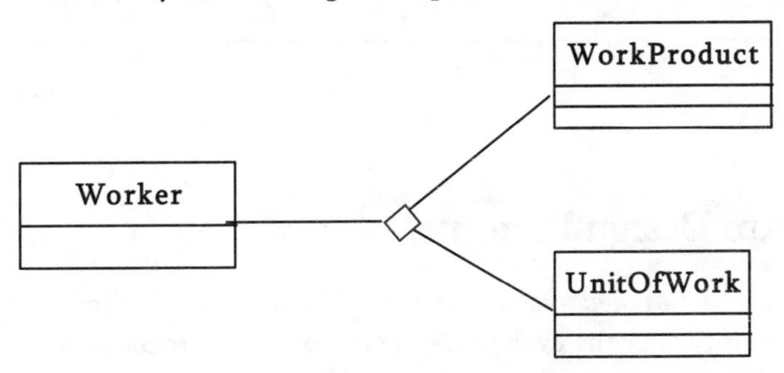

However, this is not always the case for example, the n-ary Utilization association shown in figure is described using a noun rather than a verb, because it is named from our perspective rather than the perspective of one of the classes. That is, from our perspective, we want to understand a worker's utilization relative to the other classes. From the worker's perspective, a worker is responsible for work products and performs units of work.

Chapter-3

DESIGN PATTERNS INTRODUCTION

3.1 What Are Design Patterns?

A design pattern is a *defined*, *used* and *tested* solution for a known problem. Design patterns got popularity after the evolution of object oriented programming. Object oriented programming and design patterns became inseparable.

In software engineering, a *design pattern* is a general reusable solution to a commonly occurring problem within a given context in software design.

A design pattern is *not* a finished design that can be transformed directly into code. It is a *description* for how to solve a problem that can be used in many different situations.

3.2 Brief History Of Design Patterns

Patterns originated as an *architectural* concept by *Christopher Alexander* who is a *civil* engineer. In 1987, Kent Beck and Ward Cunningham began experimenting with the idea of applying patterns to *programming* and presented their results at a conference that year. In the following years, Beck, Cunningham and others followed up on this work.

Design patterns gained popularity in computer science after the book Design Patterns: Elements of Reusable Object-Oriented Software was published in 1994 by the so-called Gang of Four (*GoF*).

3.3 Why Design Patterns?

Design patterns can speed up the development process by providing tested, proven development paradigms. Good software design requires considering issues that may not become visible until later in the implementation.

Reusing design patterns helps to prevent issues that can cause major problems, and it also improves code readability.

- Experienced designers reuse solutions that have worked in the past.
- Knowledge of the patterns that have worked in the past allows a designer to be more productive and the resulting designs to be more flexible and reusable.

3.4 Categories Of Design Patterns

There are many types of design patterns. Lot of research is going to codify design patterns in particular domains, including use of existing design patterns as well as domain specific design patterns. Examples include:

- User interface design patterns
- Secure usability patterns
- Web design patterns
- Business model design patterns
- Information visualization design patterns
- Secure design patterns

This book deals with fundamental design patterns given by *GoF*. *GoF* gave 23 design patterns and they were categorized into to *three* types as given below.

- Creational design patterns
- Structural design patterns
- Behavioral design patterns

Creational patterns: Creational design patterns are used to instantiate objects. Instead of instantiating objects directly, depending on scenario either *X* or *Y* object can be instantiated. This will give flexibility for instantiation in high complex business logic situations.

Creational design patterns (based on *GoF*):

- Abstract Factory Design Pattern
- Builder Design Pattern
- Factory Method Design Pattern
- Prototype Design Pattern
- Singleton Design Pattern

Structural patterns: Structural design patterns are used to organize our program into groups. This segregation will provide us clarity and gives us easier maintainability.

Structural design patterns (based on *GoF*):

- Adapter Design Pattern
- Bridge Design Pattern
- Composite Design Pattern
- Decorator Design Pattern
- Facade Design Pattern
- Flyweight Design Pattern
- Proxy Design Pattern

Behavioral patterns: Behavioral design patterns are used to define the communication and control flow between objects. Most of these design patterns are specifically concerned with communication between objects.

Behavioral design patterns (based on *GoF*):

- Chain of Responsibility Design Pattern
- Command Design Pattern
- Interpreter Design Pattern
- Iterator Design Pattern
- Mediator Design Pattern
- Memento Design Pattern
- Observer Design Pattern
- Strategy Design Pattern
- State Design Pattern
- Template Method Design Pattern
- Visitor Design Pattern

3.5 What To Observe For A Design Pattern?

For each of the design pattern understand the following:

- What is the name of the pattern?
- What is the type of the pattern? Whether it is a Structural, Creational or Behavioral pattern.
- What is the goal (also called *intent*) of the pattern?
- What are the other names for the pattern?
- When to use the pattern?
- What are the examples for the pattern?
- What is the UML diagram (also called *Structure*) for the pattern? A graphical representation of the pattern. Class diagrams and Interaction diagrams are used for this purpose.
- Who are the participants in the pattern? A listing of the classes and objects used in the pattern and their roles in the design.
- How classes and objects used in the pattern interact with each other.
- A description of the results, side effects, and tradeoffs (Consequences) caused by using the pattern.
- How to Implement the pattern?
- What are the related Patterns? Other patterns that have some relationship with the pattern; discussion of the differences between the pattern and similar patterns.

3.6 Using Patterns To Gain Experience

An important step in designing object-oriented system is discovering the objects. There are various techniques that help discovering the objects (for example, use cases and collaboration diagrams). Discovering the objects is the difficult step for inexperienced designers.

Lack of experience can lead to too many objects with too many interactions and therefore dependencies and that creates a system which is hard to maintain and impossible to reuse. This spoils the goal of object-oriented design.

Design patterns help overcome this problem because they teach the lessons distilled from experience by experts: patterns document expertise.

Also, patterns not only describe how software is structured, but also tell how classes and objects interact, especially at run time. Taking these interactions and their into account leads to more flexible and reusable software.

3.7 Can We Use Design Patterns Always?

Using design patterns properly gives reusable code, the consequences generally include some costs as well as benefits. Reusability is often obtained by introducing encapsulation, or indirection, which can decrease performance and increase complexity.

We should *not* try to *force* the code into a specific pattern, rather notice which patterns start to crystalise out of your code and help them along a bit. That means, writing a program that does *X* using pattern *Y* is *not* a *good idea*. It might work for hello world class programs (small programs) fit for demonstrating the code constructs for patterns, but not much more.

The main concern is that people often have a tendency to wrong design patterns. After learning a few, see the usefulness of them, and without realizing it turn those few patterns into a kind of golden hammer which they then apply to everything.

The key isn't necessarily to learn the patterns themselves. The key is to learn to identify the scenarios and problems which the patterns are meant to address. Then applying the pattern is simply a matter of using the right tool for the job. It's the job that must be identified and understood before the tool can be chosen.

The question is when did you start doing everything using patterns? Not all solutions fit neatly into an existing design pattern and adopting a pattern may mean that you muddy the cleanness of your solution. You may find that rather than the design pattern solving your problem you generate a further problem by trying to force your solution to fit a design pattern.

We should not overuse the patterns in projects where they are really not necessary. The key is *try* to keep the code clean, modular and readable and make sure the classes aren't tightly coupled.

3.8 Design Patterns vs. Frameworks

Software frameworks can be confused with design patterns. They are closely related.

Design Patterns	Frameworks
Design patterns are recurring solutions to problems that arise during the life of an application in a particular context.	A framework is a group of components that cooperate with each other to provide a reusable architecture for applications with a given domain.
The primary goal is to help improve the quality of the software in terms of the software being reusable, maintainable, extensible, etc...	The primary goal is to help improve the quality of the software in terms of the software being reusable, maintainable, extensible, etc...
Patterns are logical in nature.	Frameworks are more physical in nature, as they exist in the form of some software.
Pattern descriptions are independent of programming language.	Since frameworks exist in the form of some software, they dependent of programming language.
Patterns are more generic in nature and can be used in any kind of application.	Frameworks provide domain-specific functionality.
Patterns provide a way to do *good* design and are used to help design frameworks.	Design patterns may be used in the design and implementation of a framework.

Chapter-4

CREATIONAL PATTERNS

4.1 Creational Design Patterns

This design category is all about the class instantiation. Creational design deal with object creation methods. These design patterns tries to create objects in a manner suitable to the situation.

If we do not follow creational patterns, the basic form of object creation may create design problems and adds complexity to the design. Creational design patterns solve this problem by controlling this object creation.

4.2 Categories Of Creational Design Patterns

Creational design patterns are sub-categorized into:

- *Object-Creational* patterns: Deals with Object creation and defer part of its object creation to another object. These patterns use delegation to get the job done.
- *Class-Creational* patterns: Deals with Class-instantiation and defer its object creation to subclasses. These patterns use inheritance effectively in the instantiation process.

Creational design patterns (5 Design Patterns):

- *Abstract Factory* pattern: Provides an interface for creating related or dependent objects without specifying the objects' concrete classes.
- *Builder* pattern: It separates the construction of a complex object from its representation so that the same construction process can create different representation.
- *Factory Method* pattern: Allows a class to defer instantiation to subclasses.
- *Prototype* pattern: Specifies the kind of object to create using a prototypical instance, and creates new objects by cloning this prototype.
- *Singleton* pattern: Ensures that a class only has one instance, and provides a global point of access to it.

Object-Creational patterns	Class-Creational patterns
Abstract Factory	Factory Method

Builder Prototype Singleton	

4.3 Factory Method Design Pattern

Factory Method is just a fancy name for a method that instantiates (produces) objects. Like a factory, the job of the *factory method* is to create (or produce) objects. *Factory Method* pattern is a *creational* pattern. It is used to instantiate an object from one among a set of classes based on some *logic*.

Factory Methods have many advantages over constructors. Depending on the situation, consider providing *factory methods* instead of constructors or in addition to existing constructors.

The general approach to create new objects is by calling constructors. *Factory methods* provide alternative approach for this.

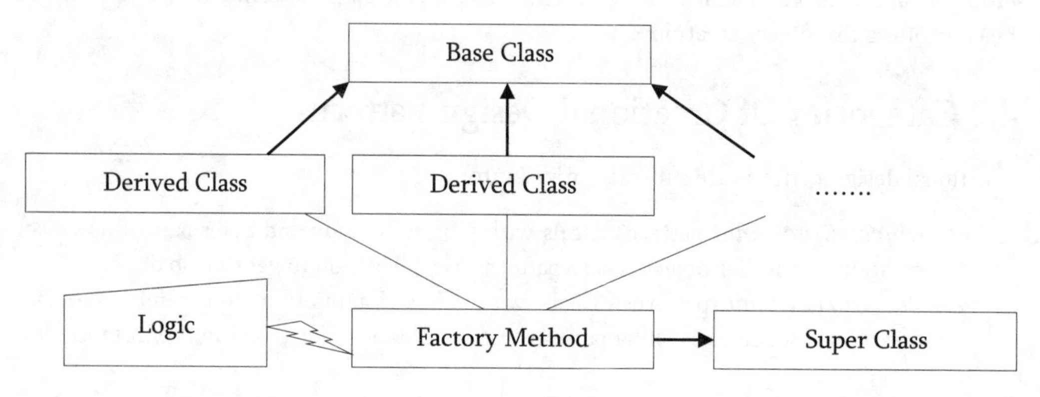

Examples For Factory Method Design Pattern

Let us consider the logging functionality in an application. In general, logging messages is one of the most commonly performed tasks in software applications. Logging appropriate messages at appropriate stages can be very useful for debugging applications.

The logging functionality could be needed by many different clients, such as file logging, database logging, console logging etc...

The common prototypes of all these clients can be kept in an *interface* and a separate *concrete* class for each of this client to provide implementation. Then, *depending* on the client request we can create its specific object for logger and send that.

UML Diagram For Factory Method Design Pattern

The participant classes in this pattern are:

- *Product* defines the interface for objects the factory method creates.
- *ConcreteProduct* implements the *Product* interface.
- *Creator* (also called as *Factory* because it creates the *Product* objects) declares the method *FactoryMethod*, which returns a *Product* object. May call the generating method for creating *Product* objects.
- *ConcreteCreator* overrides the generating method for creating *ConcreteProduct* objects

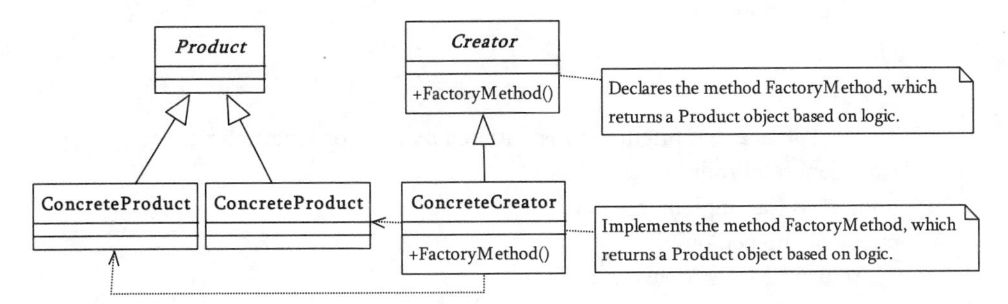

The dashed line indicates a dependency relationship between *ConcreteCreator* and *ConcreteProduct*. All concrete products are subclasses of the *Product* class, so all of them have the same basic implementation, at some extent.

The *Creator* class specifies all standard and generic behavior of the products and when a new product is needed, it sends the creation details that are supplied by the client to the *ConcreteCreator*.

Another point to note here is that (specific to $C++$), we cannot make constructors *virtual* but *factory* methods can be declared as *virtual*. For the same reason, *factory* methods design patterns are also called as *virtual constructors*.

Factory Method Design Pattern Implementation

Assume that we have a set of classes which extends a common super *class* or *interface*. Now we will create a concrete class with a method which accepts one or more arguments. This method is our *factory* method. What it does is, based on the arguments passed *factory* method does logical operations and decides on which subclass to instantiate.

This *factory* method will have the super class as its return type. *Factory* methods can not only return the object of the same type as its class, but *also* the objects of its derived class types.

Now, let us implement the factory method with a sample application. Having UML diagram in mind, it is easy for us now to produce the code related to it.

```
//Base class that serves as type to be instantiated for factory method pattern
//Pet: Product class
```

```
public interface Pet {
  public String petSound();
}
//Derived class 1 that might get instantiated by a factory method pattern
//Dog: ConcreteProduct class
public class Dog implements Pet {
  public String petSound(){
      return "Bow Bow... ";
   }
}

//Derived class 2 that might get instantiated by a factory method pattern
//Cat: ConcreteProduct class
public class Cat implements Pet {
  public String petSound(){
      return " Meaw Meaw... ";
   }
}

//Factory method pattern implementation that instantiates objects based on logic
public class PetFactory {
  public Pet getPet(String petType) {
      Pet pet = null;
     // based on logic factory instantiates an object
     if ("Bow".equals(petType))
        pet = new Dog();
     else if ("Meaw".equals(petType))
        pet = new Cat();
      return pet;
  }
}
```

Now, let us create the factory method to instantiate

```
//Client using the factory method pattern
public class SampleFactoryMethod {
  public static void main(String args[]){
      PetFactory petFactory = new PetFactory();         //creating factory
      Pet pet = petFactory.getPet("Bow");               //factory instantiates an object
     //you don't know which object factory created
      System.out.println(pet.petSound());
  }
}
```

When To Use Factory Method Design Pattern?

Based on the above discussion, we can understand that *Factory Method* pattern is useful and applicable in the following cases:

- When a class can't guess the type of the objects it is supposed to create.
- When a class wants its subclasses to be the ones to specific the type of a newly created object.
- When we want to localize the knowledge of which class gets created.

Question: For the *logger* example which we discussed in previous sections, can you come up with code?

Answer: Since the logging functionality could be needed by many different clients, such as *file* logging, *database* logging, *console* logging etc.. The common prototypes of all these clients can be kept in an interface. Let us define an interface AppLogger that declares the interface to be used by the client objects to log messages.

```
public interface AppLogger {
    public void log(String logMsg);
}
```

Now let us define concrete classes for each of these clients to provide implementation. For simplicity consider three logging concrete classes for file logging, database logging and console logging.

- *FileLogger*: Stores the messages in a log file.
- *DatabaseLogger*: Stores the messages in a database.
- *ConsoleLogger*: Displays the messages on the screen.

```
public class FileLogger implements AppLogger {
    public void log(String logMsg) {
    FileUtil futil = new FileUtil();
        futil.writeToFile("Logging.txt", logMsg, true, true);
    }
}

public class DatabaseLogger implements AppLogger {
    public void log(String logMsg) {
        //Open Database connection
        //Write log to it.
    }
}

public class ConsoleLogger implements AppLogger {
    public void log(String logMsg) {
```

```
        System.out.println(logMsg);
    }
}
```

Consider a factory class *LoggerFactory* that intends to use the services provided by the *AppLogger* implementers. For simplicity, we can take an extra argument for factory method and based on which we select which concrete class object to create.

```
public class LoggerFactory {
//Factory Method
public Logger getLogger(int value) {
    if (value == 1) {
        return new FileLogger();
    }
    else if (value == 2) {
        return new DatabaseLogger();
    }
    else if (value == 3){
        return new ConsoleLogger();
    }
  }
}
```

The below code is a sample test program which creates different logging objects based on the input sent to getLogger method.

```
public class LoggerFactoryTest {
    public static void main(String[] args) {
        LoggerFactory factory = new LoggerFactory();
        AppLogger logger = factory.getLogger(1);
        logger.log("Message to File");
        logger = factory.getLogger(3);
        logger.log("Console Message");
    }
}
```

4.4 Abstract Factory Design Pattern

Modularization is a big issue in today's programming. Programmers are trying to avoid the idea of adding code to existing classes in order to make them support encapsulating more general information.

This pattern is one level of abstraction higher than *factory method* pattern. This means that the abstract factory returns the factory of classes. Like *factory method* pattern (returns one of the several sub-classes), this returns such factory which later will return one of the sub-classes. In simple terms, the *Abstract Factory* is a factory object that returns one of several factories.

Factory patterns are examples of creational patterns. The abstract factory design pattern is an extension of the factory method pattern, which allows us to create objects without being concerned about the actual class of the objects being produced. The abstract factory pattern extends the factory method pattern by allowing more types of objects to be produced.

UML Diagram For Abstract Factory Design Pattern

The *AbstractFactory* defines the interface that all of the concrete factories will need to implement in order to products. *ConcreteFactory*1 and *ConcreteFactory*2 are the concrete classes of this interface (*AbstractFactory*) and they create two seperate families of product. Meanwhile, *AbstractProductA* and *AbstractProductB* are interfaces for the different types of product. Each factory will create one of each of these abstract products.

- *AbstractFactory*: Declares an interface for operations that create abstract product objects.
- *ConcreteFactory*: Implements the operations to create concrete product objects.
- *AbstractProduct*: Declares an interface for a type of product object.
- *ConcreteProduct*: Defines a product object to be created by the corresponding concrete factory.
- *Client*: Uses only interfaces declared by *AbstractFactory* and *AbstractProduct* classes.

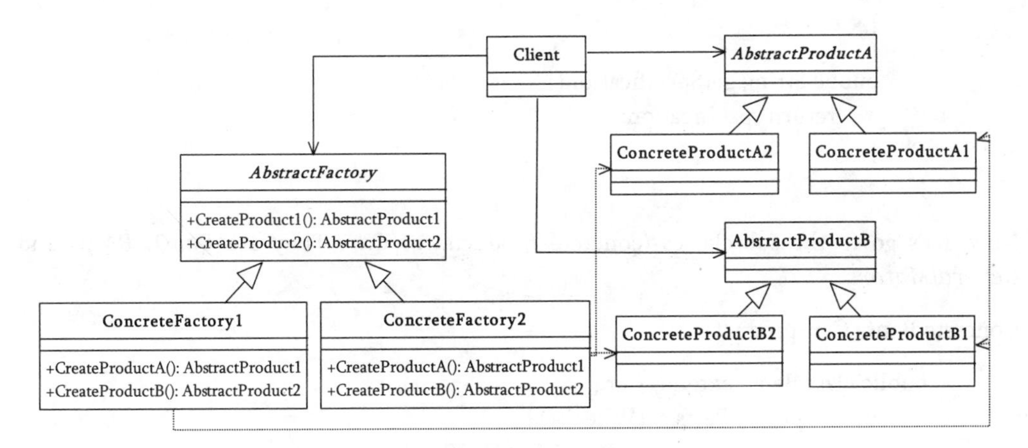

The Client class deals with *AbstractFactory*, *AbstractProductA* and *AbstractProductB*. It doesn't know anything about the implementations. The actual implementation of *AbstractFactory* that the *Client* class uses is determined at runtime.

As you can see, one of the main benefits of abstract factory pattern is that the client is totally decoupled from the concrete products. Also, new product families can be easily added into the system, by just adding in a new type of *ConcreteFactory* that implements *AbstractFactory*, and creating the specific product implementations.

Abstract Factory Design Pattern Implementation

Let's understand this pattern with the help of an example. Suppose we need to get the specification of various parts of a car. The different parts of car are, say wheels, mirrors, engine and body. The different types of cars (products) are BenQ, BMW, and GeneralMotors and so on. So, here we have an abstract base class *Car*.

```
public abstract class Car {
    public Parts getWheels();
    public Parts getMirrors();
    public Parts getEngine();
    public Parts getBody();
}
```

This class, as you can see, has four methods all returning different parts of car. They all return an object called *Parts*. The specification of *Parts* will be different for different types of cars. Let's have a look at the class *Parts*.

```
public class Parts {
    public String specification;

    public Parts(string spec) {
        specification = spec;
    }

    public String getSpecification() {
        return specification;
    }
}
```

Now, let's go to the sub-classes (concrete products) of *Car*. They are *BenQ*, *BMW* and *GeneralMotors*.

Concrete BenQ Car (product):

```
public class BenQ extends Car {
        public Parts getWheels() {
            return new Parts("BenQ Wheels");
        }
        public Parts getMirrors() {
            return new Parts("BenQ Mirrors");
        }
```

```
        public Parts getEngine() {
            return new Parts("BenQ Engine");
        }

        public Parts getBody() {
            return new Parts("BenQ Body");
        }
}
```

Concrete BMW Car (product):

```
public class BMW extends Car {
        public Parts getWheels() {
            return new Parts("BMW Wheels");
        }

        public Parts getMirrors() {
            return new Parts("BMW Mirrors");
        }

        public Parts getEngine() {
            return new Parts("BMW Engine");
        }

        public Parts getBody() {
            return new Parts("BMW Body");
        }
}
```

Concrete GeneralMotors Car (product):

```
public class GeneralMotors extends Car {
        public Parts getWheels() {
                return new Parts("GeneralMotors Wheels");
        }
        public Parts getMirrors() {
                return new Parts("GeneralMotors Mirrors");
        }

        public Parts getEngine() {
                return new Parts("GeneralMotors Engine");
        }

        public Parts getBody() {
                return new Parts("GeneralMotors Body");
        }
```

```
}
```

Now let's have a look at the *Abstract* factory which returns a factory *Car*. We call the class CarType.

```
public class CarType {
    private Car car;

    public static void main(String[] args) {
        CarType type = new CarType();
        Car car = type.getCar("BenQ");
        System.out.println(Wheels: " + car.getWheels().getSpecification());
        System.out.println("Mirrors: " + car.getMirrors().getSpecification());
        System.out.println("Engine: " + car.getEngine().getSpecification());
        System.out.println("Body: " + car.getBody().getSpecification());
    }

    public Car getCar(String carType) {
        if (carType.equals("BenQ"))
            car = new BenQ();
        else if(carType.equals("BMW"))
            car = new BMW();
        else if(carType.equals("GeneralMotors"))
            car = new GeneralMotors();
        return car;
    }
}
```

When To Use Abstract Factory Pattern?

One of the main advantages of *Abstract Factory Pattern* is that it isolates the concrete classes that are generated. The names of actual implementing classes are not needed to be known at the client side (decouples the concrete classes from the client). Because of the isolation, we can change the implementation from one factory to another.

4.5 Builder Design Pattern

Builder pattern, as the name indicates, builds complex objects from simple ones step-by-step. Builder pattern is a creational pattern used to construct a complex object step by step and the final step will return the object.

The process of constructing an object should be generic so that it can be used to create different representations of the same object.

Examples For Builder Design Pattern

As an example, we can consider construction of a car. *Car* is the final end product (object) that is to be returned as the output of the construction process. It will have many steps, like setting base, wheels, mirrors, lights, engine, roof, interior and so on. Finally, the whole car object is returned. We can build cars with different properties.

The purpose of the builder pattern is to separate the construction of a complex object from its representation so that the same construction process can create different representations.

Vehicle Manufacturer: Let us take the case of a vehicle manufacturer that, from a set of parts, can build a car, a bicycle, a motorcycle or a scooter. In this case the Builder will become the VehicleBuilder. It specifies the interface for building any of the vehicles in the list above, using the same set of parts and a different set of rules for every type of type of vehicle.

The ConcreteBuilders will be the builders attached to each of the objects that are being under construction. The Product is of course the vehicle that is being constructed and the Director is the manufacturer and its shop.

Students Exams: If we have an application that can be used by the students of a University to provide them with the list of their grades for their exams, this application needs to run in different ways depending on the user that is using it, user that has to log in. This means that, for example, the admin needs to have some buttons enabled, buttons that needs to be disabled for the student, the common user.

The Builder provides the interface for building form depending on the login information. The ConcreteBuilders are the specific forms for each type of user. The Product is the final form that the application will use in the given case and the Director is the application that, based on the login information, needs a specific form.

UML Diagram For Builder Design Pattern

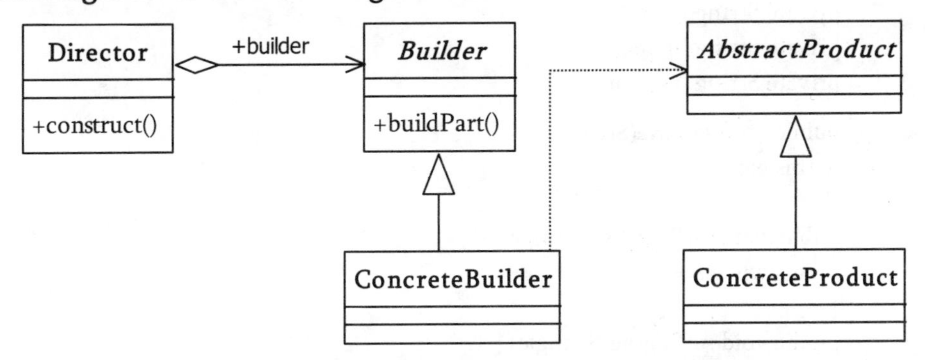

- The *Builder* provides an interface for creating the parts that make up a Product, and ConcreteBuilder provides an implementation of this interface.

- The *ConcreteBuilder* keeps track of the representation it creates, provides a way to get the result (Product) as well as constructing the product.
- The *Director* constructs the object through the Builder's interface. The *Product* is the object, usually complex, that we are constructing. This would include all the classes that define what we are constructing.

Builder Pattern Implementation

Following is the interface (*CarPlan* is the *AbstractProduct*), that will be returned as the car (*ConcreteProduct*) from the builder. Please note that, we can use abstract class as well instead of interface.

```
public interface CarPlan {
    public void setBase(String basement);
    public void setWheels(String structure);
    public void setEngine(String structure);
    public void setRoof(String structure);
    public void setMirrors(String roof);
    public void setLights(String roof);
    public void setInterior(String interior);
}
```

Concrete class (*Car* is the *ConcreteProduct*) for the above interface. The builder constructs an implementation for the following class.

```
//If we use, abstract class then we have to extend the abstract class.
public class Car implements CarPlan {
    private String base;
    private String wheels;
    private String engine;
    private String roof;
    private String mirrors;
    private String lights;
    private String interior;

    public void setBase(String b) {
        this.base = b;
    }
    public void setWheels(String w) {
        this.wheels = w;
    }
    public void setEngine(String e) {
        this.engine = e;
    }
```

```
        public void setRoof(String r) {
            this.roof = r;
        }
        public void setMirrors(String m) {
            this.mirrors = m;
        }
        public void setLights(String l) {
            this.lights = l;
        }
        public void setInterior(String i) {
            this.interior = i;
        }
    }
```

Now, we will define the builder interface (*CarBuilder*) with multiple different implementations of this interface in order to facilitate, the same construction process to create different representations.

```
public interface CarBuilder {
    public void buildBase();
    public void buildWheels();
    public void bulidEngine();
    public void bulidRoof();
    public void bulidMirrors();
    public void bulidLights();
    public void buildInterior();
    public Car getCar();
}
```

First implementation of a builder (*ConcreteBuilder*).

```
public class LowPriceCarBuilder implements CarBuilder {
        private Car car;
        public LowPriceCarBuilder() {
            car = new Car();
        }
        public void buildBase() {
            car.setBase("Low priced base");
        }
        public void buildWheels() {
            car.setWheels("Cheap Tyres");
        }
        public void bulidEngine() {
            car.setEngine("Low Quality Engine");
```

```
        }
        public void bulidRoof() {
            car.setRoof("No flexible roof");
        }
        public void bulidMirrors(){
            car.setMirrors("Cheap Mirrors");
        }
        public void bulidLights(){
            car.setLights("Cheap Lights");
        }
        public void buildInterior(){
            car.setInterior("Cheap Interior");
        }
        public Car getCar() {
            return this.car;
        }
    }
```

Second implementation of a builder (*ConcreteBuilder*).

```
    public class HighEndCarBuilder implements CarBuilder {
        private Car car;
        public HighEndCarBuilder() {
            car = new Car();
        }

        public void buildBase() {
            car.setBase("Quality base");
        }

        public void buildWheels() {
            car.setWheels("Quality Tyres");
        }

        public void bulidEngine() {
            car.setEngine("High-end Engine");
        }

        public void bulidRoof() {
            car.setRoof("Flexible roof");
        }

        public void bulidMirrors(){
            car.setMirrors("Quality Mirrors");
        }
```

```
        public void bulidLights(){
            car.setLights("Quality Lights");
        }

        public void buildInterior(){
            car.setInterior("High-end Interior");
        }

        public Car getCar() {
            return this.car;
        }
    }
```

Following class (*MechanicalEngineer* is the *Director* for this example) constructs the *car* and most importantly, this maintains the building sequence of object.

```
    public class MechanicalEngineer {
        private CarBuilder carBuilder;
        public MechanicalEngineer(CarBuilder carBuilder){
            this.carBuilder = carBuilder;
        }

        public Car getCar() {
            return carBuilder.getCar();
        }
        public void buildCar() {
            carBuilder.buildBase();
            carBuilder.buildWheels();
            carBuilder.bulidEngine();
            carBuilder.bulidRoof();
            carBuilder.bulidMirrors();
            carBuilder.bulidLights();
            carBuilder.buildInterior();
        }

    }
```

Testing the sample builder design pattern.

```
    int main() {
        CarBuilder lowPriceCarBuilder = new LowPriceCarBuilder();
        MechanicalEngineer engineer = new MechanicalEngineer(lowPriceCarBuilder);
        engineer.buildCar();
        Car car = engineer.getCar();
        System.out.println("Builder Constructed Car: " + car);
```

```
}
```

The Builder pattern hides the internal details of how the product is built. Each builder is independent of others. This improves modularity and makes the building of other builders easy. Because, each builder builds the final product step by step, we have more control on the final product.

In Java API, *StringBuffer* and *StringBuilder* are some examples of builder pattern.

Question: Let us consider the construction of a house. For instance to build a house, we will take several steps: build floor, build walls, Build roof etc.. Can you come up with implementation of builder pattern for house?

Answer: Let's use an abstract class *HouseBuilder* to define these three steps (build floor, build walls, Build roof). Any subclass of *HouseBuilder* will follow these three steps to build house (that is to say to implement these three methods in the subclass).

Then we use a *HouseDirector* class to force the order of these three steps (that is to say that we have to build walls after finished building floor and before building roof).

The *HouseClient* orders the building of two houses, one wood house and one brick house. Even though the houses are of different types (wood and brick) they are built the same way, The construction process allows different representations for the object that is constructed.

```
public abstract class HouseBuilder {
    protected House house;
    protected Floor floor;
    protected Walls walls;
    protected Roof roof;
    public abstract House createHouse();
    public abstract Floor createFloor();
    public abstract Walls createWalls();
    public abstract Roof createRoof();
}

public class WoodBuilder extends HouseBuilder {
    public Floor createFloor() {
        floor = new WoodFloor();
        return floor;
    }

    public House createHouse() {
        house = new WoodHouse();
        return house;
    }
```

```
    public Roof createRoof() {
        roof = new WoodRoof();
        return roof;
    }

    public Walls createWalls() {
        walls = new WoodWalls();
        return walls;
    }
}

public class BrickBuilder extends HouseBuilder {
    //similar to WoodBuilder
}

public class HouseDirector {
    public House constructHouse(HouseBuilder builder) {
        House house = builder.createHouse();
        System.out.println(house.getRepresentation());
        house.setFloor(builder.createFloor());
        System.out.println(house.getFloor().getRepresentation());
        house.setWalls(builder.createWalls());
        System.out.println(house.getWalls().getRepresentation());
        house.setRoof(builder.createRoof());
        System.out.println(house.getRoof().getRepresentation());
        return house;
    }
}

public abstract class House {
    protected Floor floor;
    protected Walls walls;
    protected Roof roof;
    public Floor getFloor() {
        return floor;
    }

    public void setFloor(Floor floor) {
        this.floor = floor;
    }

    public Walls getWalls() {
        return walls;
    }
    public void setWalls(Walls walls) {
```

```
        this.walls = walls;
    }

    public Roof getRoof() {
        return roof;
    }
    public void setRoof(Roof roof) {
    this.roof = roof;
    }
    public abstract String getRepresentation();
}
public interface Floor {
    public String getRepresentation();
}
public interface Walls {
    public String getRepresentation();
}
public interface Roof {
    public String getRepresentation();
}
public class WoodHouse extends House {
    public String getRepresentation() {
        return "Building a wood house";
    }
}

public class WoodFloor implements Floor {
    public String getRepresentation() {
        return "Finished building wood floor";
    }
}
public class WoodWalls implements Walls {
    //similar to WoodFloor
}
public class WoodRoof implements Roof {
    //similar to WoodFloor
}
// Similar structure for Brick family
public class BrickHouse extends House …
public class BrickFloor implements Floor …
```

```
public class BrickWalls implements Walls ...
public class BrickRoof implements Roof ...

public class HouseClient {
    public static void main(String[] args) {
        HouseDirector director = new HouseDirector();
        HouseBuilder woodBuilder = new WoodBuilder();
        BrickBuilder brickBuilder = new BrickBuilder();
        // Build a wooden house
        House woodHouse = director.constructHouse(woodBuilder);
        System.out.println();
        // Build a brick house
        House brickHouse = director.constructHouse(brickBuilder);
    }
}
```

Question: What is the difference between *abstract factory* and *builder* patterns?

Answer: Abstract factory may also be used to construct a complex object, then what is the difference with builder pattern? In builder pattern emphasis is on *step by step*. Builder pattern will have many number of small steps. Those every steps will have small units of logic enclosed in it.

There will also be a sequence involved. It will start from step-1 and will go on up to step$-n$ and the final step is returning the object. In these steps, every step will add some value in construction of the object. That is you can imagine that the object grows stage by stage. Builder will return the object in last step. But in abstract factory how complex the built object might be, it will not have step by step object construction.

In the Factory pattern, the factory is in charge of creating various subtypes of an object depending on the needs.

The user of a factory method doesn't need to know the exact subtype of that object. An example of a factory method could be *createCar* might return a *Ford* or a *Honda* typed object.

The builder design pattern describes an object that knows how to craft another object of a specific type over several steps.

Note: The above reasoning works for Factory Method as well.

4.6 Singleton Design Pattern

Singleton pattern is the most commonly used design pattern. This is one of favorite interview questions and has lots of interesting follow-up to dig into details. This not only check the knowledge of design pattern but also check coding, multithreading concepts which are very important while working for a real life application.

The singleton design pattern is used when only one instance of an object is needed throughout the lifetime of an application. The singleton class is instantiated at the time of first access and the same instance is used thereafter till the application quits.

There are only two points in the definition of a singleton design pattern,

- There should be only one instance allowed for a class and
- We should allow global point of access to that single instance.

In singleton pattern, trickier part is implementation and management of that single instance.

Strategy for Singleton instance creation: We suppress the constructor (by making it *private*) and *don't* allow even a single instance for the class. But we *declare* an *attribute* for that *same* class inside, create instance for that and return it.

UML Diagram For Singleton Design Pattern

UML diagram for the same is given below. This implementation provides global access to the object through static method *getInstance*.

Singleton
-singleton: Singleton
-Singleton() +getInstance(): Singleton

Singleton Design Pattern Implementation

```
public class Singleton {
    private static Singleton instance;

    private Singleton() {
    }

    public static Singleton getInstance() {
        if (instance == null) {
                instance = new Singleton();
        }
        return instance;
    }
}
```

The singleton implemented above is easy to understand. The Singleton class maintains a *static* reference to the lone singleton *instance* and returns that reference from the static *getInstance*() method.

There are several interesting points concerning the *Singleton* class. First, *Singleton* employs a technique known as *lazy instantiation* to create the singleton. As a result, the singleton instance is not created until the *getInstance*() method is called for the first time. This technique ensures that singleton instances are created only when needed.

We need to be careful with multiple threads. In a single-threaded environment, this works fine. If we don't synchronize the method which is going to return the instance, there is a possibility of allowing multiple instances in a multi-threaded scenario.

If two threads (say, *Thread* 1 and *Thread* 2) call *getInstance*() at the same time, two Singleton instances can be created if *Thread* 1 is preempted just after it enters the *if* block and control is subsequently given to *Thread* 2.

Making the classic *Singleton* implementation thread safe is easy. Just *synchronize* the *getInstance*() method.

```
public class Singleton {
    private static Singleton instance;
    private Singleton() {
    }
    public synchronized static Singleton getInstance() {
        if (instance == null) {
                instance = new Singleton();
        }
        return instance;
    }
}
```

The problem with this solution is that it may be expensive. Each access to the *Singleton* requires acquisition of a lock, but in reality, we need a lock only when initializing *instance*. That should occur only the first time instance is called. If *instance* is called n times during the course of a program run, we need the lock only for the first call. To solve this problem, instead of synchronizing the entire method, the below code only synchronizes the *critical* code.

```
public class Singleton {
    private static Singleton instance;

    private Singleton() {
    }

    public static Singleton getInstance() {
        if (instance == null) {
            synchronized(Singleton.class) {
                instance = new Singleton();
            }
```

```
        }
        return instance;
    }
}
```

Double-Checked Locking

However, the above code is not thread-safe. Consider the following scenario: *Thread* 1 enters the synchronized block, and, before it can assign the singleton member variable, the thread is preempted. Subsequently, another thread can enter the if block. The second thread will wait for the first thread to finish, but we will still wind up with two distinct singleton instances.

To solve this problem, we generally go for *double-checked locking* mechanism. Double-checked locking is a technique that, at first glance, appears to make *lazy* instantiation thread-safe. What happens if two threads simultaneously access *getInstance*()? Assume *Thread* 1 enters the synchronized block and is preempted. Subsequently, a second thread enters the *if* block.

When *Thread* 1 exits the synchronized block, *Thread* 2 makes a second check to see if the singleton instance is still null. Since *Thread* 1 set the singleton member variable, *Thread* 2's second check will fail, and a second singleton will not be created.

```
public class Singleton {
    private static Singleton instance;

    private Singleton() {
    }

    public synchronized static Singleton getInstance() {
        if (instance == null) {
            synchronized(Singleton.class) {
                if (instance == null) {
                    instance = new Singleton();
                }
            }
        }
        return instance;
    }
}
```

Early and Lazy Instantiation In Singleton Pattern

The above example code is a sample for *lazy* instantiation for singleton design pattern. The single instance will be created at the time of first call of the *getInstance*() method. We can also implement the same singleton design pattern in a simpler way but that would instantiate the single instance early at the time of loading the class (*early* instantiation). Following example code describes how we can instantiate early. It also takes care of the multithreading scenario.

```
public class Singleton {
    private static Singleton instance = new Singleton();
    private Singleton() {}

    public static Singleton getInstance() {
        return instance;
    }
}
```

Question: Given a large program how can we find Singletons in it?

Answer: In a large, complex program it may not be simple to discover where in the code a Singleton has been instantiated. Remember that in Java, global variables do not really exist, so we can't save these Singletons in a single place.

One solution is to create such singletons at the beginning of the program and pass them as arguments to the major classes that might need to use them.

```
instance = Singleton.getInstance();
Processor p = new Processor(instance);   //some class which uses Singleton instance
```

Question: Are there any other consequences of the Singleton Pattern?

Answer:

- It can be difficult to subclass a Singleton, since this works only if the base Singleton class has not yet been instantiated.
- We can easily change a Singleton to allow a small number of instances where this is allowable and meaningful.

Question: Given an online book store, can you think of classes where we can use Singleton?

Answer: The following code fragment shows a Catalog class which could be part of an online book store. It collaborates with a servlet, which shows the customer the entire catalog. Every shop can only have one catalogue it makes sense to design the catalogue class as Singleton. Doing it this way it is more save because the Singleton guarantees that every client sees the same catalogue.

```
public class Catalog {
    private static Singleton catalog = null;
    private ArrayList catalogList;

    private Catalog() {
    }
```

```
        public static Catalog getInstance() {
            if (catalog == null) {
                catalog = new Catalog();
            }
            return catalog;
        }
        ....
    }
```

This example shows a possible design for a Singleton class in Java. The static variable catalog holds the single existing object of the class. To get it another class cannot access the constructor as it is set to private.

It must call the public method *getInstance*() which returns the object. Inside *getInstance*() it is first checked if the variable catalog was already instantiated and has a reference; if not the constructos is called – which may only happen once.

4.7 Prototype Design Pattern

As we know today's programming is all about costs (time and memory). Saving time and memory is a big issue when it comes to using computer resources, so programmers are doing their best to find ways of improving the performance. When we talk about *object creation* we can find a better way to have new objects and that is subject of our discussion for this section.

When creation of an object is *time consuming* and a costly affair and if we already have a most similar object instance in hand, then we go for *prototype* pattern. Instead of going through a time consuming process to create a complex object, just copy the existing similar object and modify it according to our needs.

The prototype means making a clone. *Cloning* is the operation of replicating an object. The cloned object, the copy, is initialized with the current state of the object on which clone was invoked. This implies cloning of an object avoids creation. If the cost of creating a new object is large and creation is resource intensive, we clone the object.

For example, we can consider construction of a home. *Home* is the final end product (object) that is to be returned as the output of the construction process. It will have many steps, like basement construction, wall construction, roof construction and so on. Finally the whole *home* object is returned.

Cloning an object is based on the concepts of *shallow* and *deep* copying.

- *Shallow* Copying: When the original object is changed, the new object is changed as well. This is due to the fact that the shallow copy makes copies of only the references, and not the objects to which they refer.

- *Deep* Copying: When the original object is modified, the new object remains unaffected, since the entire set of objects to which the original object refers to were copied as well.

When copying involves primitive types, i.e. a byte, modifying either the original or the new copy will not modify the other object. This occurs because shallow copying of primitive types values result in separate values being stored in the cloned object.

However, when a clone involves reference types, the pointer is copied. As a result, the original and the copy objects will contain pointers to the same object.

To implement the prototype design pattern, we just have to copy the existing instance in hand. A simple way is to clone the existing instance in hand and then make the required update to the cloned instance so that you will get the object you need.

Always remember while using clone to copy, whether you need a *shallow* copy or *deep* copy and decide based on your business needs. Using clone to copy is entirely a design decision while implementing the prototype design pattern. *Clone* is not a mandatory choice for prototype pattern.

UML Diagram

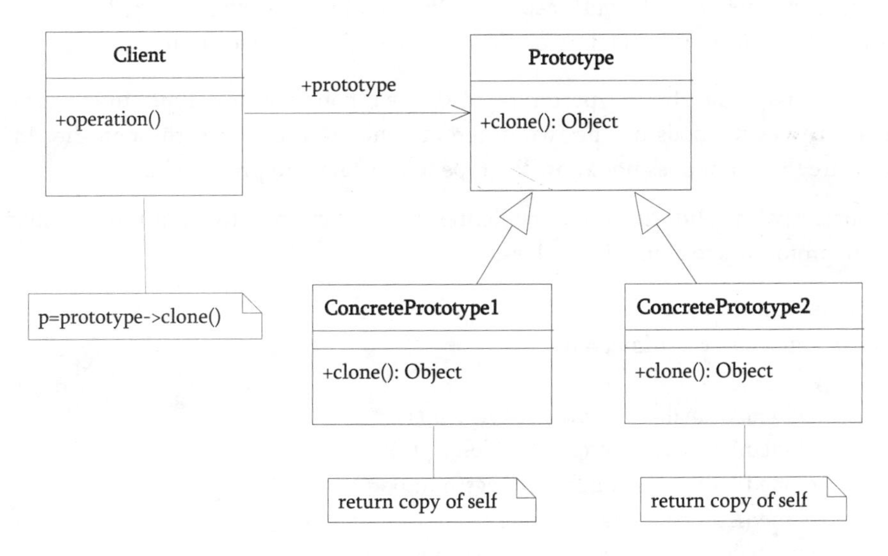

The classes participating to the prototype pattern are:

- *Client* - creates a new object by asking a prototype to clone itself.
- *Prototype* - declares an interface for cloning itself.
- *ConcretePrototype* - implements the operation for cloning itself.

Java has a built-in clone method in native code. We use the interface *Cloneable* and call its method *clone*() to clone the object. This method is defined by the parent class, *Object*, and presents the following behavior: *clone*() takes a block of memory from the *Java* heap.

The block size is the same size as the original object. It then performs a bitwise copy of all fields from the original object into fields in the cloned object. This kind of operation is known as a *shallow* copy.

The process of cloning starts with an initialized and instantiated class. We declare an abstract base class (*Prototype*) that specifies a *clone*() method. The *Client* asks for a new object of that type and sends the request to the *Prototype* class.

A *ConcretePrototype*, depending on the type of object needed, will handle the cloning through the *clone*() method, making a new instance of itself.

Prototype Design Pattern Implementation

The following is an example of the *prototype* pattern. The prototype object is an *Animal* (abstract base class) object. The *Animal* prototype (abstract class) contains two concrete prototype subclasses called *Sheep* and *Chicken*. The *AnimalCreator* (client) class contains references to the two concrete prototypes.

During the initialization of the *AnimalCreator* class the two concrete prototypes, *Sheep* and *Chicken* are created and stored as the two concrete prototypes members of the *AnimalCreator* class. The *AnimalCreator* class contains a *retrieveAnimal* method that clones a prototype *Animal* depending on the parameter that is passed to it.

The *Animal* class is the abstract prototype of the two concrete prototypes in the example. The client invokes methods on the two different concrete prototypes through the *Animal* type to ensure the client does not know the type of the concrete prototypes.

Most importantly, the *Animal* prototype defines a *clone* method to assist the two subtypes or concrete prototypes to clone themselves.

```
public Animal clone() {
   Animal clonedAnimal = null;
   try {
      clonedAnimal = (Animal) super.clone();
      clonedAnimal.setDescription(description);
      clonedAnimal.setNumberOfLegs(numberOfLegs);
      clonedAnimal.setName(name);
   } catch (CloneNotSupportedException e) {
      e.printStackTrace();
   } // catch
   return clonedAnimal;
} // method clone
```

The *Sheep* object is a concrete prototype that extends the *Animal* prototype. The *Sheep* prototype has a clone method to clone itself to create a new object.

```
public class Sheep  extends Animal {
```

The *Chicken* object is a concrete prototype that extends the *Animal* prototype. The *Chicken* prototype has a clone method to clone itself to create a new object.

```
public class Chicken extends Animal {
```

The *AnimalCreator* class is used to create and manage prototype objects. The *AnimalCreator* class contains two concrete prototypes that are initialized during the initialization of the class. The *AnimalCreator* class forms part of the *prototype* pattern by returning a cloned object (Animal) to the client without the client knowing the type of the prototype.

```
public Animal retrieveAnimal(String kindOfAnimal) {
   if ("Chicken".equals(kindOfAnimal)) {
      return (Animal) chicken.clone();
   } else if ("Sheep".equals(kindOfAnimal)) {
      return (Animal) sheep.clone();
   } // if

   return null;
} // method retrieveAnimal
```

The *AnimalClient* class makes use of the *AnimalCreator* class to create a concrete prototypes of type *Animal*. The AnimalClient class does not know the type of the concrete prototypes but references them through the *Animal* prototype.

```
AnimalCreator animalCreator = new AnimalCreator();
Animal[] animalFarm = new Animal[8];
animalFarm[0] = animalCreator.retrieveAnimal("Chicken");
animalFarm[1] = animalCreator.retrieveAnimal("Chicken");

animalFarm[4] = animalCreator.retrieveAnimal("Sheep");
animalFarm[5] = animalCreator.retrieveAnimal("Sheep");

for (int i= 0; i<=7; i++) {
        System.out.println(animalFarm[i].helloAnimal());
} // for
```

Consequences Of The Prototype Pattern

- Using the Prototype pattern, we can add and remove classes at run time by cloning them as needed. We can revise the internal data representation of a class at run time based on program conditions.
- One difficulty in implementing the *Prototype* pattern in Java is that if the classes already exist, we may not be able to change them to add the required clone or *deep*

clone methods. Also, classes that have circular references to other classes cannot really be cloned.

- Finally, the idea of having prototype classes to copy implies that we have sufficient access to the data or methods in these classes to change them after cloning. This may require adding data access methods to these prototype classes so that we can modify the data once we have cloned the class.

Notes On Prototype Design Pattern

- The prototype means making a clone. *Cloning* is the operation of replicating an object. Instead of going through a time consuming process to create a complex object, just copy the existing similar object and modify it according to our needs.
- *Prototype* (look at UML diagram) → declares an *interface* for cloning itself.
- *ConcretePrototype*→ implements an *operation* for cloning itself.
- *Client* → creates a new object by *asking* a prototype to clone itself.
- A client can *install* and *remove* prototypes at *run − time*.
- Specifying new objects by varying values: Highly dynamic systems let us define new behavior through *object composition*—by specifying values for an object's variables, for example—and not by defining new classes. We effectively define new kinds of objects by instantiating existing classes and registering the instances as prototypes of client objects. A client can exhibit new behavior by delegating responsibility to the prototype. This kind of design lets users define new *classes* without programming. In fact, cloning a prototype is similar to instantiating a class. The *Prototype* pattern can greatly reduce the number of classes a system needs.
- Specifying new objects by varying structure: Many applications build objects from parts and subparts. Editors for circuit design, for example, build circuits out of subcircuits.1 For convenience, such applications often let us instantiate complex, user-defined structures, say, to use a specific sub circuit again and again. The Prototype pattern supports this as well. We simply add this sub circuit as a prototype to the palette of available circuit elements.
- Use the Prototype pattern
    - When a system should be independent of how its products are created, composed, and represented; and
    - When the classes to instantiate are specified at run-time, for example, by dynamic loading; or to avoid building a class hierarchy of factories that parallels the class hierarchy of products; or
    - When instances of a class can have one of only a few different combinations of state. It may be more convenient to install a corresponding number of prototypes and clone them rather than instantiating the class manually, each time with the appropriate state.
- The main liability of the Prototype pattern is that

- Each subclass of Prototype must implement the Clone operation, which may be difficult. For example, adding Clone is difficult when the classes under consideration already exist.
- Implementing Clone can be difficult when their internals include objects that don't support copying or have circular references.

Question: What is the difference between *Abstract Factory* and *prototype* patterns?

Answer: *Prototype* and *Abstract Factory* are competing patterns in some ways.. They can also be used together, however. An *Abstract Factory* might store a set of prototypes from which to *clone* and return product objects. Designs that make heavy use of the *Composite* and *Decorator* patterns often can benefit from *Prototype* as well.

Question: What is the difference between *Factory Method* and *Prototype* patterns?

Answer: *Factory Method* produces a hierarchy of *creator* classes that parallels the product class hierarchy. The *Prototype* pattern lets us clone a prototype instead of asking a factory method to make a new object. Hence we don't need a *creator* class hierarchy at all.

STRUCTURAL PATTERNS

Chapter-5

5.1 Structural Design Patterns

Structural Patterns describe how objects and classes can be combined to form larger structures. In software engineering, structural design patterns are design patterns that help the design by identifying a simple way to realize relationships between entities.

Structural design patterns are used to organize our program into groups. This segregation will provide us clarity and gives us easier maintainability. Structural design patterns are used for structuring code and objects.

5.2 Categories Of Structural Design Patterns

Structural design patterns are used to organize our program into groups. This segregation will provide us clarity and gives us easier maintainability. Structural design patterns are sub-categorized into:

- Object-Structural patterns: Deals with how objects can be associated and composed to form larger, more complex structures.
- Class-Structural patterns: Deals with abstraction using inheritance and describe how it can be used to provide more useful program interface.

Structural design patterns (7 Design Patterns):

- *Adapter* pattern: Allows us to provide a new interface for a class that already exists, allowing reuse of a class where our client requires a different interface.
- *Bridge* pattern: Allows us to decouple a class from its interface. This allows the class and its interface to be changed independently over time which can lead to more reuse and less future shock. It also allows us to dynamically switch between implementations at runtime allowing more runtime flexibility.
- *Composite* pattern: It allows the client to deal with complex and flexible tree structures. The trees can be built from various types of containers or leaf nodes, and its depth or composition can be adjusted or determined at runtime.
- *Decorator* pattern: Allows us to dynamically modify an object at runtime by attaching new behaviors, or by modifying existing ones.

- *Facade* pattern: This pattern allows us to simplify the client by creating a simplified interface for a subsystem.
- *Flyweight* pattern: This pattern optimizes memory use when we need a design a class with which our client will need to create huge number runtime of objects.
- *Proxy* pattern: This pattern provides a surrogate object that controls access to some other object. The aim of this pattern is to simplify the client when it needs to use an object that has complications.

Object-Structural patterns	Class-Structural patterns
Bridge Composite Decorator Facade Flyweight Object Adapter Proxy	Class Adapter

5.3 Adapter Design Pattern

The first among the structural design patterns is *Adapter*. The name for it is totally appropriate, because it does exactly what any other real-life thing called adapter does. Have you ever faced any problem with power sockets of 2 pin and 3 pin? If we have a 3-pin plug and a 2-pin power socket, then we use an intermediate adapter and fit the 3-pin cable to it and attach the adapter to 2-pin power socket. In similar way this adapter design pattern works.

The software adapters work exactly like the outlet adapters. Consider the case of having a class or module we need to use in our application. Assume it is poorly coded and it would pollute our nicely designed code. But there's no other way, we need its functionality and don't have time to write it from scratch. The best practice is to write our own adapter and wrap the old code inside of it. Then we can use our own interface and therefore reduce our dependence on the old ugly code.

Adapter pattern converts the existing interfaces to a new interface to achieve compatibility and reusability of the unrelated classes in one application. Adapter pattern is also known as *Wrapper* pattern. An adapter allows classes to work together that normally could not because of incompatible interfaces.

The adapter is also responsible for transforming data into appropriate forms. When a client specifies its requirements in an interface, we can usually create a new class that implements the interface and subclasses an existing class. This approach creates a class adapter that translates a client's calls into calls to the existing class's methods.

UML Diagram For Adapter Design Pattern

Here is an example class diagram of adapter use. You see there is some old interface which the adapter *uses*. On the other end, there is new *target interface* that the adapter implements. The *client* (i.e. application) then uses the daisy fresh new interface.

Now, let's consider the roles in the pattern:

- *Client*: the class which tries to use *Target*
- *Target*: The interface that the *Client* wants to use
- *Adaptee*: An implementation that needs adapting
- *Adapter*: The class that implements the Target interface in terms of the *Adaptee*
- *request*: An operation that the *Client* wants to perform
- *specificRequest*: The implementation of request's functionality in the *Adaptee*

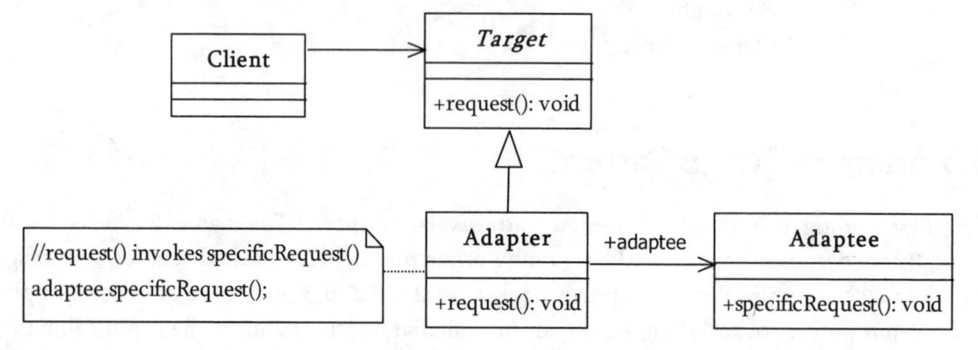

The *Target* interface defines the domain specific interface that the *Client* used, so the client collaborates with objects that implement the *Target* interface. On the other side of things, the *Adaptee* is the existing interface that needs adapting in order for our client to interact with it. The Adapter adapts the *Adaptee* to the *Target* interface - in other words, it translates the request from the client to the adaptee.

The purpose of *Target* interface is to enable objects of adaptee types to be interchangeable with any other objects that might implement the same interface. However, the adaptees might not conform to the operation names and signatures of Target, so an interface alone is not a sufficiently powerful mechanism. That is why we need the Adapter pattern.

An *Adaptee* offers similar functionality to request, but under a different name and with possibly different parameters. The Adaptee is completely independent of the other classes and is oblivious to any naming conventions or signatures that they have.

Let's take a look at the interactions in a sequence diagram. In this example, as far as the *Client* is concerned it's just calling the request method of the Target interface, which the Adapter has implemented. In the background however, the Adapter knows that to return the right result, it needs to call a different method, specificAdapteeRequest, on the *Adaptee*.

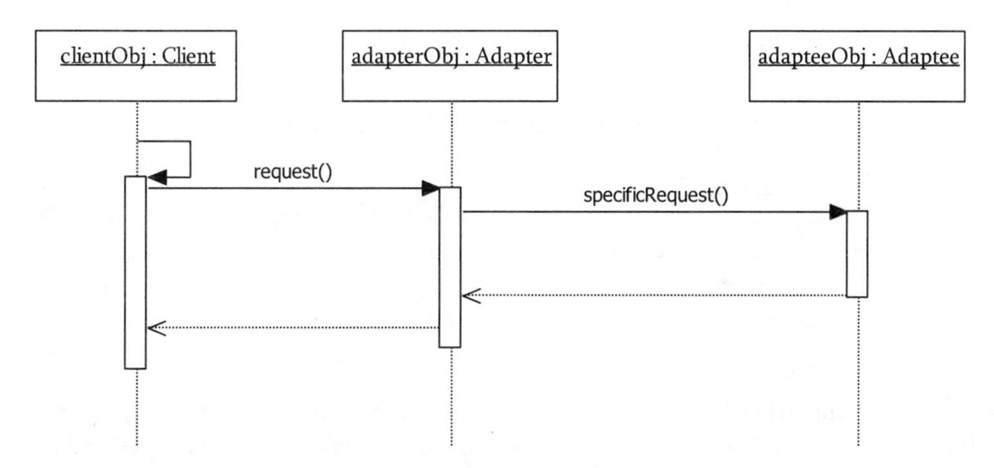

There are two ways of implementing the *Adapter* pattern:

- Using inheritance [class adapters]
- Using composition [object adapters]

Adapter Implementation Using Inheritance

First, let us do it with *inheritance* approach. When a class with incompatible method needs to be used with another class we can use inheritance to create an adapter class. The adapter class which is inherited will have new compatible methods. Using those new methods from the adapter the core function of the base class will be accessed. This is called $is - a$ relationship.

The first step in implementation is defining the *Plug*(Adaptee) class which has the different specification ($3 - Pin$) to that of *Socket*.

```
public class Plug {
   private String specification;

   private String getInput() {
      return specification;
   }

   public Plug(){
      specification = "3-Pin";
   }
}
```

At very minimal, we can define the Socket interface (Target) and a sample concrete adapter (Adapter) for it as:

```
public interface Socket {
```

```
    public String getInput();   //expects power to 2-Pin
}

public class ExpansionAdapter implements Socket, extends Plug {

    public String getInput() {
        String input = super.getInput();        //Calling base class getInput
        input = input + " power converted to 2-Pin";
        return input;
    }
}
```

Observe that, getInput() of *ExpansionAdapter* converts the 3-Pin (input from Plug) power to 2-Pin (input to Socket) power. To test the pattern, we can simply create a *Socket* and use adapter class to convert the interface.

```
public class Client {
    private Socket socket;

    public void funtionTest() {
        socket = new ExpansionAdapter();
        socket.getInput();
    }
}
```

Adapter Implementation Using Composition

The above implementation can also be done using composition. Instead of inheriting the base class, create adapter by having the base class as attribute inside the adapter. We can access all the methods by having it as an attribute. This is nothing but *has – a* relationship (*Composition*). Following example illustrates this approach.

Difference is only in the adapter class and other two classes are same. In most scenarios, prefer composition over inheritance. Using composition we can change the behavior of class easily if needed. It enables the usage of tools like dependency injection.

The difference is that an object adapter *contains* (composition) the adaptee while the class adapter *inherits* from the adaptee. Which one to use is dependent on the specific requirements of application. For example, if there are multiple adaptees, then we would use the object adapter.

```
public class Plug {
    private String specification;

    private String getInput() {
        return specification;
```

```
    }

    public Plug(){
        specification = "3-Pin";
    }
}

public interface Socket {
    public String getInput();   //expects power to 2-Pin
}

public class ExpansionAdapter implements Socket {
    //Plug object is now part of Adapter
    private Plug plug;

    ExpansionAdapter(Plug p){
            plug = p;
    }

    public String getInput() {
        String input = plug.getInput();
        input = input + " power converted to 2-Pin";
        return input;
    }
}

public class Client {
    private Socket socket;

    public void funtionTest() {
        socket = new ExpansionAdapter(new Plug());
        socket.getInput();
    }
}
```

When To Use Adapter Design Pattern?

The main use of this pattern is when a class that you need to use doesn't meet the requirements of an interface. As mentioned before, adapters are common across *Eclipse* plug-ins.

For a particular object to contribute to the Properties view, adapters are used display the objects data. The view itself doesn't need to know anything about the object properties it is displaying for.

Drawbacks Of Adapters

Due to the additional layer of code added, and so to maintain. But if rewriting existing code is not an option, adapters provide a good option.

Types Of Adapters

Class Adapters:

- They adapt Adaptee to Target by committing to a *concrete Adapter* class. As a consequence, a class adapter won't work when we want to adapt a class and all its subclasses.
- Lets *Adapter* override some of *Adaptee's* behavior, since *Adapter* is a subclass of Adaptee.
- Introduces only one object and no additional pointer indirection is needed to get to the adaptee.

Object Adapters:

- Lets a *single Adapter work with many Adaptees* that is, the *Adaptee* itself and all of its subclasses (if any). The *Adapter* can also add functionality to all Adaptees at once.
- Makes it harder to override *Adaptee* behavior. It will require subclassing Adaptee and making Adapter refer to the subclass rather than the *Adaptee* itself.

Pluggable Adapters:

These are the *C*lasses with built-in interface adaptation. A class is more reusable when we minimize the assumptions other classes must make to use it. Interface adaptation lets us incorporate our class into existing systems that might expect different interfaces to the class.
Two – way adapters:

These are used to provide transparency. An adapted object no longer conforms to the Adaptee interface, so it can't be used as is wherever an Adaptee object can. Two-way adapters can provide such transparency. Specifically, they're useful when two different clients need to view an object differently.

Notes On Adapter Design Pattern

- This pattern is also known as *Wrapper*.
- The intention of this pattern is to convert the interface of a class into another interface that the clients expect.
- Adapter lets classes work together that couldn't otherwise because of *incompatible interfaces*.
- Participants in UML diagram are:
    - *Target*: Defines the domain-specific interface that *Client* uses.

- *Client*: Collaborates with objects conforming to the Target interface.
- *Adaptee*: Defines an existing interface that needs adapting.
- *Adapter*: Adapts the interface of Adaptee to the Target interface.

- Clients call operations on an *Adapter* instance. In turn, the adapter calls Adaptee operations that carry out the request.
- We can use the *Adapter* pattern when
  - We want to use an existing class, and its interface does not match the one we need.
  - We want to create a reusable class that cooperates with unrelated or unforeseen classes, that is, classes that don't necessarily have compatible interfaces.
  - (Object adapter only) we need to use several existing subclasses, but it's impractical to adapt their interface by subclassing every one. An object adapter can adapt the interface of its parent class.

Question: What is the difference between Decorator and Adapter design patterns?

Answer: *Decorator* enhances another object *without* changing its interface. A decorator is thus *more transparent* to the application than an adapter is. As a consequence, *Decorator supports recursive composition*, which isn't possible with pure adapters.

5.4 Bridge Design Pattern

The *Bridge* pattern is an example for *structural* pattern. The Bridge pattern is used to separate out the interface from its implementation. Doing this gives the flexibility so that both can vary independently.

As an example, let us consider the electrical equipments we have at home and their switches. For example, switch of the fan. The switch is the interface and the actual implementation is the *running* of the fan once it's switched-on.

Still, both the switch and the fan are independent of each other. Another switch can be plugged in for the fan and this switch can be connected to light bulb.

UML Diagram For Bridge Design Pattern

- *Abstraction* – core of the bridge design pattern and defines the crux. Contains a reference to the implementer.
- *Refined Abstraction* – Extends the abstraction takes the finer detail one level below. Hides the finer elements from implemetors.
- *Implementor* - This interface is the higer level than abstraction. Just defines the basic operations.

- *Concrete Implementation* – Implements the above implementer by providing concrete implementation.

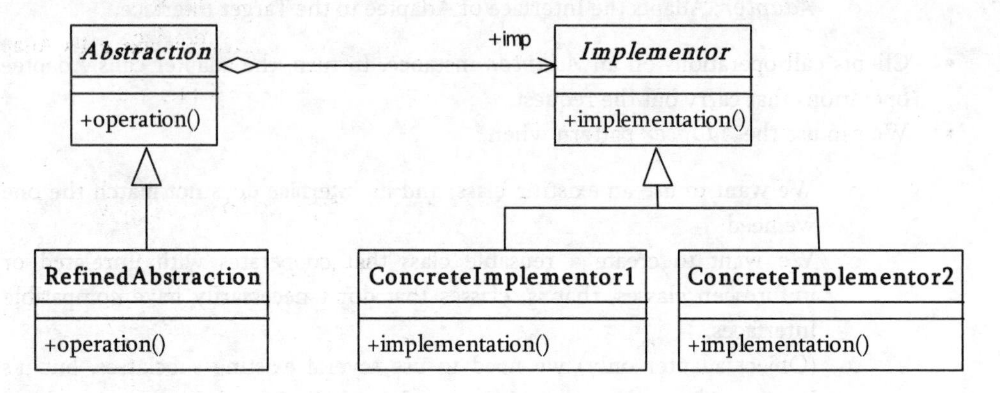

The *Abstraction* defines the abstraction, and maintains the reference to the *implementor*. *RefinedAbstraction* provides an extension to the *Abstraction*, by adding extra methods that provide different ways of getting at the same functionality. The *Implementor* interface defines an interface for the implementation classes (the *ConcreateImplementor* classes).

RefinedAbstractions are implemented in terms of the abstraction, and not that implementation interface. This means, implementation details are hidden from the client.

Bridge Design Pattern Implementation

The pattern is similar to the Adapter pattern, except the Bridge pattern separates the interface from implementation. First, we have our TV implementation interface:

```
//Implementor
public interface TV{
    public void powerOn();
    public void powerOff();
    public void changeChannel(int channel);
}
```

And then we create two specific implementations - one for *Google* and one for *Apple*:

```
//Concrete Implementor
public class Google implements TV{
    public void powerOn() {
        //Google specific on code
    }

    public void powerOff() {
        //Google specific off code
    }
```

```
    public void changeChannel(int channel){
        //Google specific changeChannel code
    }
}

//Concrete Implementor
public class Apple implements TV{
    public void powerOn() {
        //Apple specific on code
    }

    public void powerOff() {
        //Apple specific off code
    }

    public void changeChannel(int channel){
        //Apple specific changeChannel code
    }
}
```

Assume that above two classes deal with the specific implementations of the TV from each vendor. Now, we create a remote control abstraction to control the TV:

```
//Abstraction
public abstract class TVRemoteControl{
    private TV implementor;
    public void powerOn() {
        implementor.powerOn();
    }

    public void powerOff() {
        implementor.powerOff();
    }

    public void setChannel(int channel){
        implementor.changeChannel(channel);
    }
}
```

As the remote control holds a reference to the TV, it can delegates the methods through to the interface. But what is we want a more specific remote control - one that has the + / - buttons for moving through the channels? All we need to do is extend our RemoteControl abstraction to contain these concepts:

```
//Refined abstraction
```

```
public class ConcreteTVRemoteControl extends TVRemoteControl{
   private int currentChannel;

   public void nextChannel()  {
      currentChannel++;
      setChannel(currentChannel);
   }

   public void prevChannel()  {
      currentChannel--;
      setChannel(currentChannel);
   }
}
```

When To Use Bridge Design Pattern?

The Bridge pattern should be used when both the class as well as what it does very often. The bridge pattern can also be thought of as two layers of abstraction. When the abstractions and implementations should not be bound at compile time, and should be independently extensible the pattern should be used.

Bridge pattern is useful in times when you need to switch between multiple implementations at runtime.

Problems With Bridge Design Pattern

One of the major drawbacks of this pattern is that, in providing flexibility, it increases complexity. There are also possible performance issues with the indirection of messages - the abstraction needs to pass messages along to the implementer for the operation to get executed.

Notes On Bridge Design Pattern

- Bridge pattern is also known as *Handle/Body*
- *Decouple* an abstraction from its implementation so that the two can vary independently.
- Inheritance binds an implementation to the abstraction permanently, which makes it difficult to modify, extend, and reuse abstractions and implementations independently
- *Abstraction* forwards client requests to its *Implementor* object.
- An *Abstract Factory* can create and configure a particular Bridge.
- The *Adapter* pattern is geared toward making unrelated classes work together. It is usually applied to systems *after they're designed*. *Bridge*, on the other hand, is *used up – front* in a design to let *abstractions* and *implementations* vary independently.

Question: What is the difference between Bridge and Adapter design patterns?

Answer: *Bridge* has a structure similar to an object adapter, but Bridge has a different purpose. The adapter design pattern helps two incompatible classes to work together. But, bridge design pattern decouples the abstraction and implementation by creating two different hierarchies.

That means, *Bridge* is meant to separate an interface from its implementation so that they can be varied easily and independently. An adapter is meant to change the interface of an existing object.

5.5 Composite Design Pattern

Frequently programmers develop systems in which a component may be an individual object or it may represent a collection of objects. The *Composite* pattern is designed to accommodate both cases. In simple terms, a composite is a collection of objects and they may be either a composite, or just a primitive object.

The composite pattern is a *structural* design pattern. In the composite pattern, a tree structure exists where identical operations can be performed on leaves and nodes. A node in tree structure is a class that can have children. A node class is a *composite* class.

A leaf in a tree structure is a *primitive* class that does not have children. The children of a composite can be leaves or other composites.

The goal of *Composite* pattern is to be able to *treat* individual objects (individual nodes or leaves) and compositions of objects (sub-trees) the same way. All objects in the *Composite* are derived from *Composite* itself.

The *Composite* pattern allows us to build complex objects by recursively composing similar objects in a tree-like manner.

Examples For Composite Design Pattern

The *Composite* composes objects into tree structures and lets clients treat individual objects and compositions uniformly. Arithmetic expressions are Composites: an arithmetic expression consists of an operand, an operator (+ - * /), and another operand. The operand can be a number, or another arithmetic expression. Thus, 2 + 3 and (2 + 3) + (4 * 6) are both valid expressions.

UML Diagram For Composite Design Pattern

The Composite pattern consist of *Component*, *Leaf* and *Composite* classes as shown in class diagram. In *Composite* pattern we need to define an abstract base class (*Component*) that specifies the behavior that needs to be exercised uniformly across all primitive and composite objects.

- *Component*: (structure)
    - Component is at the top of hierarchy. It is an abstraction for the composite.
    - It declares the interface for objects in composition.
    - Optionally defines an interface for accessing a component's parent in the recursive structure, and implements it if that is appropriate.
- *Leaf*: (primitive)
    - The end nodes of the tree and will not have any child.
    - Defines the behavior for single objects in the composition
- *Composite*: (group)
    - Consists of child components and defines behavior for them
    - Implements the child related operations.

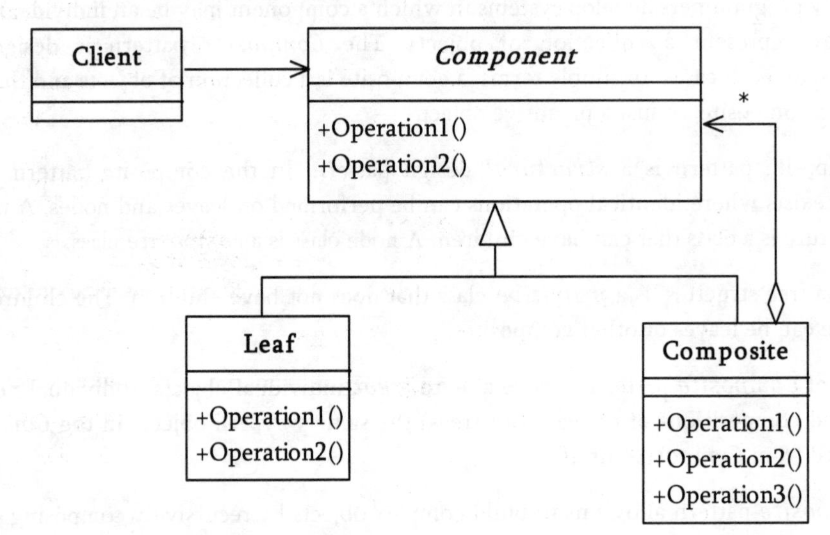

The *Leaf* class and the *Composite* class share a common *component* interface that defines the common operations that can be performed on leaves and composites. When an operation on a composite is performed, this operation is performed on all children of the composite, whether they are leaves or composites. Thus, the composite pattern can be used to perform common operations on the objects that compose a tree.

It makes more sense to define the common leaf/composite operations on a *Component* interface, but to put the composite operations in a separate interface or to simply implement them in the composite class.

When To Use Composite Design Pattern?

- If the collection of objects should be treated similarly as a single object.
- Manipulating a single object should be as similar to manipulating a group of objects.

- Recursive formation and tree structure for composite should be noted.
- Clients access the whole hierarchy through the components and they are not aware about if they are dealing with leaf or composites.

Composite Design Pattern Implementation

Another classic example is a file structure in an operating system (either *Linux* or *Windows*). As we know, any file system can have files, directories or combination of both. First, we'll declare a *FileComponent* interface that declares the operations that are common for the composite class and the leaf class. This allows us to perform operations on composites and leaves using one standard interface.

```
public interface FileComponent {
        public void printName();
}
```

The *LeafFile* class has name field and implements *printName*() method of the *FileComponent* interface by outputting messages to standard output. To define the *LeafFile* object, we can simply create a concrete class for *FileComponent* and implement the *printName* function.

```
class LeafFile implements FileComponent{
   public LeafFile(String name){
      fileName = name;
   }

   public void printName(){
      System.out.println("File Name: " + fileName);
   }

   private String fileName;
}
```

Since directory is a collection of file objects, we can use a list to store them. In the below code observe that, we have a list which stores *FileComponents* .

```
class Directory implements FileComponent{
   public Directory(String name) {
      fileName = name;
   }

   public void add(FileComponent obj) {
      files.add(obj);
   }

   public void printName() {
```

```
            System.out.println("Directory Name: " + fileName);
            for (int i = 0; i < files.size(); ++i) {
                FileComponent obj = (FileComponent) files.get(i);
                obj.printName();
            }
        }
        private String fileName;
        private List files = new ArrayList();
    }
```

Sample client code for testing could be: note that we are adding *directories* as *children* to *other* directory.

```
    publicclass CompositeDemo{
        public static void main(String[] args) {
            Directory one = new Directory("test123"),
                        two = new Directory("test456"),
                        thr = new Directory("test789");
            LeafFile  a = new LeafFile ("a.txt"),
                        b = new LeafFile ("b.txt"),
                        c = new LeafFile ("c.txt"),
                        d = new LeafFile ("d.txt"),
                        e = new LeafFile ("e.txt");
            one.add(a);
            one.add(two);
            one.add(b);
            two.add(c);
            two.add(d);
            two.add(thr);
            thr.add(e);
            one.printName();
        }
    }
```

Notes On Composite Design Pattern

- Compose objects into *tree structures* to represent *part – whole hierarchies.*
- Composite lets clients treat individual objects and compositions of objects uniformly using recursive composition.
- Defines *class hierarchies* consisting of primitive objects and composite objects. Primitive objects can be composed into more complex objects, which in turn can be

composed, and so on recursively. Wherever client code expects a primitive object, it can also take a composite object.

- *Makes the client simple*. Clients can treat composite structures and individual objects uniformly. Clients normally don't know (and shouldn't care) whether they're dealing with a leaf or a composite component.
- Makes it *easier to add new kinds of components*. Newly defined Composite or Leaf subclasses work automatically with existing structures and client code. Clients don't have to be changed for new Component classes.
- *Can make your design overly general*. The disadvantage of making it easy to add new components is that it makes it *harder to restrict the components of a composite*. With Composite, we can't rely on the type system to enforce those constraints for you. You'll *have to use run – time checks instead*.
- Participants of Composite pattern:
  - Component
    - declares the interface for objects in the composition.
    - implements default behavior for the interface common to all classes, as appropriate.
    - declares an interface for accessing and managing its child components.
    - Optionally defines an interface for accessing a component's parent in the recursive structure, and implements it if that's appropriate.
  - Leaf
    - represents leaf objects in the composition. A leaf has no children.
    - defines behavior for primitive objects in the composition.
  - Composite
    - defines behavior for components having children.
    - stores child components.
    - implements child-related operations in the Component interface.
  - Client → manipulates objects in the composition through the Component interface.
- Often the component-parent link is used for a *Chain of Responsibility*.
- *Decorator* is often used with *Composite*. When decorators and composites are used together, they will usually have a common parent class. So decorators will have to support the Component.
- *Flyweight* lets you share components, but they can no longer refer to their parents.
- *Iterator* can be used to traverse composites.

Question: Can you come-up with an example where we can use Composite design pattern?

Answer: Consider the structure of a document. A document consists of various levels of sections. Each type of a section can have either none or several sections on the level below. A section has a name and also a special size. Nodes have their own quantity of pages, but also the amount of pages from their entire child - nodes and - leaves has to be taken into account.

```
import java.util.*;
class Section {
    String title;
    int pages;
    List subsections;

    public Section(String title, int pages) {
        this.title = title;
        this.pages = pages;
        subsections = new ArrayList();
    }
    public int getAllPages() {
        int p = pages;
        Section s;
        for(int i = 0; i<subsections.size(); i++) {
            s = (Section) subsections.get(i);
            p += s.getAllPages();
        }
        return p;
    }

    public String getTitle() {
        return title;
    }

    public int getPages() {
        return pages;
    }
    public void add(Section s) {
        subsections.add(s);
    }

    public void remove(Section s) {
        subsections.remove(s);
    }
}
```

The class has two attributes to save the section text as a String and the number of pages in an integer attribute. Both are set inside the constructor and to get the values the class offers two *get*() – methods. These features are what leave and nodes have in common. But the class also includes an ArrayList – named subsections. It is used to save all child nodes and leaves.

The ArrayList also gets initialized inside the constructor. As the ArrayList saves objects from the same type – Sections – it makes no difference if the actual object is a node or a leaf. For all children nodes can be added simply by calling *add*() and also removed by calling *remove*(). For all leaves the method is not called and the ArrayList remains empty. The *Composite* pattern makes it easy to add and remove children. The following code builds the document tree shown above.

```
class CompositeTest {
  public static void main(String args[]) {
      Section s1, s2, s3, s11, s12, s13, s21, s22, s23, s31;
      Section title = new Section("Peeling Design Patterns", 2);
      title.add(s1=new Section("UML Basics", 1));
      title.add(s2=new Section("UML Diagrams", 1));
      title.add(s3=new Section("UML Notations", 1));
      s1.add(s11=new Section("Definition and History", 1));
      s1.add(s12=new Section("The pattern concept", 2));
      s2.add(s21=new Section("Introduction to UML Diagrams", 10));
      s2.add(s22=new Section("Singleton", 1));
      s2.add(s23=new Section("Factory Method", 1));
      s3.add(s31=new Section("Introduction", 1));
      int ap = s23.getAllPages();
      System.out.println(s23.getTitle() + " has " + ap + " pages!");
  }
}
```

Since nodes and leaves are handled in the same way, the Test – program doesn't have to distinguish between them. This makes it also much easier to add new sections in case of a new version. In the main part of the program all objects get instantiated and the nodes get built using the *add*() method.

5.6 Decorator Design Pattern

Decorator design pattern is used to extend or modify the behavior of an *instance* at runtime. Inheritance can be used to extend the *abilities*of a *class* (for all instances of class).

Unlike inheritance, we can choose any single object of a class and modify its behavior leaving the other instances unmodified. *Inheritance* adds functionality to classes, whereas the decorator pattern adds functionality to objects by wrapping objects in other objects.

UML Diagram For Decorator Design Pattern

In implementing the decorator pattern we construct a wrapper around an object by extending its behavior. The wrapper will do its job either before or after and delegate the call to the wrapped instance. Each time additional functionality is required, the object is wrapped in another object.

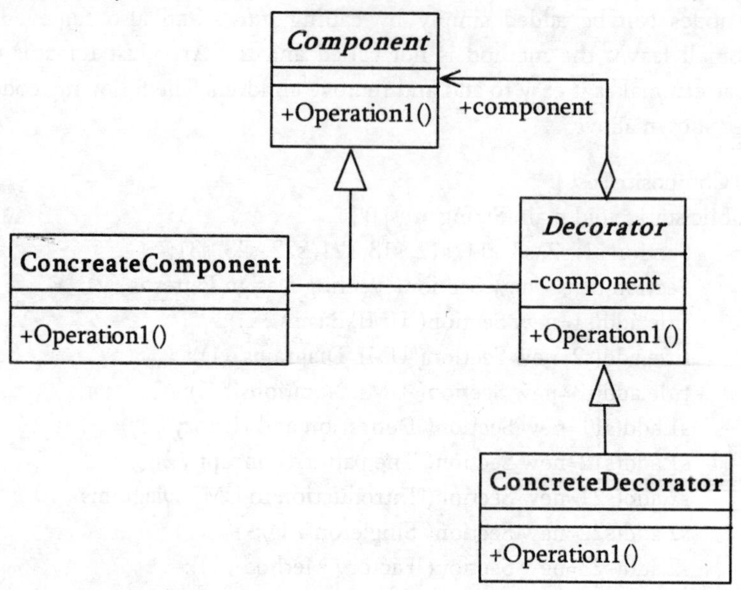

Let us see the roles in decorator pattern:

- *Component*: Interface for the objects that can have responsibilities added to it dynamically.
- *ConcreteComponent*: Defines an object implementing Component interface. This is the object that is going to be decorated, but it doesn't have any knowledge of decoration.
- *Decorator*: Maintains a reference to the Component object, and defines an interface that conforms to the Component interface. So it contains a reference to the base behavior, and also implements the same interface, hence can be treated as the Component itself. The client code expecting the Component will deal with Decorator without even noticing the difference.
- *ConcreteDecorator*: This actually adds responsibility to the component. The class that inherits from Decorator and may add some additional specific functionality in the form of new public methods.

Steps For Creating Decorator Design Pattern

- Subclass the original *Decorator* class into a *Component* class
- In the *Decorator* class, add a *Component object* as a field
- Pass a *Component* to the *Decorator constructor* to initialize the *Component object*
- In the *Decorator* class, redirect all *Component* methods to the *Component object*

- In the *ConcreteDecorator* class, override any *Component method(s)* whose behavior needs to be modified

When To Use Decorator Pattern?

Decorator design pattern is used to extend or modify the behavior of an *instance* at runtime. Inheritance can be used to extend the *abilities*of a *class* (for all instances of class). Unlike inheritance, we can choose any single object of a class and modify its behavior leaving the other instances unmodified. Inheritance adds functionality to classes, whereas the decorator pattern adds functionality to objects by wrapping objects in other objects.

Decorator Design Pattern Implementation

We start with an interface which creates a blue print for the class which will have decorators. Then implement that interface with basic functionalities. Till now we have got an interface and an implementation concrete class. Now, create an abstract class that contains (aggregation relationship) an attribute type of the interface. The constructor of this class assigns the interface type instance to that attribute. This class is the decorator base class. Now we can extend this class and create as many concrete decorator classes we want.

The concrete decorator class will add its own methods. Either after or before executing its own method the concrete decorator will call the base instance's method. Key to this decorator design pattern is the binding of method and the base instance happens at runtime based on the object passed as parameter to the constructor. It dynamically customizes the behavior of that specific instance alone.

Following given example is an implementation of decorator design pattern. *House* is a classic example for decorator design pattern. We create a basic *House* and then add decorations like colors, lights etc. to it as we prefer. The added decorations change the look and feel of the basic house. We can add as many decorations as we want. This sample scenario is implemented below.

```
public interface House {
    public String makeHouse();
}
```

The above is an interface depicting a house. I have kept things as simple as possible so that the focus will be on understanding the design pattern. Following class is a concrete implementation of this interface. This is the base class on which the decorators will be added.

```
public class SimpleHouse implements House {
    public String makeHouse () {        @Override
        return "Base House ";
    }
```

```
}
```

Following class is the decorator base class. It is the core of the decorator design pattern. It contains an attribute for the type of interface (*House*). Instance is assigned dynamically at the creation of decorator using its constructor. Once assigned that instance method will be invoked.

```
abstract class HouseDecorator implements House{
    protected House house;
    public HouseDecorator (House house) {
        this.house = house;
    }

    public String makeHouse) {
        return house.makeHouse();
    }
}
```

Following two classes are similar. These are two decorators, concrete class implementing the abstract decorator. When the decorator is created the base instance is passed using the constructor and is assigned to the super class. In the *makeHouse* method we call the base method followed by its own method *addColors*(). This *addColors*() extends the behavior by adding its own steps.

```
public class ColorDecorator extends HouseDecorator {
        private String addColors() {
                return " + Colors";
        }

        public ColorDecorator(House house) {
                super (house);
        }

        public String makeHouse() {
                return house.makeHouse() + addColors();
        }
}
public class LightsDecorator extends HouseDecorator {
        private String addLights() {
                return " + Lights";
        }

        public LightsDecorator(House house) {
                super (house);
        }
```

```
        public String makeHouse() {
                return house.makeHouse() + addLights();
        }
}
```

Execution of the decorator pattern: To test the pattern we can create a simple house and decorate that with colors and lights. We can use as many decorators in any order we want. This excellent flexibility and changing the behavior of an instance of our choice at runtime is the main advantage of the decorator design pattern.

```
public class TestDecorator {
   public static void main(String args[]) {
      House house = new LightsDecorator(new ColorDecorator( new SimpleHouse()));
      System.out.println(house.makeHouse());
   }
}
```

Question: Can you give any example decorator classes in Java API?

Answer: The Decorator Pattern is used for adding additional functionality to a particular object as opposed to a class of objects. It is easy to add functionality to an entire class of objects by subclassing (inheritance) an object, but it is impossible to extend a single object this way. With the Decorator Pattern, we can add functionality to a single object and leave others like it unmodified.

Examples of the *Decorator* pattern in the Java API can be found in the classes for processing input and output streams. *BufferedReader*(), for example, makes reading text from a file convenient and efficient:

```
BufferedReader in = new BufferedReader(new FileReader("File.txt"));
```

Another classical example of the decorator pattern is:

```
FileReader       frdr = new FileReader(filename);
LineNumberReader lrdr = new LineNumberReader(frdr);
```

The preceding code creates a reader *lrdr* that reads from a file and tracks line numbers. Line 1 creates a file reader (*frdr*), and line 2 adds line-number tracking.

Question: What is the difference between inheritance and decorator patterns? Can't we add extra functionality with inheritance?

Answer: In the previous problem, to add colors and lights for decoration we can simply create a subclasses to *House*. If we wish to add colors and lights to all houses then it make sense to create a subclass to *House*. Decorator pattern is an alternative to subclassing. Subclassing associates behavior at compile time, and the change affects all instances of the original class, decorating can provide new behavior at run-time for individual objects.

The major point of the pattern is to enable run-time changes: we may not know how we want the house to look until the program is running, and this allows us to easily modify it. Granted, this can be done via the sub classing, but not as nicely.

Question: Can you give any example where we can use decorator pattern in daily life?

Answer: The following example illustrates the use of decorators using coffee making scenario. In this example, the scenario only includes cost and ingredients. The *Coffee* interface defines the functionality of Coffee implemented by decorator.

```
public interface Coffee {
    public double getCost();          // returns the cost of the coffee
    public String getIngredients(); // returns the ingredients of the coffee
}
```

The following *SimpleCoffee* class provides the implementation of a simple coffee without any extra ingredients.

```
public class SimpleCoffee implements Coffee {
    public double getCost() {
        return 1;
    }
    public String getIngredients() {
        return "Coffee";
    }
}
```

The following classes contain the decorators for all Coffee classes, including the decorator classes themselves. *CoffeeDecorator* is an abstract decorator class and note that it implements Coffee interface.

```
public abstract class CoffeeDecorator implements Coffee {
    protected final Coffee decoratedCoffee;
    protected String ingredientSeparator = ", ";

    public CoffeeDecorator(Coffee decoratedCoffee) {
        this.decoratedCoffee = decoratedCoffee;
    }
    public double getCost() { // implementing methods of the interface
        return decoratedCoffee.getCost();
    }
    public String getIngredients() {
        return decoratedCoffee.getIngredients();
    }
```

```
}
```

Milk decorator mixes milk with coffee: note it extends CoffeeDecorator

```
public class Milk extends CoffeeDecorator {
    public Milk(Coffee decoratedCoffee) {
        super(decoratedCoffee);
    }
    public double getCost() { // overriding methods defined in the abstract superclass
        return super.getCost() + 0.5;
    }
    public String getIngredients() {
        return super.getIngredients() + ingredientSeparator + " Milk ";
    }
}
```

Whip decorator mixes whip with coffee: note it extends CoffeeDecorator

```
public class Whip extends CoffeeDecorator {
    public Whip(Coffee decoratedCoffee) {
        super(decoratedCoffee);
    }
    public double getCost() {
        return super.getCost() + 0.7;
    }
    public String getIngredients() {
        return super.getIngredients() + ingredientSeparator + " Whip ";
    }
}
```

Sprinkles decorator mixes sprinkles with coffee: note it extends CoffeeDecorator

```
public class Sprinkles extends CoffeeDecorator {
    public Sprinkles(Coffee decoratedCoffee) {
        super(decoratedCoffee);
    }
    public double getCost() {
        return super.getCost() + 0.2;
    }

    public String getIngredients() {
        return super.getIngredients() + ingredientSeparator + " Sprinkles ";
    }
```

```
}
```

Below is a test program that creates a Coffee instance which is fully decorated (i.e., with milk, whip, and sprinkles), and calculate cost of coffee and prints its ingredients:

```
public class DecoratorTest{
    public static void main(String[] args)  {
        Coffee c = new SimpleCoffee();
        System.out.println("Cost: " + c.getCost() + ",Ingredients: " + c.getIngredients());

        c = new Milk(c);
        System.out.println("Cost: " + c.getCost() + ", Ingredients: " + c.getIngredients());

        c = new Sprinkles(c);
        System.out.println("Cost: " + c.getCost() + ", Ingredients: " + c.getIngredients());

        c = new Whip(c);
        System.out.println("Cost: " + c.getCost() + ", Ingredients: " + c.getIngredients());

        // Note that we can also stack more than one decorator of the same type
        c = new Sprinkles(c);
        System.out.println("Cost: " + c.getCost() + ", Ingredients: " + c.getIngredients());
    }
}
```

5.7 Facade Design Pattern

Let us consider a simple example for understanding the pattern. While walking past the road, we can only see this glass face of the building. We do not know anything about it, the wiring, the pipes and other complexities.

The face hides all the complexities of the building and displays a good looking front. This is how facade pattern is used. It hides the complexities of the system and provides a simple interface to the client from where the client can access the system.

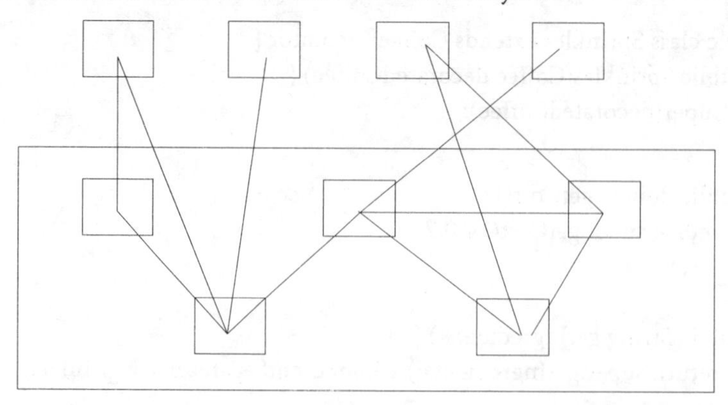

In Java, the interface JDBC is an example of facade pattern. We as users or clients create connection using the *java.sql.Connection* interface, the implementation of which we are not concerned about. The implementation is left to the vendor of driver.

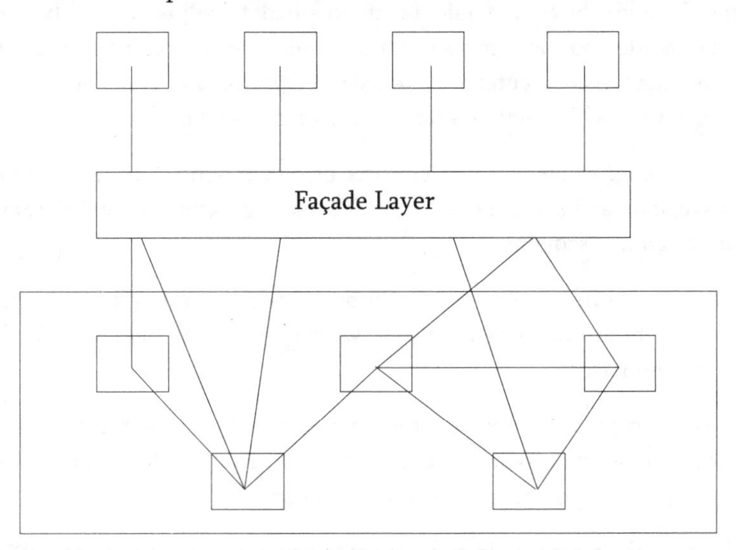

Many business processes involve complex manipulations of business classes (as shown in figure). Complex processes that involve multiple business objects can lead to tight coupling between those classes. This reduces the flexibility and design clarity. Complex relationships between low-level business components make clients difficult to write.

Facade design pattern simplifies the interface to a complex system. For that it is usually composed of all the classes, which make up the subsystems of the complex system.

A Facade shields the user from the complex details of the system and provides them with a *simplified* view of it which is *easy to use*. It also decouples the code that uses the system from the details of the subsystems, making it easier to modify the system later.

Think of a component that solves a complex business problem. That component may expose lot of interfaces to interact with it. To complete a process flow we may have to interact with multiple interfaces.

To simplify that interaction process, we introduce facade layer. Facade exposes a simplified interface (in this case a single interface to perform that multi-step process) and internally it interacts with those components and gets the job done for you. It can be taken as one level of abstraction over an existing layer.

Facade design pattern is one among the other design patterns that promote loose coupling. It emphasizes one more important aspect of design which is abstraction. By hiding the complexity behind it and exposing a simple interface it achieves abstraction.

Examples For Facade Design Pattern

I wish to give you couple of real world examples. Let's take a car; starting a car involves multiple steps. Imagine how it would be if you had to adjust n number of valves and controllers. The facade you have got is just a key hole. On turn of a key it sends instruction to multiple subsystems and executes a sequence of operation and completes the objective. All you know is a key turn which acts as a facade and simplifies your job.

Similarly consider microwave oven, it consists of components like transformer, capacitor, magnetron, waveguide and some more. To perform an operation these different components needs to be activated in a sequence.

Every component has different outputs and inputs. Imagine you will have separate external controller for all these components using which you will heat the food. It will be complicated and cumbersome.

In this scenario, oven provides you preprogrammed switches which can be considered as a facade. On click on of a single switch the job gets done. That single menu switch works as an abstraction layer between you and the internal components.

Let us consider another example. In software scenario, we can have interfaces which act as a facade. Methods in these interfaces contain the interaction sequence, formatting and converting data for input for components. As such it will not hold the business logic.

UML Diagram For Facade Design Pattern

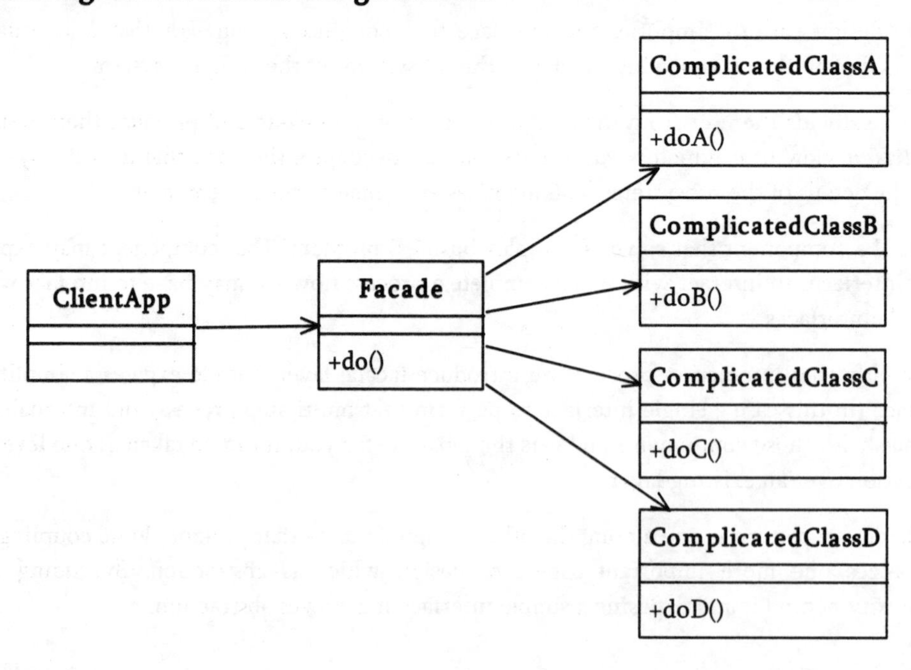

This UML diagram shows that, there can be any number of classes involved in this *Facade* system. There is one client, one facade, and multiple classes underneath the facade. In a typical situation, the facade would have a limited amount of actual code, making calls to lower layers most of the time.

Provide a simplified interface to a set of interfaces in a subsystem. Facade defines a higher-level interface that makes the subsystem easier to use.

The classes and/or objects participating in this pattern are:

- *Facade*: It knows which subsystem classes are responsible for a request and delegates client requests to appropriate subsystem objects.
- *Subsystem classes*: They implement subsystem functionality and handles work assigned by the Facade object. They have no knowledge of the facade and keep no reference to it.

Facade Design Pattern Implementation

Let's try to understand the facade pattern using a simple example (Graphical User Interface, GUI). Any typical GUI will have a title, menu items and content to be shown in the middle content area. To provide these features we can have different classes as shown below.

```
public class GUIMenu{
    public void drawMenuButtons() { }
}
public class GUITitleBar{
    public void showTitleBar(String caption) { }
}
public class GUIContent{
    public void showButtons() { }
    public  void showTextFields() { }
    public  void setDefaultValues() { }
}
```

Now, to create a simple GUI the users have to think about all these classes. To make it simple, what we can do is create another class which combines all these into a single interface (facade).

```
public class MyGUI{
   private GUIMenu menu;
   private GUITitleBar titleBar;
   private GUIContent content;
   public MyGUI(){
        menu = new GUIMenu();
```

```
        titleBar = new GUITitleBar();
        content = new GUIContent();
    }
      public void drawGUI()   {
        content.showButtons();
        content.showTextFields();
        content.setDefaultValues();
        menu.drawMenuButtons();
        titleBar.showTitleBar("Title of the GUI");
      }
  }
```

To create a GUI, users can simply use the MyGUI class with one simple call as shown below.

```
public class TestFacade {
    public static void main(String args[]) {
        MyGUI facade = new MyGUI();
        facade.drawGUI();
    }
}
```

In this way the implementation is left to the façade. The client is given just one interface and can access only that. This hides all the complexities. All in all, the *Façade* pattern hides the complexities of system from the client and provides a simpler interface.

Looking from other side, the facade also provides the implementation to be changed without affecting the client code.

When To Use Facade Design Pattern?

Use Facade design pattern when:

- You want to provide a simple interface to a complex subsystem. Subsystems often get more complex as they evolve. Most patterns, when applied, result in more and smaller classes. This makes the subsystem more reusable and easier to customize, but it also becomes harder to use for clients that don't need to customize it. A facade can provide a simple default view of the subsystem that is good enough for most clients. Only clients needing more customizability will need to look beyond the facade.
- There are many dependencies between clients and the implementation classes of an abstraction. Introduce a facade to decouple the subsystem from clients and other subsystems, thereby promoting subsystem independence and portability.

- You want to layer your subsystems. Use a facade to define an entry point to each subsystem level. If subsystems are dependent, then you can simplify the dependencies between them by making them communicate with each other solely through their facades.

Notes On Facade Design Pattern

- Just for the sake of introducing a facade layer do not create additional classes. Layered architecture is good but assesses the need for every layer. Just naming a class as TestFacade.java doesn't really make it a facade.
- Creating a java class and *forcing* the UI to interact with other layers through it and calling it a facade layer is one more popular mistake. Facade layer should not be forced and it's always optional. If the client wishes to interact with components directly it should be allowed to bypass the facade layer.
- Methods in facade layer have only one or two lines which calls the other components. If facade is going to be so simple it invalidates its purpose and clients can directly do that by themselves.
- A controller is not a facade.
- Facade is *not* a layer that imposes security and hides important data and implementation.
- Don't create a facade layer in advance. If you feel that in future the subsystem is going to evolve and become complicated to defend that do not create a stub class and name it a facade. After the subsystem has become complex you can implement the facade design pattern.
- Subsystems are not aware of facade and there should be no reference for facade in subsystems.
- Provides a unified interface to a set of interfaces in a subsystem.
- Defines a higher-level interface that makes the subsystem easier to use.
- Provides a single, simplified interface to the more general facilities of a subsystem.
- Clients communicate with the subsystem by sending requests to Facade, which forwards them to the appropriate subsystem object(s).
- Although the subsystem objects perform the actual work, the facade may have to do work of its own to translate its interface to subsystem interfaces.
- Clients that use the facade don't have to access its subsystem objects directly.

Summary Of Facade Design Pattern

- Facade provides a single interface.

- Programmers comfort is a main purpose of facade.
- Simplicity is the aim of facade pattern.
- Facade design pattern is used for promoting subsystem independence and portability.
- Subsystem may be dependent with one another. In such case, facade can act as a coordinator and decouple the dependencies between the subsystems.
- Translating data to suit the interface of a subsystem is done by the facade.

Question: What is the difference between Mediator and Façade design patterns?

Answer: Mediator is similar to Facade in that it abstracts functionality of existing classes. Mediator design pattern may look very similar to facade design pattern in terms of abstraction.

However, Mediator's purpose is to abstract arbitrary communication between colleague objects, often centralizing functionality that doesn't belong in any one of them. A mediator's colleagues are aware of and communicate with the mediator instead of communicating with each other directly.

In contrast, a facade abstracts the interface to subsystem objects to make them easier to use; it doesn't define new functionality, and subsystem classes don't know about it.

In the implementation of mediator pattern, subsystem or peers components are aware of the mediator and that interact with it. In the case of facade pattern, subsystems are not aware of the existence of facade. Only facade talks to the subsystems.

Question: What is the difference between Adapter and Facade Patterns?

Answer: Facade defines a new interface, whereas Adapter uses an old interface. Remember that Adapter makes two existing interfaces work together as opposed to defining an entirely new one. Adapter and Facade are both wrappers; but they are different kinds of wrappers.

The intent of Facade is to produce a simpler interface, and the intent of Adapter is to design to an existing interface. While Facade generally wraps multiple objects and Adapter wraps a single object; Facade could front-end a single complex object and Adapter could wrap several objects.

5.8 Proxy Design Pattern

Proxy means *in place of*. In attendance call, we give proxy for our friends in college, right? *Representing* or *in place of* or *on behalf of* are literal meanings of proxy and that directly explains proxy design pattern. It is one of the simplest and straight forward design patterns. Proxy pattern is an example of *structural* design patterns.

There are many different flavors of *proxy*, depending on its purpose. We may have a *protection* proxy, to control access rights to an object. A *virtual* proxy handles the case where an object might be expensive to create, and a *remote* proxy controls access to a remote object.

Examples For Proxy Design Pattern

There are many cases where we can use the proxy pattern. Let's take a scenario. Say, we want to attach an image with the E-Mail. Now, suppose this email has to be sent to millions of consumers in an E-Mail campaign. Attaching the image and sending along with the E-Mail will be a very heavy operation.

What we can do instead is, send the image as a link to one of the servlet. The place holder of the image will be sent. Once the email reaches the consumer, the image place holder will call the servlet and load the image at run time straight from the server.

Let us consider another example. Let' say we need to withdraw money to make some purchase. The way we will do it is, go to an ATM and get the money, or purchase straight with a cheque. In old days when ATMs and cheques were not available, what used to be the way?

Well, get your passbook, go to bank, get withdrawal form there, stand in a queue and withdraw money. Then go to the shop where you want to make the purchase. In this way, we can say that ATM or cheque in modern times act as proxies to the Bank.

UML Diagram For Proxy Design Pattern

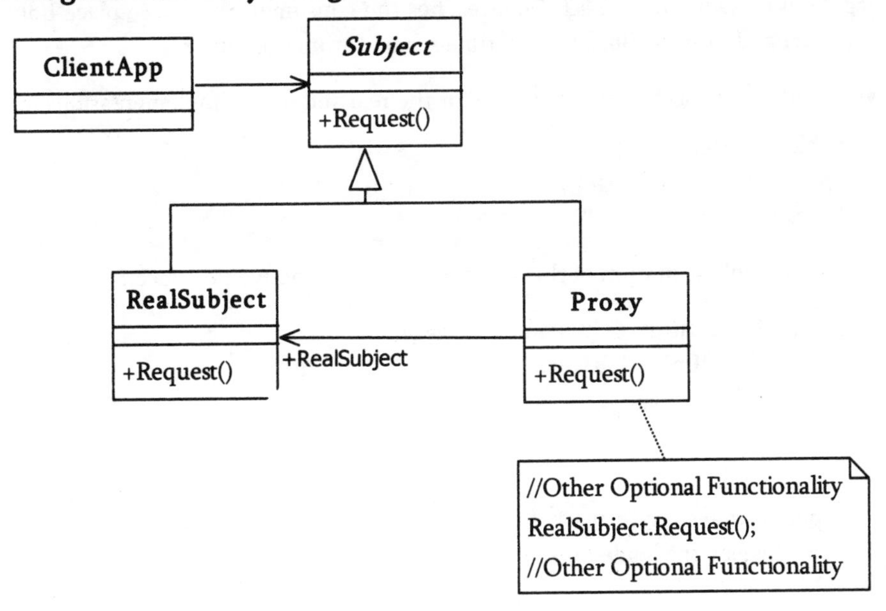

The participant's classes in the proxy pattern are:

- *Subject*: It is an interface implemented by the *RealSubject* and representing its services. The interface must be implemented by the proxy as well so that the proxy can be used in any location where the RealSubject can be used.
- *Proxy*: It maintains a reference that allows the Proxy to access the RealSubject. Proxy implements the same interface implemented by the RealSubject so that the Proxy can be substituted for the RealSubject and controls access to the RealSubject and may be responsible for its creation and deletion. Other responsibilities depend on the kind of proxy.
- *RealSubject*: It is the real object that the proxy represents.

When To Use Proxy Design Pattern?

The proxy pattern is used when we need to represent a complex object with a simpler one. If creation of object is expensive, its creation can be postponed till the very need arises and till then, a simple object can represent it. This simple object is called the *Proxy* for the complex object.

Proxy Design Pattern Implementation

For better understanding, let's take an example for implementation. Say, we want to attach an image with the E-Mail (as discussed above). Now, suppose this E-Mail has to be sent to millions of consumers in an ad-campaign. Attaching the image and sending along with the E-Mail will be a very heavy operation.

What we can do instead is, send the image as a link to one of the servlet. The place holder of the image will be sent. Once the E-Mail reaches the consumer, the image place holder will call the servlet and load the image at run time straight from the server.

First, we should create a common interface for the real and proxy implementations to use:

```
public interface Image{
  public void showImage();
}
```

The RealImage implementation of this interface works as you would expect:

```
public class RealImage implements Image{
   public RealImage(URL url)   {
      //load the image
      loadImage(url);
   }
   public void showImage()  {
      //display the loaded image
   }
```

```
        //a method that only the real image has
        public void loadImage(URL url){
            // complex operations to load image
        }
    }
```

Now the Proxy implementation can be written, which provides access to the RealImage class. Note that it's only when we call the displayImage() method that it actually uses the RealImage. Until then, we don't need the data.

```
    public class ProxyImage implements Image{
        private URL url;
        public ProxyImage(URL url)   {
            this.url = url;
        }
        //this method delegates to the real image
        public void showImage() {
            RealImage real = new RealImage(url);
            Real.showImage();
        }
    }
```

The code below illustrates a sample program; the program simply loads three images, and renders only one image, once using the proxy pattern. Note that when using the proxy pattern, the images are not loaded into memory until they needs to be rendered.

```
    public class ProxyTest {
        public static void main(String[] args) {
            // assuming that the user selects a folder that has 3 images
            //create the 3 images
            Image img1 = new ProxyImage ("TestFolder/Image1.jpeg");
            Image img2 = new ProxyImage ("TestFolder/Image2.jpeg");
            Image img3 = new ProxyImage ("TestFolder/Image3.jpeg");
            // assume that the user clicks on Image one item in a list
            // this would cause the program to call showImage() for that image only
            // note that in this case only image one was loaded into memory
            img1.showImage();
        }
    }
```

Notes On Proxy Design Pattern

- Also Known As *surrogate*

- One reason for controlling access to an object is to defer the full cost of its creation and *initialization* until we actually need to use it.
- Proxy is applicable whenever there is a need for *sophisticated reference to an object* than a simple pointer.
- Remote proxy can hide the fact that an object resides in a different address space.
- *Virtual* proxy creates expensive objects on demand.
- *Protection proxy* controls access to the original object. Protection proxies are useful when objects should have different access rights.
- Provides an interface *identical* to Subject's so that a proxy can be substituted for the real subject.
- Controls access to the *real subject* and may be *responsible* for creating and deleting it.
- Proxy *forwards* requests *to* RealSubject when appropriate, depending on the kind of proxy.

Question: What is the difference between decorator and proxy patterns?

Answer: Decorator, like Proxy, is also a stand-in for another class, and it also has the same interface as that class, usually because it is a subclass. The intent is different, however. The purpose of the Decorator pattern is to extend the functionality of the original class in a way that is transparent to the client class.

Question: What is the difference between adapter and proxy patterns?

Answer: An adapter provides a different interface to the object it adapts. In contrast, a proxy provides the same interface as its subject. However, a proxy used for access protection might refuse to perform an operation that the subject will perform, so its interface may be effectively a subset of the subject's.

5.9 Flyweight pattern

Flyweight reduces the cost of creating and manipulating a large number of similar objects. Flyweight is used when there is a need to create large number of objects which are in similar nature. Large number of objects consumes high memory and flyweight design pattern gives a solution to reduce the load on memory by sharing objects. It is achieved by isolating object properties into two types *intrinsic* and *extrinsic*.

Consider, for example, a game of war, where there are a large number of soldier objects. Assume a *Soldier* object maintain the graphical representation of a soldier, soldier behavior such as motion, and firing weapons, in addition soldiers health and location on the war terrain. Creating a large number of soldier objects is a necessity however it would incur a huge memory cost. To solve these kind of issues Flyweight pattern is used.

Sharing is the key in flyweight pattern and we need to decide if this pattern can be applied or not.

How To Apply Flyweight?

The object which we are going to create in large number should be analyzed before going for flyweight. Idea is to create lesser number of objects by reusing the same objects. Create smaller groups of objects and they should be reused by sharing. Closely look at objects properties and they can be isolated as two types intrinsic and extrinsic. Sharing is judged with respect to a context.

Let's take the example of editors. Consider a simple text editor where we can use only alphabet set A to Z. If we are going to create 100 page document using this editor we may have 200000 (2000 X 100) characters (assuming 2000 characters / page). Without flyweight we will create 200000 objects to have fine grained control. With such fine control, every character can have its own characteristics like color, font, size, etc. How do we apply flyweight here?

Intrinsic and Extrinsic State

Create only 26 objects for (A to Z) mapping every unique characters. These 26 objects will have intrinsic state as its character. That is object *'a'* will have state as character *'a'*. Then what happens to color, font and size? Those are the extrinsic state and will be passed by client code. 26 objects will be in store; client code will get the needed character/object and pass the extrinsic state to it with respect to the context. With respect to context means, *'a'* in first line may come in red color and the same character may come in blue color in different line.

UML For Flyweight Design Pattern

The participant's classes in the proxy pattern are:

- *Flyweight* - Declares an interface through which flyweights can receive and act on extrinsic state.
- *ConcreteFlyweight* - Implements the Flyweight interface and stores intrinsic state. A ConcreteFlyweight object must be sharable. The Concrete flyweight object must maintain state that it is intrinsic to it, and must be able to manipulate state that is extrinsic.
- *FlyweightFactory* - The factory creates and manages flyweight objects. In addition the factory ensures sharing of the flyweight objects. The factory maintains a pool of different flyweight objects and returns an object from the pool if it is already created, adds one to the pool and returns it in case it is new.
- *Client* - A client maintains references to flyweights in addition to computing and maintaining extrinsic state.

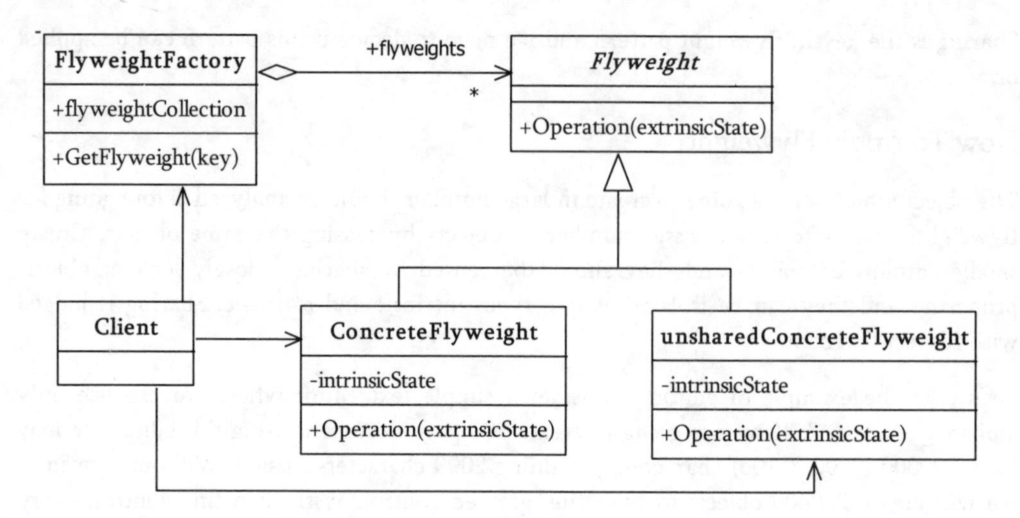

Flyweight Design Pattern Implementation

The object with intrinsic state is called flyweight object. When we implement flyweight we create concrete objects and have the intrinsic state stored in that. To create those concrete objects we will have factory and that is called Flyweight factory. This factory is to ensure that the objects are shared and we don't end up creating duplicate objects.

Let us take an example scenario of drawing. We need to draw different geometrical shapes like rectangles and ovals in huge number. Every shape may vary in color, size, fill type, font used. For implementation sake let's limit our shapes to two rectangle and oval. Every shape will be accompanied by a label which directly maps it with the shape. That is all rectangles will have label as '*R*' and all ovals will have label as '*O*'.

Now our flyweight will have intrinsic state as label only. Therefore we will have only two flyweight objects. The varying properties color, size, fill type and font will be extrinsic. We will have a flyweight factory that will maintain the two flyweight objects and distribute to client accordingly. There will be an interface for the flyweights to implement so that we will have a common blueprint and that is the flyweight interface.

Client code will use random number generators to create extrinsic properties. We are not storing the extrinsic properties anywhere; we will calculate on the fly and pass it. Use of random number generator is for convenience.

```
public interface MyShape {
  public void draw(Graphics g, int x, int y, int width, int height,
                    Color color, boolean fill, String font);
}

public class MyOval implements MyShape {

  private String label;
```

```
  public MyOval(String label) {
    this.label = label;
  }

  public void draw(Graphics oval, int x, int y, int width, int height,
                   Color color, boolean fill, String font) {
    oval.setColor(color);
    oval.drawOval(x, y, width, height);
    oval.setFont(new Font(font, 12, 12));
    oval.drawString(label, x + (width / 2), y);
    if (fill)
      oval.fillOval(x, y, width, height);
  }
}

public class MyRectangle implements MyShape {
  private String label;

  public MyRectangle(String label) {
    this.label = label;
  }

  public void draw(Graphics rectangle, int x, int y, int width, int height,
                   Color color, boolean fill, String font) {
    rectangle.setColor(color);
    rectangle.drawRect(x, y, width, height);
    rectangle.setFont(new Font(font, 12, 12));
    rectangle.drawString(label, x + (width / 2), y);
    if (fill)
      rectangle.fillRect(x, y, width, height);
  }
}

public class ShapeFactory {
  private static final HashMap shapes = new HashMap();

  public static MyShape getShape(String label) {
    MyShape concreteShape = (MyShape) shapes.get(label);
    if (concreteShape == null) {
      if (label.equals("R")) {
        concreteShape = new MyRectangle(label);
      } else if (label.equals("O")) {
        concreteShape = new MyOval(label);
      }
```

```
            shapes.put(label, concreteShape);
        }
        return concreteShape;
    }
}

public class Client extends JFrame {
    private static final int WIDTH = 300;
    private static final int HEIGHT = 300;
    private static final String shapes[] = { "R", "O" };
    private static final Color colors[] = { Color.red, Color.green, Color.blue };
    private static final boolean fill[] = { true, false };
    private static final String font[] = { "Arial", "Courier" };

    public Client() {
        Container contentPane = getContentPane();

        JButton startButton = new JButton("Draw Shapes");
        final JPanel panel = new JPanel();

        contentPane.add(panel, BorderLayout.CENTER);
        contentPane.add(startButton, BorderLayout.SOUTH);
        setSize(WIDTH, WIDTH);
        setDefaultCloseOperation(JFrame.EXIT_ON_CLOSE);
        setVisible(true);

        startButton.addActionListener(new ActionListener() {
            public void actionPerformed(ActionEvent event) {

                Graphics g = panel.getGraphics();
                for (int i = 0; i < 100; ++i) {
                    MyShape shape = ShapeFactory.getShape(getRandomShape());
                    shape.draw(g, getRandomX(), getRandomY(), getRandomWidth(),
                        getRandomHeight(), getRandomColor(),
                        getRandomFill(), getRandomFont());
                }
            }
        });
    }

    private String getRandomShape() {
        return shapes[(int) (Math.random() * shapes.length)];
    }

    private int getRandomX() {
        return (int) (Math.random() * WIDTH);
```

```
    }
    private int getRandomY() {
      return (int) (Math.random() * HEIGHT);
    }
    private int getRandomWidth() {
      return (int) (Math.random() * (WIDTH / 7));
    }
    private int getRandomHeight() {
      return (int) (Math.random() * (HEIGHT / 7));
    }
    private Color getRandomColor() {
      return colors[(int) (Math.random() * colors.length)];
    }
    private boolean getRandomFill() {
      return fill[(int) (Math.random() * fill.length)];
    }
    private String getRandomFont() {
      return font[(int) (Math.random() * font.length)];
    }
    public static void main(String[] args) {
      Client client = new Client();
    }
}
```

When To Use Flyweight Design Pattern?

We need to consider following factors when choosing flyweight,

- Need to create large number of objects.
- Because of the large number when memory cost is a constraint.
- When most of the object attributes can be made external and shared.
- The application must not mandate unique objects, as after implementation same object will be used repeatedly.
- Its better when extrinsic state can be computed rather than stored.

Flyweight is all about memory and sharing. Nowadays an average desktop comes with 500 GB hard disk, 4GB RAM and with this we can stuff our whole home inside and will still have remaining space to put an elephant in it.

Do we really need to bother about memory and usage? Since the cost has come down there is no restriction to use it effectively. Think about mobile devices that are increasing every day and they still have memory constraint.

Even if we have huge memory, in some cases the application may need efficient use of it. For example assume we are working with an application that maps stars from universe. In this application if we are going to create an object for every star then think of it how much memory we will need.

As an example, consider text editors. If we create an object for every character in a file, think of it how many objects we will create for a long document. What will be the application performance?

Notes On Flyweight Design Pattern

- A *flyweight* object is a shared object that can be used in multiple contexts simultaneously.
- Flyweights cannot make assumptions about the context in which they operate.
- *Intrinsic* state is stored in the flyweight and that information is *independent* of the flyweight's context and sharable.
- *Extrinsic* state depends on and varies with the *flyweight's* context and can't be shared. Client objects are responsible for passing extrinsic state to the flyweight when it needs it.
- The *Flyweight* pattern's effectiveness depends heavily on how and where it's used. Apply the Flyweight pattern when <u>all</u> of the following are true:
    - An application uses a large number of objects.
    - Storage costs are high because of the sheer quantity of objects.
    - Most object state can be made extrinsic.
    - Many groups of objects may be replaced by relatively few shared objects once extrinsic state is removed.
    - The application doesn't depend on object identity. Since flyweight objects may be shared, identity tests will return true for conceptually distinct objects.
- The *more* flyweights are shared, the *greater* the storage savings. The savings increase with the amount of shared state.
- *Sharability* also implies some form of *reference* counting or *garbage* collection to reclaim a flyweight's storage when it's no longer needed.

Question: What is the difference between Flyweight, Façade and Composite patterns?

Answer:

- Flyweight shows how to make lots of little objects, whereas *Facade* shows how to make a single object represent an entire subsystem.
- Flyweight is often combined with *Composite* to implement shared leaf nodes.

Chapter-6

BEHAVIORAL PATTERNS

6.1 Behavioral Design Patterns

Behavioral patterns are those patterns which are specifically concerned with communication (interaction) between the objects. The interactions between the objects should be such that they are talking to each other and still are loosely coupled.

Tight coupling occurs when a group of classes are highly dependent on one another. In object oriented design, the amount of coupling refers to how much the design of one class depends on the design of another class. In other words, how often do changes in one class force related changes in other classes class?

Loose coupling is the key for architectures. In behavioral patterns, the implementations and the client which uses them should be loosely coupled in order to avoid hard-coding and dependencies.

Behavioral design patterns deals with relationships among communications using different objects. They find common communication patterns and provide a well-known solution to implement this communication giving more flexibility.

6.2 Categories Of Behavioral Design Patterns

Behavioral patterns describe not just patterns of objects or classes but also the patterns of communication between them. Behavioral patterns are used to avoid hard-coding and dependencies. Behavioral design patterns are sub-categorized into:

- Object-Behavioral patterns: Behavioral object patterns use object composition rather than inheritance. Describes how a group of objects collaborate to perform some task that no single object can perform alone.
- Class-Behavioral patterns: Behavioral class patterns uses *inheritance* rather than inheritance to describe algorithms and flow of control.

Behavioral design patterns (11 Design Patterns):

- *Chain* of *Responsibility* Pattern (CoR): A way of passing a request between a chain of objects.

- *Command* Pattern: The *Command* pattern is used when there is a need to issue requests to objects without knowing anything about the operation being requested or the receiver of the request.
- *Interpreter* Pattern: *Interpreter* provides way to include language elements in a program. Interpreter pattern is a design pattern that specifies how to evaluate sentences in a language.
- *Iterator* Pattern: Iterators are used to access elements of an aggregate (collection) object sequentially without exposing its underlying representation.
- *Mediator* Pattern: Defines simplified communication between classes.
- *Momento* Pattern: Capture and restore an object's internal state.
- *Observer* Pattern: A way of notifying change to a number of classes.
- *State* Pattern: Changes an object's behavior when its state changes.
- *Strategy* Pattern: Encapsulates an algorithm inside a class.
- *Template Method* Pattern: Defer the exact steps of an algorithm to a subclass.
- *Visitor* Pattern: Defines a new operation to a class without change.

Object-Behavioral Patterns	Class-Behavioral Patterns
Chain of Responsibility Command Iterator Mediator Memento Observer State Strategy Visitor	Interpreter Template Method

6.3 Chain of Responsibility Design Pattern

Chain of Responsibility (CoR) is an example for behavioral design patterns. Chain of responsibility is a design pattern where a sender sends a request to a chain of objects, where the *objects* in the *chain* decide themselves who to honor the request. If an object in the chain decides not to serve the request, it forwards the request to the next object in the chain.

Chain of responsibility helps to decouple sender of a request and receiver of the request with some trade-offs. Decoupling is one of the important aspect in software design. This allows us to achieve complete decoupling between the sender and the receiver. A *sender* is an object that invokes an operation, and a *receiver* is an object that receives the request to execute a certain operation. With decoupling, the sender has no knowledge of the receivers interface.

In CoR, responsibility is outsourced. In a chain of objects, the responsibility of deciding who to serve the request is left to the objects participating in the chains. It is similar to passing the question in a quiz scenario. When the quiz master asks a question to a person, if he/she doesn't know the answer, he/she passes the question to next person and so on. When one person answers the question, the passing flow stops. Sometimes, the passing might reach the last person and still nobody gives the answer.

Problems With Chain of Responsibility

There may be scenarios where a node is capable of solving the request but may not get a chance for it. Though there is a candidate who can solve the problem, but since nobody forwarded the request to it, it was not given a chance to serve and final result is the request goes unattended failure. This happens because of improper chain sequence. A chain sequence may not be suitable for all scenarios.

In object oriented design generally, every object is responsible for all its behavior. Behavior of an object is not transferred to other objects and is enclosed within itself. In chain of responsibility, some percentage of behavior is offloaded to third party objects.

Examples For Chain of Responsibility

Few examples for chain of responsibility patterns are: Coin sorting machine, ATM money dispenser, Servlet Filter and finally Javas own Exception Handling mechanism. We know exception handling better than anybody else and we are daily living with it. This qualifies as the best example for chain of responsibility.

In Java, we may have sequence of exceptions listed in catch statements and when there is an exception thrown, the catch list is scanned one by one from top. If first exception in catch can handle it the job is done, else the responsibility is moved to next in line and so on till it reaches finally block if we have one.

```
try {
    FileInputStream fin = new FileInputStream(f);
    BufferedReader br = new BufferedReader(new InputStreamReader(fin), "ASCII");
    String line = br.readLine();
    line = line.trim();
    int number = Integer.parseInt(line);
    br.close();
    //Few other actions
    return number;
} catch (FileNotFoundException fnf) {
    displayErrorMessage(fnf.getMessage());
} catch (IOException ioex) {
```

```
        displayErrorMessage(ioex.getMessage());
    } catch (NumberFormatException nfe) {
        displayErrorMessage("The file contained invalid data");
    }
    return -1; // If we get here, we didn't read a number from the file
```

In this example, the first line of the try block can throw a *FileNotFoundException* and some of the later lines can throw an *IOException*. Additionally, there is one line that can throw a *NumberFormatException*. The call to line.trim() can't actually throw any of these exceptions, but it doesn't matter: we can still include it in the same try block to avoid having to make our code messy with multiple try/catch blocks.

Unix operating system has many cool features and one of the most well-known is the pipe, which lets us create combinations of commands by piping one command's output to another's input. For example, suppose we want to list all source files from the given directory that invoke or define a method named *execute*(). Here is one way to do that with a pipe:

```
grep "execute(" `find $DIR_NAME -name "*.java"` | awk -F: '{print }'
```

The *grep* command searches files for regular expressions; here, we used it to find occurrences of the string *execute*(in files unearthed by the find command. grep's output is piped into awk, which prints the first token—delimited by a colon—in each line of grep's output (a vertical bar signifies a pipe). That token is a filename, so we end up with a list of filenames that contain the string *execute*(.

Now that we have a list of filenames, we can use another pipe to sort the list:

```
grep "execute(" `find $STRUTS_SRC_DIR -name "*.java"` | awk -F: '{print }' | sort
```

This time, we have piped the list of filenames to sort. What if we want to know how many files contain the string *execute*(? It is easy with another pipe:

```
grep "execute(" `find $STRUTS_SRC_DIR -name "*.java"` | awk -F: '{print }' | sort -u | wc -l
```

The *wc* command counts words, lines, and bytes. In this case, we specified the $-l$ option to count lines, one line for each file. We also added a $-u$ option to sort to ensure uniqueness for each filename (the $-u$ option filters out duplicates).

Pipes are powerful because they let us dynamically compose a chain of operations. Software systems often employ the equivalent of pipes (e.g., email filters or a set of filters for a servlet). At the heart of pipes and filters lies a design pattern: Chain of Responsibility (CoR).

UML Diagram For Chain of Responsibility Design Pattern

In the diagram above some explanations are needed on what is the role of every class:

- *Handler* - defines an interface for handling requests
- *ConcreteHandler* - handles the requests it is responsible for. If it can handle the request it does so, otherwise it sends the request to its successor.
- *Client* - sends commands to the first object in the chain that may handle the command.

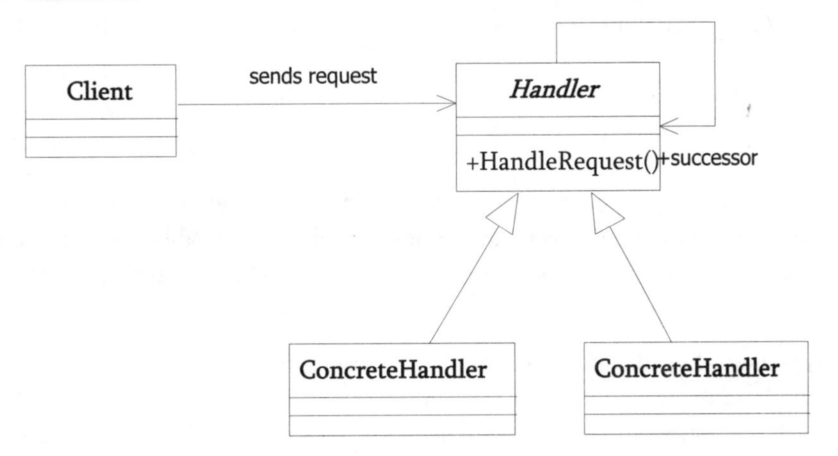

CoR Implementation

The Chain of Responsibility pattern uses a chain of objects to handle a request, which is typically an event. Objects in the chain forward the request along the chain until one of the objects handles the event. Processing stops after an event is handled.

Those restrictions, of course, are for a classic CoR implementation. In practice, those rules are bent; for example, servlet filters are a CoR implementation that allows multiple filters to process an HTTP request.

Typically, request handlers are extensions of a base class that maintains a reference to the next handler in the chain, known as the successor. The base class might implement handleRequest () like this:

```
public abstract class HandlerBase {
    ...
    public void handleRequest(SomeRequestObject sro) {
      if(successor != null)
          successor.handleRequest(sro);
    }
}
```

So by default, handlers pass the request to the next handler in the chain. A concrete extension of HandlerBase might look like this:

```
public class SpamFilter extends HandlerBase {
```

```
    public void handleRequest(SomeRequestObject mailMessage) {
      if(isSpam(mailMessage))   { // If the message is spam
        // take spam-related action. Do not forward message.
      }
      else { // Message is not spam.
        super.handleRequest(mailMessage); // Pass message to next filter in chain.
      }
    }
  }
```

The SpamFilter handles the request if the message is spam, and therefore, the request goes no further; otherwise, messages are passed to the next handler, presumably another email filter looking to weed them out. Eventually, the last filter in the chain might store the message after it passes muster by moving through several filters.

Note the hypothetical email filters discussed above are mutually exclusive: Ultimately, only one filter handles a request. We might opt to turn that inside out by letting multiple filters handle a single request, which is a better analogy to UNIX pipes. Either way, the underlying engine is the CoR pattern.

Now let us consider the following example code which gives a sample implementation of chain of responsibility. The following code illustrates the pattern with the example of a logging class. Each logging handler decides if any action is to be taken at this log level and then passes the message on to the next logging handler. Note that this example should not be seen as a recommendation on how to write logging classes.

Also, note that in a *pure* implementation of the chain of responsibility pattern, a logger would not pass responsibility further down the chain after handling a message. In this example, a message will be passed down the chain whether it is handled or not.

```
abstract class Logger {
    public static int ERR = 3;
    public static int NOTICE = 5;
    public static int DEBUG = 7;
    protected int mask;

    // The next element in the chain
    protected Logger next;

    public Logger setNext(Logger log) {
        next = log;
        return log;
    }

    public void message(String msg, int priority) {
        if (priority <= mask) {
```

```
            writeMessage(msg);
        }
        if (next != null) {
            next.message(msg, priority);
        }
    }

    abstract protected void writeMessage(String msg);
}

class StdoutLogger extends Logger {
    public StdoutLogger(int mask) {
        this.mask = mask;
    }

    protected void writeMessage(String msg) {
        System.out.println("Writing to stdout: " + msg);
    }
}

class EmailLogger extends Logger {
    public EmailLogger(int mask) {
        this.mask = mask;
    }

    protected void writeMessage(String msg) {
        System.out.println("Sending via email: " + msg);
    }
}

class StderrLogger extends Logger {
    public StderrLogger(int mask) {
        this.mask = mask;
    }

    protected void writeMessage(String msg) {
        System.err.println("Sending to stderr: " + msg);
    }
}

public class ChainOfResponsibilityExample {
    public static void main(String[] args) {

        // Build the chain of responsibility
        Logger logger, logger1,logger2;
        logger = new StdoutLogger(Logger.DEBUG);
        logger1 = logger.setNext(new EmailLogger(Logger.NOTICE));
```

```
        logger2 = logger1.setNext(new StderrLogger(Logger.ERR));

        // Handled by StdoutLogger
        logger.message("Entering function y.", Logger.DEBUG);

        // Handled by StdoutLogger and EmailLogger
        logger.message("Step1 completed.", Logger.NOTICE);

        // Handled by all three loggers
        logger.message("An error has occurred.", Logger.ERR);
    }
}
```

When To Use Chain Of Responsibility?

- Sender will not know which object in the chain will serve its request.
- Everyone (object) in chain will have the responsibility to decide, if they can serve the request.
- If object (or node) decides to forward the request, it should be capable of choosing the next node and forward it.
- There is a possibility where none of the node may serve the request (some requests might not get handled).
- Multiple objects, determined at runtime, are candidates to handle a request.

6.4 Command Design Pattern

Command pattern (also known as *Action, Transaction*) is an object behavioral pattern. This allows us to achieve complete decoupling between the sender and the receiver. A *sender* is an object that invokes an operation, and a *receiver* is an object that receives the request to execute a certain operation. With decoupling, the sender has no knowledge of the receivers interface. The term *request* refers to the command that is to be executed.

UML Diagram For Command Design Pattern

Three terms always associated with the command pattern are *client*, *invoker* and *receiver*.

- *Command*: It declares an interface for executing an operation.
- *ConcreteCommand:* Defines a binding between a receiver object and an action. It implements *Execute*() by invoking the corresponding operation(s) on receiver.
- *Client*: The *client* instantiates the command object and provides the information required to call the method at a later time.
- *Invoker*: The *invoker* decides when the method should be called.
- *Receiver*: The *receiver* is an instance of the class that contains the method's code. That means, it knows how to perform the operations associated with carrying out a request. Any class may serve as a receiver.

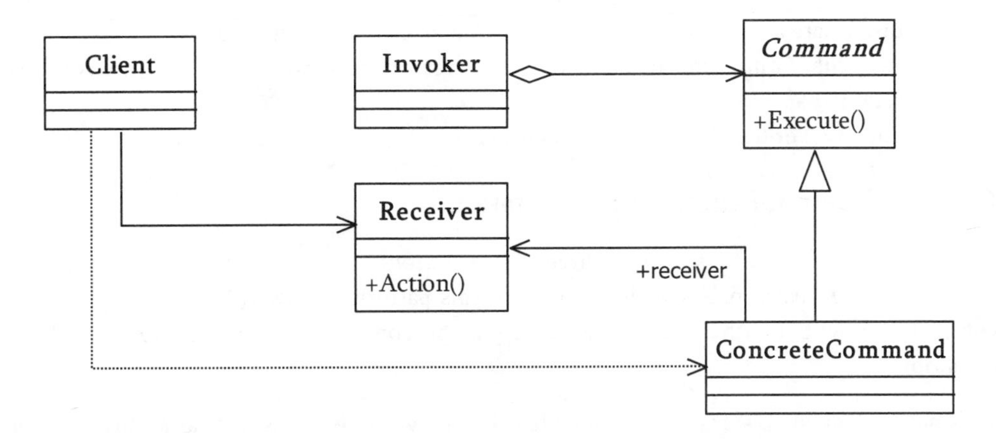

Examples For Command Design Pattern

- *Multi – level undo*: If all user actions in a program are implemented as command objects, the program can keep a stack of the most recently executed commands. When the user wants to undo a command, the program simply pops the most recent command object and executes its undo () method.
- *Transactional behavior*: Similar to *undo*, a database engine or software installer may keep a list of operations that have been or will be performed. Should one of them fail, all others can be reverted or discarded (usually called *rollback*). For example, if two database tables which refer to each other must be updated, and the second update fails, the transaction can be rolled back, so that the first table does not now contain an invalid reference.
- *Progress bars*:Suppose a program has a sequence of commands that it executes in order. If each command object has a getEstimatedDuration() method, the program can easily estimate the total duration. It can show a progress bar that meaningfully reflects how close the program is to completing all the tasks.
- *Networking*: It is possible to send whole command objects across the network to be executed on the other machines, for example player actions in computer games.

Steps For Creating Command Design Pattern

The client creates a *ConcreteCommand* object and specifies its *receiver*. An *Invoker* object stores the ConcreteCommand object. The invoker issues a request by calling *Execute* on the command. When commands are undoable, *ConcreteCommand* stores state for undoing the command prior to invoking *Execute*. The *ConcreteCommand* object invokes operations on its receiver to carry out the request. Command decouples the invoker from the receiver (and the request it carries out).

1. Define a *Command* interface with a method signature like execute().
2. Create one or more derived classes that encapsulate some subset of the following: a *receiver* object, the method to invoke, the arguments to pass.

3. Instantiate a *Command* object for each deferred execution request.
4. Pass the *Command* object from the creator (aka *client*) to the invoker (aka *receiver*).
5. The invoker decides when to *execute*().

Command Design Pattern Implementation

In this section we will design the three classes (*client*, *invoker* and *receiver*) related to command design pattern. A classic example of this pattern is a *switch*. In this example we configure the switch with 2 commands: to turn an air conditioner *on* and to turn *off* the air conditioner.

Let's have a look at this example with code. The below *Switch* class acts as an invoker. Our objective is to develop a *Switch* that can turn either object on or off. We see that the *AirConditioner* have different interfaces, which means the *Switch* has to be independent of the *receiver* interface.

When the *start*() and *stop*() operations are called, they will simply make the appropriate command to *execute*( ). The *Switch* will have no idea what happens as a result of *execute*( ) being called. *Switch* is called the invoker because it invokes the execute operation in the command interface.

```
/* Invoker class: Switch */
public class Switch {
  private List<Command> commandHistory = new ArrayList<Command>();

  public Switch() {
  }

  public void storeAndExecute(Command cmd) {
    this.commandHistory.add(cmd); // optional
    cmd.execute();
  }
}
```

Below code shows the *receiver* class and contains the method's code.

```
/*Receiver class: AirConditioner */
public class AirConditioner {
  public AirConditioner() { }

  public void start() {
    System.out.println("The Air Conditioner is on");
  }

  public void stop() {
    System.out.println("The Air Conditioner is off");
```

```
    }
}
```

The *Command* pattern convert the request itself into an object. This object can be stored and passed like other objects. The key to command pattern is a *Command* interface. Command interface declares an interface for executing operations.

```
/*Command interface*/
public interface Command {
  void execute();
}
```

Each concrete *Command* class specifies a receiver-action by storing the receiver (*AirConditioner*) as an instance variable. It provides different implementations of the *execute*() method to invoke the request. The receiver has the knowledge required to carry out the request.

The concrete commands, *StartCommand* and *StopCommand*, implements the execute operation of the command interface. It has the knowledge to call the appropriate receiver object's operation. It acts as an adapter in this case.

By the term adapter, I mean that the concrete *Command* object is a simple connector, connecting the *invoker* and the *receiver* with different interfaces.

Concrete Command for turning on the air conditioner:

```
/*Concrete Command for turning on the Air Conditioner*/
public class StartCommand implements Command {
  private AirConditioner theAirConditioner;

  public StartCommand(AirConditioner airConditioner) {
    this.theAirConditioner = airConditioner;
  }

  public void execute(){
    theAirConditioner.start();
  }
}
```

Concrete Command for turning off the air conditioner:

```
/*Concrete Command for turning off the Air Conditioner*/
public class StopCommand implements Command {
  private AirConditioner theAirConditioner;

  public StopCommand(AirConditioner airConditioner) {
    this.theAirConditioner = airConditioner;
  }
```

```
        public void execute() {
            theAirConditioner.stop();
        }
    }

    public class PressSwitch {
        public static void main(String[] args){
            AirConditioner  lamp = new AirConditioner();
            Command switchOn = new StartCommand(lamp);
            Command switchOff = new StopCommand(lamp);

            Switch sw = new Switch();

            try {
                if (args[0].equalsIgnoreCase("ON")) {
                    sw.storeAndExecute(switchOn);
                    System.exit(0);
                }
                if (args[0].equalsIgnoreCase("OFF")) {
                    sw.storeAndExecute(switchOff);
                    System.exit(0);
                }

                System.out.println("Argument \"ON\" or \"OFF\" is required.");
            } catch (Exception e) {
                System.out.println("Arguments required.");
            }
        }
    }
```

A benefit of this implementation of the command pattern is that the switch can be used with any device, not just an air conditioner - the Switch in the following example turns an air conditioner on and off, but the Switch's constructor can accept any subclasses of Command. For example, we could configure the *Switch* to start an engine or to turn a light *on*.

Notice in the code example above that the *Command* pattern completely decouples the object that invokes the operation (*Switch*) from the ones having the knowledge to perform it (*AirConditioner*).

When To Use Command Design Pattern?

Use the Command pattern when you want to:

- *Parameterize objects* by an action to perform. Commands are an object-oriented replacement for callbacks.

- *Specify, queue, and execute requests at different times*. A Command object can have a lifetime independent of the original request. If the receiver of a request can be represented in an address space-independent way, then you can transfer a command object for the request to a different process and fulfill the request there.
- *Support undo*. The Command's Execute operation can store state for reversing its effects in the command itself. The Command interface must have an added *Unexecute* operation that reverses the effects of a previous call to Execute. Executed commands are stored in a history list. Unlimited-level undo and redo is achieved by traversing this list backwards and forwards calling *Unexecute* and *Execute*, respectively.
- *Support logging changes* so that they can be reapplied in case of a *system crash*. By augmenting the Command interface with load and store operations, you can keep a persistent log of changes. Recovering from a crash involves reloading logged commands from disk and re-executing them with the Execute operation.
- *Structure a system around high-level operations built on primitives operations*. Such a structure is common in information systems that support transactions. A transaction encapsulates a set of changes to data. The Command pattern offers a way to model transactions. Commands have a common interface, letting you invoke all transactions the same way. The pattern also makes it easy to extend the system with new transactions.

Notes On Command Design Pattern

- *Intent*: Encapsulate a request as an object, thereby letting you parameterize clients with different requests, queue or log requests, and support undoable operations.
- To issue requests to objects without knowing anything about the operation being requested or the receiver of the request.
- *Consequences*:
  - Command *decouples* the object that invokes the operation from the one that knows how to perform it. i.e. decouple invoker from receiver
  - *Commands are first – class objects*. They can be manipulated and extended like any other object.
  - We can assemble commands into a *composite command*. In general, composite commands are an instance of the Composite pattern.
  - It's easy *to add new Commands*, because we don't have to change existing classes.

Question: What is the difference between *Command* and *Chain of Responsibility* patterns?

Answer: *Command* pattern is different from the *Chain of Responsibility* in a way that, in the CoR (*Chain of Responsibility*), the request passes through each of the objects (in the chain) before finding an object that can take the responsibility. The command pattern however finds the particular object according to the command and invokes only that one.

6.5 Interpreter Design Pattern

Interpreter pattern is an example for behavioral design patterns. Interpreter pattern is a design pattern that specifies how to evaluate sentences in a language. Interpreter pattern is an application of Composite.

Given a language, Interpreter pattern defines a representation for its grammar along with an interpreter that uses the representation to interpret sentences in the language.

Example For Interpreter Design Pattern

The classical example for the interpreter pattern is the one of interpreting the roman numerals. The expression to be interpreted is a string which is put in the context. The context consists of the remaining unparsed Roman numeral string and of the result of the numeral that are already parsed.

The context is passed to one of sub-interpreters based on the type of interpreting (*Thousand*, *Hundred*, *Ten* and *One*). In this example it is using only *TerminalExpressions*. The following participant classes are involved in this example:

- *Context*: This keeps the current string that has to be parsed and the decimal that contains the conversion already done. Initially the context keeps the full string that has to be converted and 0 for the output decimal.
- *Expression*: Consists of the interpret method which receives the context. Based on the current object it uses specific values for Thousand, Hundred, Ten, One and a specific multiplier.
- *ThousandExpression*, *HundredExpression*, *TenExpression*, *OneExpression* (*TerminalExpression*): These classes are usued to define each specific expression. Ussualy, the TerminalExpression classes implement the interpret method. In our case the method is already defined in the base Expression class and each TerminalExpression class defines its behavior by implementing the abstract methods: one, four(), five(), nine(), multiplier(). It is a template method pattern.
- *Main* (Client): In our example this class is responsible to build the syntax tree representing a specific sentence in the language defined by the grammar. After the syntax tree is built the *main* method invoks the interpret method.

UML Diagram For Interpreter Design Pattern

The UML class diagram below describes the *Interpreter* method design pattern. The items in the diagram are described below:

- *Context*: Contains information that is global to the interpreter

- *Expression*: An abstract class with an abstract method called *interpret*. It declares an interface for executing an operation
- *TerminalExpression*: This is the terminal expression.
- *NonTerminalExpressions*: Implements logical operators (OR, AND) between two terminal or non-terminal expressions.
- *Client*: Builds the abstract tree and invokes the *interpret* method of the Interpreter tree.

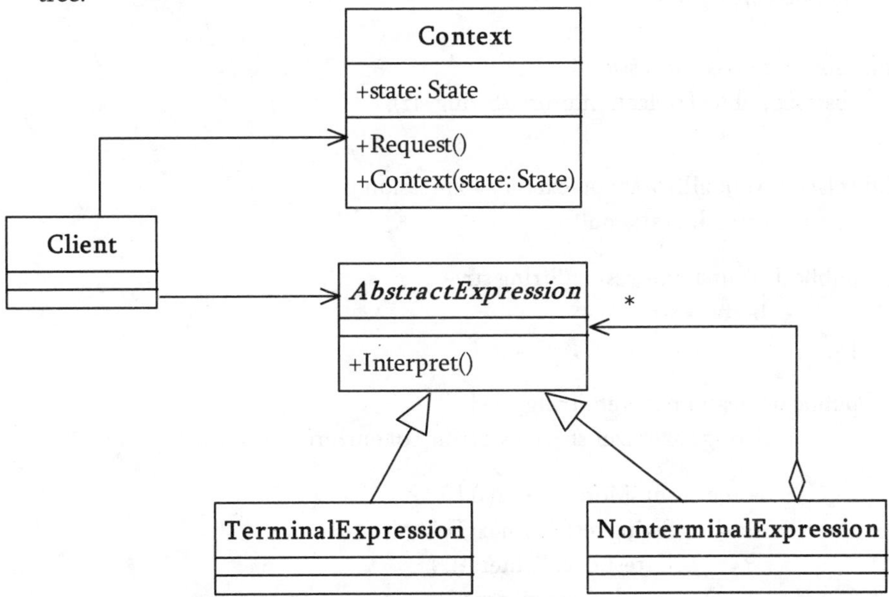

Steps for Creating Interpreter Design Pattern

- Define a grammar for the language.
- Relate each production in the grammar to a class.
- Organize the classes similar to the structure of *Composite* pattern.
- Define an *interpret*(Context) method in the *Composite* hierarchy.
- The *Context* object encapsulates the current state of the input and output as the former is parsed and the latter is accumulated. It is manipulated by each grammar class as the *interpreting* process transforms the input into the output.

Interpreter Design Pattern Implementation

As an example let us consider the rule validator. This example can be used to validate some conditions. Each expression is interpreted and the output for each expression is a boolean value. The following classes and entities are involved:

- *String* (Context): The String is used as a context. The string that has to be interpreted is parsed.
- *Expression*: An abstract class with an abstract method called *interpret*.

- *TerminalExpression*: This is the terminal expression. Only one terminal expression class is defined in our example and it returns true if a token was found there.
- *NonTerminalExpressions*: Implements logical operators(OR, AND) between 2 terminal or non terminal expressions.
- *InterpreterTest(Client)*: Builds the abstract tree and call the interpret method of the Interpreter tree.

```
public abstract class Expression {
    abstract public boolean interpret(String str);
}

public class TerminalExpression extends Expression {
    private String literal = null;

    public TerminalExpression(String str) {
        literal = str;
    }

    public boolean interpret(String str) {
        StringTokenizer st = new StringTokenizer(str);

        while (st.hasMoreTokens()) {
            String test = st.nextToken();
            if (test.equals(literal)) {
                return true;
            }
        }
        return false;
    }
}
public class OrExpression extends Expression{
    private Expression expression1 = null;
    private Expression expression2 = null;

    public OrExpression(Expression expression1, Expression expression2) {
        this.expression1 = expression1;
        this.expression2 = expression2;
    }

    public boolean interpret(String str) {
        return expression1.interpret(str) || expression2.interpret(str);
    }
}
```

```
public class AndExpression extends Expression{
        private Expression expression1 = null;
        private Expression expression2 = null;

        public AndExpression(Expression expression1, Expression expression2) {
                this.expression1 = expression1;
                this.expression2 = expression2;
        }

        public boolean interpret(String str) {
                return expression1.interpret(str) && expression2.interpret(str);
        }
}
```

This class builds the interpreter tree and defines the rule Name1 and (Name2 or (Name3 or Name4))

```
public class InterpreterTest {
        static Expression buildInterpreterTree() {
                // Literal
                Expression terminal1 = new TerminalExpression("Name1");
                Expression terminal2 = new TerminalExpression("Name2");
                Expression terminal3 = new TerminalExpression("Name3");
                Expression terminal4 = new TerminalExpression("Name4");

                // Name1 or Name3
                Expression alternation1 = new OrExpression(terminal2, terminal3);

                // Name1 or (Name2 or Name3)
                Expression alternation2 = new OrExpression(terminal1, alternation1);

                // Name1 and (Name2 or (Name3 or Name4))
                return new AndExpression(terminal4, alternation2);
        }

        public static void main(String[] args) {
                String context = "Name1 Name3";
                Expression define = buildInterpreterTree();
                System.out.println(context + " is " + define.interpret(context));
        }
}
```

Summary Of Interpreter Design Pattern

The Interpreter pattern has a limited area where it can be used. We can discuss the Interpreter pattern only in terms of formal grammars but in this area there are better solutions and this is the reason why this pattern is not so frequently used. This pattern can be applied for parsing expressions defined in simple grammars and sometimes in simple rule engines.

6.6 Iterator Design Pattern

The *Iterator* pattern is one of the most frequently used design patterns (for example programs in *Java, refer problems* of this section). The *Iterator* pattern is a behavioral object design pattern. The *Iterator* pattern allows the traversal through the elements in a group of objects (also called *collection*).

Examples For Iterator Design Pattern

The *Iterator* pattern is very useful for allowing iteration through data structures without having to worry about how the data structure is stored. In *Java*, there are iterator types associated with each container (for example, Stack, Queue, Vector, ArrayList etc...). Using these types is fine if we are iterating inside the class which defined the data structure. However, clients of class should not be exposed to the underlying data structure.

```
Vector<String> items = new Vector<String>();
  items.add("Item1");
  items.add("Item2");

  Iterator itr = items.iterator();
  while (itr.hasNext()) {
   System.out.println(itr.next());
  }
}
```

Why Iterator Design Pattern?

For example, if a class returned a list of names, stored as a vector, the client of that class might iterate through the vector like this:

```
Vector<String> items = myClassObj.getItems();
for(Iterator itr = items.iterator(); itr.hasNext();){
   System.out.println(itr.next());
}
```

In this case, the client of class now depends on the underlying data structure of *items*. If the data structure should ever change, the client must also be changed. The *Iterator* pattern makes the client loosely coupled to the *myClassObj*, and the code for iterating through a list of items might look like this:

```
NameIterator nameItr = myClassObj.getNameIterator();
```

```
while(nameItr.hasNext()){
    // Do Something
}
```

UML Diagram For Iterator Design Pattern

The participant's classes in this pattern are:

- *Iterator*: This interface represents the *AbstractIterator*, defining the iterator.
- *ConcreteIterator*: This is the implementation of Iterator (implements the Iterator interface).
- *Container*: This is an interface defining the Aggregate.
- *ConcreteContainer*: An implementation of the collection.

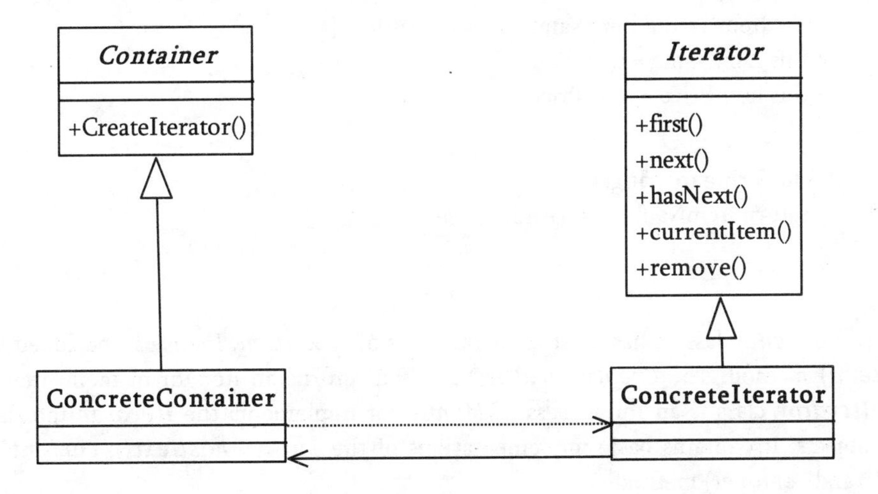

Steps For Creating Iterator Design Pattern

- Add a *createIterator*() method to the *container* class (also called *collection* class), and grant the *iterator* class privileged access.
- Design an *iterator* class that can encapsulate traversal of the *container* class.
- Clients ask the collection object to create an iterator object.
- Clients use the *first*(), *hasNext*(), *next*(), and *currentItem*() protocol to access the elements of the collection class.

When To Use Iterator Design Pattern?

Use the Iterator pattern when:

- To *access* an aggregate (also called container) object's contents *without* exposing its internal representation.
- To support *multiple traversals* of aggregate objects.

- To provide a *uniform interface* for traversing different aggregate structures (that is, to support polymorphic iteration).

Iterator Design Pattern Implementation

When writing an iterator for a class, it is very common for the iterator class to be an inner class of the class that we would like to iterate through. Let's look at an example of this. Assume that, we have an *Item* class, which represents an item on a menu. An item has a name and a price.

```
public class Item {
        String itemName;
        float itemPrice;

        public Item(String itemName, float itemPrice) {
            this.itemName = itemName;
            this.itemPrice = itemPrice;
        }

        public String toString() {
            return itemName + ": " + itemPrice;
        }
}
```

Here is the *Menu* class. It has a list of menu items of type *Item*. Items can be added via the *addItem*() method. The *CreateIterator*() method returns an iterator of menu items. The *MenuIterator* class is an inner class of *Menu* that implements the *Iterator* interface for *Item* objects. It contains basic implementations of the *first*(), *hasNext*(), *currentItem*(), *next*(), and *remove*() methods.

```
import java.util.ArrayList;
import java.util.Iterator;
import java.util.List;
public class Menu {
        List<Item> menuItems;
        public Menu() {
            menuItems = new ArrayList<Item>();
        }

        public void addItem(Item item) {
            menuItems.add(item);
        }

        public Iterator<Item> CreateIterator() {
            return new MenuIterator();
        }
```

```
        class MenuIterator implements Iterator<Item> {
            int currentIndex = 0;
            public boolean hasNext() {
                    if (currentIndex >= menuItems.size()) {
                        return false;
                    } else {
                        return true;
                    }
                }

                public Item first() {
                    return menuItems.get(0);
                }

                public Item currentItem() {
                    return menuItems.get(currentIndex);
                }

                public Item next() {
                    return menuItems.get(currentIndex++);
                }

                public void remove() {
                    menuItems.remove(--currentIndex);
                }
        }
    }
```

The *IteratorTest* class demonstrates the iterator pattern. It creates three items and adds them to the menu object. Next, it gets an Item iterator from the menu object and iterates over the items in the menu. After this, it calls *remove*() to remove the last item obtained by the iterator. Following this, it gets a new iterator object from the menu and once again iterates over the menu items.

```
import java.util.Iterator;
public class IteratorTest {
        public static void main(String[] args) {
                Item i1 = new Item("Item1", 10f);
                Item i2 = new Item("Item2", 20f);
                Item i3 = new Item("Item3", 30f);

                Menu menu = new Menu();
                menu.addItem(i1);
                menu.addItem(i2);
                menu.addItem(i3);
```

```
                System.out.println("Displaying Menu:");
                Iterator<Item> iterator = menu.CreateIterator();
                while (iterator.hasNext()) {
                        Item item = iterator.next();
                        System.out.println(item);
                }

                System.out.println("Removing last item returned");
                iterator.remove();

                System.out.println("Displaying Menu:");
                iterator = menu.iterator();
                while (iterator.hasNext()) {
                    Item item = iterator.next();
                    System.out.println(item);
                }
        }
}
```

Notes On Iterator Design Pattern

- Also known as *Cursor*.
- Provide a way to access the elements of a container object sequentially without exposing its underlying representation.
- The key idea in this pattern is to take the responsibility for access and traversal out of the container object and put it into an iterator object
- The Iterator class defines an interface for accessing the aggregate's elements.
- An *iterator* object is responsible for keeping track of the current element; that is, it knows which elements have been traversed already.
- *External iterator* (also called *Active iterator*): Client controls the iteration. Clients that use an external iterator must advance the traversal and request the next element explicitly from the iterator and it is more flexible e.g.: easy to compare two collections for equality.
- *Internal iterator*(also called *Passive Iterator*): The iterator controls iteration. The client hands an internal iterator an operation to perform, and the iterator applies that operation to every element in the aggregate and it is easier to use, because they define the iteration logic for us..

Summary Of Iterator Design Pattern

- The iterator pattern allows us to access contents of a collection without exposing its internal structure of data.
- Supports multiple simultaneous traversals of a collection. That means we can create multiple independent iterators on same collection.

- Provides a uniform interface for traversing different collection.

Question: Explain Java iterators in detail.

Answer: Often, we will want to go through the elements in a collection. For example, we might want to display each element. The easiest way to do this is to create an iterator, which is an object that implements either the *Iterator* or the *ListIterator* interface.

Iterator enables us to go through a collection, obtaining or removing elements. ListIterator extends Iterator to allow *bidirectional* traversal of a list, and the modification of elements.

Before we can access a collection through an iterator, we must obtain one. Each of the collection classes provides an *iterator*() method that returns an iterator to the start of the collection. By using this iterator object, we can access each element in the collection, one element at a time.

In general, to use an iterator to cycle through the contents of a collection, follow these steps:

1. Obtain an iterator to the start of the collection by calling the collection's *iterator*( ) method.
2. Set up a loop that makes a call to *hasNext*(). Have the loop iterate as long as *hasNext*() returns true.
3. Within the loop, obtain each element by calling *next*( ).

For collections that implement List, we can also obtain an iterator by calling *ListIterator*. The methods declared by *Iterator* are:

- *boolean hasNext*( ): Returns true if there are more elements. Otherwise, returns false.
- *Object next*( ): Returns the next element. Throws *NoSuchElementException* if there is not a next element.
- *void remove*( ): Removes the current element. Throws *IllegalStateException* if an attempt is made to call *remove*( ) that is not preceded by a call to *next*( ).

The methods declared by *ListIterator*:

- *void add*(*Object obj*): Inserts obj into the list in front of the element that will be returned by the next call to *next*( ).
- *boolean hasNext*( ): Returns true if there is a next element. Otherwise, returns false.
- *boolean hasPrevious*( ): Returns true if there is a previous element. Otherwise, returns false.
- *Object next*( ): Returns the next element. A *NoSuchElementException* is thrown if there is not a next element.
- *int nextIndex*( ): Returns the index of the next element. If there is not a next element, returns the size of the list.

- *Object previous*( ): Returns the previous element. A *NoSuchElementException* is thrown if there is not a previous element.
- *int previousIndex*( ): Returns the index of the previous element. If there is not a previous element, returns -1.
- *void remove*( ): Removes current element from the list. An *IllegalStateException* is thrown if *remove*( ) is called before *next*( ) or *previous*( ) is invoked.
- *void set*(*Object obj*): Assigns obj to the current element. This is the element last returned by a call to either *next*( ) or *previous*( ).

Here is an example demonstrating both *Iterator* and *ListIterator*. It uses an *ArrayList* object, but the general principles apply to any type of collection. Of course, *ListIterator* is available only to those collections that implement the List interface.

```
import java.util.*;
class IteratorDemo {
  public static void main(String args[]) {
    ArrayList collectn = new ArrayList();
    collectn.add("C");
    collectn.add("O");
    collectn.add("W");
    collectn.add("B");
    collectn.add("O");
    collectn.add("Y");

    // Use iterator to display contents of collectn
    System.out.print("Original contents of collection: ");
    Iterator itr = collectn.iterator();
    while(itr.hasNext()) {
      Object element = itr.next();
      System.out.print(element + " ");
    }
    System.out.println();

    // Modify objects being iterated
    ListIterator litr = collectn.listIterator();
    while(litr.hasNext()) {
      Object element = litr.next();
      litr.set(element + "+");
    }
    System.out.print("Modified contents of collection: ");
    itr = collectn.iterator();
    while(itr.hasNext()) {
      Object element = itr.next();
      System.out.print(element + " ");
```

```
            }
            System.out.println();

            System.out.print("Modified list backwards: ");
            while(litr.hasPrevious()) {
              Object element = litr.previous();
              System.out.print(element + " ");
            }
            System.out.println();
        }
    }
```

6.7 Mediator Design Pattern

The mediator pattern is all about communication. The Mediator design pattern is easy to understand but tricky to implement. At the core of the Mediator pattern is a Mediator class that coordinates a set of different requests that are sent by objects. The objects are called Colleagues.

The Colleagues let the Mediator know that they want to change, and the Mediator handles the change taking into account what effect the changes will have on the other colleagues.

For example, in a car when we turn on the headlights, the panel lights dim (assume even if it does not happen in your car). Something in the car tells the panel lights to dim when the headlights are switched on. The headlights represent one colleague and the panel lights, another.

A *Mediator* tells the panel lights to turn on as soon as we start the car, and then when the headlights are switched on, the Mediator tells the panel lights to dim. If we turn off the headlight, the *Mediator* tells the panel lights to brighten up again. The colleagues never communicate directly with one another but instead through the mediator. The idea is to reduce the complexity by handling all of the requests in one place. This also insures loose coupling between the colleagues.

UML Diagram For Mediator Design Pattern

The participant's classes in this pattern are:

- *Mediator*: It defines an interface for communicating with *Colleague* objects.
- *ConcreteMediator*: It knows the colleague classes and keeps a reference to the colleague objects. It implements the communication and transfer the messages between the colleague classes
- *Colleague* classes: These classes keep a reference to its *Mediator* object. They communicates with the *Mediator* whenever it would have otherwise communicated with another *Colleague*.

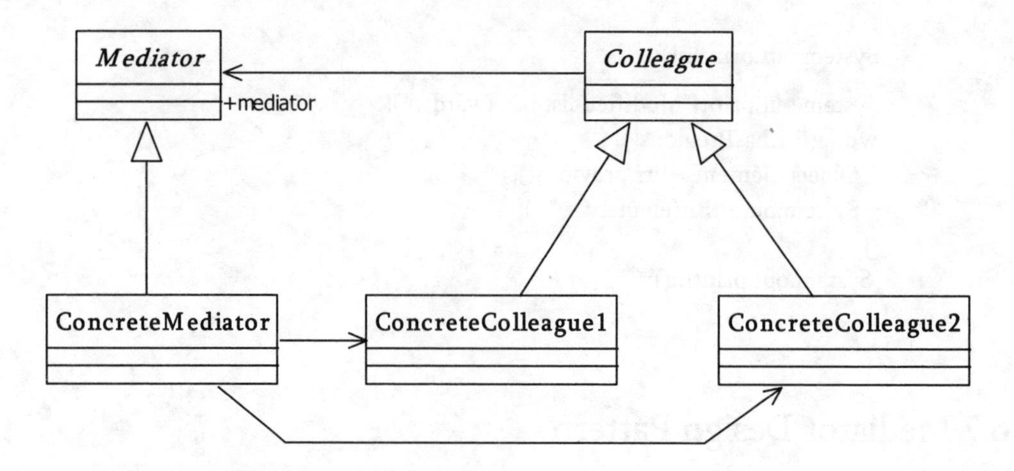

Examples For Mediator Design Pattern

When we begin with development of any product, we have a few classes and these classes interact with each other producing results.

Now, consider slowly, the logic becomes more complex and functionality increases. Then what happens? We add more classes and they still interact with each other but it gets really difficult to maintain this code now.

Mediator pattern takes care of this problem. It makes the code more maintainable. It promotes loose-coupling of classes such that only one class (*Mediator*) has the knowledge of all the classes, rest of the classes have their responsibilities and they only interact with the Mediator.

The chat application is another example of the mediator pattern. In a chat application we can have several participants. It's not a good idea to connect each participant to all the others because the number of connections would be really high. The most appropriate solution is to have a mediator where all participants will connect.

Participants in Chat application:

- *Chatroom* (Mediator: Defines the interface for interacting with participants
- *ChatroomImpl* (ConcreteMediator): implements the operations defined by the *Chatroom* interface. The operations are managing the interactions between the objects: when one participant sends a message, the message is sent to the other participants.
- *Participant* (Colleague): Defines an interface for the participants.
- *HumanParticipant* (ConcreteCollegue): Implements participants; the participant can be a human, each one having a distinct implementation but implementing the same interface. Each participant will keep only a reference to the mediator.

When To Use Mediator Design Pattern?

Mediator design pattern is preferred when:

- A set of objects communicate in well-defined but complex ways. The resulting interdependencies are unstructured and difficult to understand.
- Reusing an object is difficult because it refers to and communicates with many other objects.
- A behavior that's distributed between several classes should be customizable without a lot of subclassing.

Mediator Design Pattern Implementation

Now, let's take a look at an example of this pattern. We will create a *Mediator* class (without mediator interface). This mediator will mediate the communication between two buyers (an Indian buyer and a French buyer), an American seller, and a currency converter.

The Mediator has references to the two buyers, the seller, and the converter. It has methods so that objects of these types can be registered. It also has a *placeBid*() method. This method takes a bid amount and a unit of currency as parameters. It converts this amount to a dollar amount via communication with the *dollarConverter*. It then asks the seller if the bid has been accepted, and it returns the answer.

```
public class Mediator {
    Buyer indianBuyer;
    Buyer frenchBuyer;
    AmericanSeller americanSeller;
    DollarConverter dollarConverter;

    public Mediator() { }

    public void registerIndianBuyer(IndianBuyer indianBuyer) {
        this.indianBuyer = indianBuyer;
    }

    public void registerFrenchBuyer(FrenchBuyer frenchBuyer) {
        this.frenchBuyer = frenchBuyer;
    }

    public void registerAmericanSeller(AmericanSeller americanSeller) {
        this.americanSeller = americanSeller;
    }

    public void registerDollarConverter(DollarConverter dollarConverter) {
        this.dollarConverter = dollarConverter;
    }

    public boolean placeBid(float bid, String unitOfCurrency) {
```

```
            float dollarAmount = dollarConverter.convertCurrencyToDollars(bid,
                                                                    unitOfCurrency);
            return americanSeller.isBidAccepted(dollarAmount);
        }
    }
```

Here is the *Buyer* class. The *IndianBuyer* and *FrenchBuyer* classes are subclasses of *Buyer*. The buyer has a unit of currency as a field, and it also has a reference to the mediator. The *Buyer* class has a *attemptToPurchase*() method. This method submits a bid to the mediator's *placeBid*() method. It returns the mediator's response.

```
    public class Buyer {
        Mediator mediator;
        String unitOfCurrency;
        public Buyer(Mediator mediator, String unitOfCurrency) {
            this.mediator = mediator;
            this.unitOfCurrency = unitOfCurrency;
        }
        public boolean attemptToPurchase(float bid) {
          System.out.println("Buyer attempting a bid of " + bid + " " + unitOfCurrency);
          return mediator.placeBid(bid, unitOfCurrency);
        }
    }
```

The *IndianBuyer* class is a subclass of *Buyer* and in the constructor, we set the *unitOfCurrency* to be "INR". We also register the *IndianBuyer* with the mediator so that the mediator knows about the *IndianBuyer* object.

```
    public class IndianBuyer extends Buyer {
        public IndianBuyer(Mediator mediator) {
            super(mediator, "INR");
            this.mediator.registerIndianBuyer(this);
        }
    }
```

The *FrenchBuyer* class is similar to the *IndianBuyer* class, except the *unitOfCurrency* is "EURO", and it registers with the mediator as the FrenchBuyer.

```
    public class FrenchBuyer extends Buyer {
        public FrenchBuyer(Mediator mediator) {
            super(mediator, "EURO");
            this.mediator.registerFrenchBuyer(this);
        }
    }
```

In the constructor of the *AmericanSeller* class, the class gets a reference to the mediator and the *priceInDollars* gets set. This is the price of some good being sold. The seller registers with the mediator as the *AmericanSeller*.

The seller's *isBidAccepted*() method takes a bid (in dollars). If the bid is over the price (in dollars), bid is accepted and true is returned. Otherwise, false is returned.

```
public class AmericanSeller {
    Mediator mediator;
    float priceInDollars;

    public AmericanSeller(Mediator mediator, float priceInDollars) {
        this.mediator = mediator;
        this.priceInDollars = priceInDollars;
        this.mediator.registerAmericanSeller(this);
    }

    public boolean isBidAccepted(float bidInDollars) {
        if (bidInDollars >= priceInDollars) {
            System.out.println("Seller accepts bid of " + bidInDollars + " dollars\n");
                return true;
        } else {
            System.out.println("Seller rejects bid of " + bidInDollars + " dollars\n");
            return false;
        }
    }
}
```

The *DollarConverter* class is another colleague class. When created, it gets a reference to the mediator and registers itself with the mediator as the *DollarConverter*. This class has methods to convert amounts in *euros* and *inr* to dollars.

```
public class DollarConverter {
    Mediator mediator;
    public static final float DOLLAR_UNIT = 1.0f;
    public static final float EURO_UNIT = 0.7f;
    public static final float INR_UNIT = 45.0f;

    public DollarConverter(Mediator mediator) {
            this.mediator = mediator;
            mediator.registerDollarConverter(this);
    }

    private float convertEurosToDollars(float euros) {
            float dollars = euros * (DOLLAR_UNIT / EURO_UNIT);
```

```
            System.out.println("Converting " + euros + " euros to " + dollars + " dollars");
            return dollars;
        }

        private float convertInrToDollars(float inr) {
            float dollars = inr * (DOLLAR_UNIT / INR_UNIT);
            System.out.println("Converting " + inr + " inr to " + dollars + " dollars");
            return dollars;
        }

        public float convertCurrencyToDollars(float amount, String unitOfCurrency) {
            if ("INR".equalsIgnoreCase(unitOfCurrency)) {
                    return convertIntToDollars(amount);
            } else {
                    return convertEurosToDollars(amount);
            }
        }
    }
```

The *MediatorTest* class demonstrates our mediator pattern. It creates a *IndianBuyer* object and a *FrenchBuyer* object. It creates an *AmericanSeller* object with a selling price set to 10 dollars. It then creates a *DollarConverter*. All of these objects register themselves with the mediator in their constructors.

The Indian buyer starts with a bid of 55 *inr* and keeps bidding up in increments of 15 *inr* until the bid is accepted. The French buyer starts bidding at 3 *euros* and keeps bidding in increments of 1.50 *euros* until the bid is accepted.

```
    public class MediatorTest {
        public static void main(String[] args) {
            Mediator mediator = new Mediator();
            Buyer indianBuyer = new IndianBuyer(mediator);
            Buyer frenchBuyer = new FrenchBuyer(mediator);
            float sellingPriceInDollars = 10.0f;
            AmericanSeller americanSeller = new AmericanSeller(mediator,
                                                    sellingPriceInDollars);
            DollarConverter dollarConverter = new DollarConverter(mediator);
            float indianBidInInr = 55.0f;
            while (!indianBuyer.attemptToPurchase(indianBidInInr)) {
                    indianBidInInr += 15.0f;
            }

            float frenchBidInEuros = 3.0f;
            while (!frenchBuyer.attemptToPurchase(frenchBidInEuros)) {
```

```
                frenchBidInEuros += 1.5f;
            }
        }
    }
```

Problems With Mediator Design Pattern

In practice the mediators tends to become more complex and complex. A good practice is to take care to make the mediator classes responsible only for the communication part.

Notes On Mediator Design Pattern

- Define an object that encapsulates how a set of objects interact.
- Colleagues *send* and *receive* requests from a Mediator object.
- It *decouples* colleagues. A mediator promotes loose coupling between colleagues. You can vary and reuse Colleague and Mediator classes independently.
- It simplifies object protocols. A mediator *replaces* many-to-many interactions with one-to-many interactions between the mediator and its colleagues. One-to-many relationships are easier to understand, maintain, and extend.
- It *centralizes* control. The Mediator pattern trades complexity of interaction for complexity in the mediator. Because a mediator encapsulates protocols, it can become more complex than any individual colleague. This can make the mediator itself a monolith that's hard to maintain.
- Facade differs from Mediator in that it abstracts a subsystem of objects to provide a more convenient interface. Its protocol is unidirectional; that is, Facade objects make requests of the subsystem classes but not vice versa. In contrast, Mediator enables cooperative behaviour that colleague objects don't or can't provide, and the protocol is multidirectional.
- There's no need to define an abstract Mediator class when colleagues work with only one mediator. The abstract coupling that the Mediator class provides lets colleagues work with different Mediator subclasses, and vice versa

Question: What is the difference between Mediator and Façade design patterns?

Answer: Mediator design pattern may look very similar to facade design pattern in terms of abstraction. Mediator abstracts the functionality of the subsystems in this way it is similar to the facade pattern. In the implementation of mediator pattern, subsystem or peers components are aware of the mediator and that interact with it. In the case of facade pattern, subsystems are not aware of the existence of facade. Only facade talks to the subsystems.

A simplified mediator becomes a facade pattern if the mediator is the only active class and the colleagues are passive classes. A facade pattern is just an implementation of the mediator pattern where mediator is the only object triggering and invoking actions on passive colleague classes. The Facade is being called by some external classes.

Question: What is the difference between Mediator and Adapter design patterns?

Answer: The mediator patterns just *mediate* the requests between the colleague classes. It is not supposed to change the messages it receives and sends. If it alters those messages then it is an Adapter pattern.

Question: What is the difference between Mediator and Observer design patterns?

Answer: The observer and mediator are similar patterns, solving the same problem. The main difference between them is the problem they address. The observer pattern handles the communication between observers and subjects or subject. It is very probable to have new observable objects added. On the other side in the mediator pattern the mediator class is the most likely class to be inherited.

6.8 Memento Design Pattern

We all use this pattern at least once every day. *Memento* pattern provides an ability to restore an object to its previous state (undo via *rollback*). *Memento* pattern is implemented with two objects: originator and a caretaker. The originator is some object that has an internal state. *Caretaker* is going to perform some action to the originator, but wants to be able to undo the change.

Examples For Memento Design Pattern

Suppose we have an object which stores form information and we would like to allow the user to make changes in the form and then if they make a mistake later we can put back in the original form values. Well, we could serialize the form object and then deserialize it later but this is obviously messy and not a good solution.

Another possible solution would be to have an outside object use the form's access methods to pull out what we need to save the state but this causes high coupling between the class saving the state and the form. Any changes in the form would require changes in the other class. We need something that will allow you to save the state and restore it later without having to get involved in the details. This is where the memento pattern comes in.

UML Diagram For Memento Design Pattern

Let's take a look at each of the participants in this pattern.

- *Originator*: The Originator is the object that knows how to save itself. This is the class that we want to make stateful.
- *Caretaker*: The Caretaker is an object that deals with when, and why, the *Originator* needs to save or restore itself. The caretaker is going to do something to the originator, but wants to be able to undo the change.

- *Memento*: The Memento holds the information about the Originator's state, and *cannot* be modified by the Caretaker.

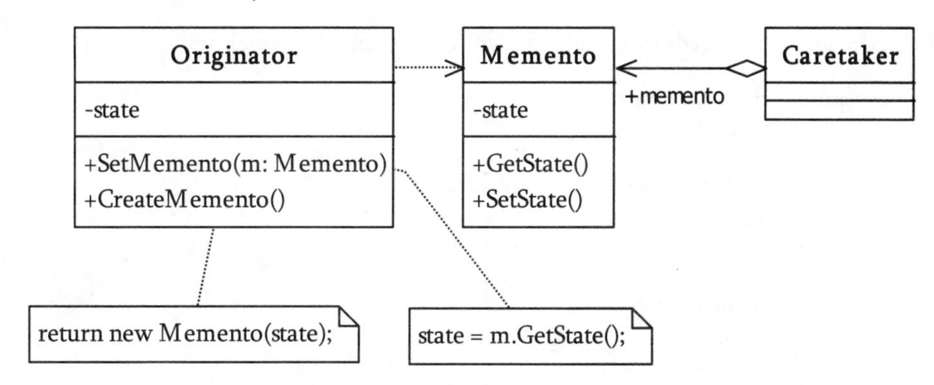

Steps For Creating Memento Design Pattern

The caretaker first asks the originator for a memento object. Then it does whatever operation (or sequence of operations) it was going to do. To roll back to the state before the operations, it returns the memento object to the originator. The memento object is the one which the caretaker cannot, or should not, change.

- Identify the roles of *caretaker* and *originator*.
- Design a Memento class and declare the originator a friend. This class does nothing more than accept and return this snapshot (memento role).
- Caretaker knows when to *check point*(saving state) the originator.
- Originator creates a *Memento* and copies its state to that Memento.
- Caretaker holds on to the Memento.
- Caretaker knows when to roll back the originator.
- Originator reinstates itself using the saved state in the Memento.
- Caretaker role asks the Originator to return a Memento and because the Originator's previous state to be restored of desired.

When To Use Memento Design Pattern?

The Memento pattern is useful when we need to provide an undo mechanism in applications, when the internal state of an object may need to be restored at a later stage. Using serialization along with this pattern, it is easy to preserve the object state and bring it back later on.

Memento Design Pattern Implementation

Client requests a *Memento* from the source object when it needs to checkpoint the source object's state. Source object initializes the *Memento* with its state. The client is the care taker of the *Memento*, but only the source object can store and retrieve information from the *Memento*. If the client subsequently needs to "rollback" the source object's state, it hands the *Memento* back to the source object for reinstatement.

First, the memento needs to be able to save editor contents, which will just be plain text:

```
public class Memento {
    private String state;

    public Memento(String stateToSave) {
        state = stateToSave;
    }

    public String getSavedState() {
        return state;
    }
}
```

The Caretaker is that object that deals with when, and why, the Originator needs to save or restore itself.

```
public class Caretaker {
    private List<Memento> savedStates = new ArrayList<Memento>();

    public void addMemento(Memento m) {
        savedStates.add(m);
    }

    public  Memento getMemento(int index) {
        return savedStates.get(index);
    }
}
```

Now our Originator class can use the memento. The class could also contain additional data that is not part of the state saved in the memento.

```
class Originator {
    private String state;
    public  void setState(String state) {
        System.out.println("Setting state to ");
        this.state = state;
    }

    public Memento saveToMemento() {
        System.out.println("Saving to Memento.");
        return new Memento(state);
    }
```

```
        public void restoreFromMemento(Memento m) {
            state = m.getSavedState();
            System.out.println("Restoring state from Memento:");
        }
    }
```

Sample Client Code:

```
    public class MementoTest {
        public static void main(String[] args) {
            Caretaker caretaker = new Caretaker();
            Originator originator=new Originator();
            originator.setState("State1");
            originator.setState("State2");
            caretaker.addMemento(originator.saveToMemento() );
            originator.setState("State3");
            caretaker.addMemento( originator.saveToMemento());
            originator.restoreFromMemento(caretaker.getMemento(1));
        }
    }
```

An unlimited "*undo*" and "*redo*" capability can be readily implemented with a stack of command objects and a stack of *Memento* objects.

Summary and Notes On Memento Design Pattern

- Also known as *Token*.
- A memento is an object that stores a snapshot of the internal state of another object—the memento's originator.
- The undo mechanism will request a memento from the originator when it needs to checkpoint the originator's state. The originator initializes the memento with information that characterizes its current state. Only the originator can store and retrieve information from the memento.
- Use the Memento pattern when a snapshot of an object's state must be saved so that it can be restored to that state later.
- Participants in Memento pattern:
    - *Memento*: It stores internal state of the Originator object. The memento may store as much or as little of the originators internal state as necessary at its originator's discretion. Memento protects against access by objects other than the originator. Mementos have effectively two interfaces. Caretaker sees a narrow interface to the Memento—it can only pass the memento to other objects. Originator, in contrast, sees a wide interface, one that lets it access all the data necessary to restore itself to its previous state.

  - Ideally, only the originator that produced the memento would be permitted to access the memento's internal state.
  - *Originator*: It creates a memento containing a snapshot of its current internal state. Originator uses the memento to restore its internal state.
  - *Caretaker*: It is responsible for the memento's safekeeping. It never operates on or examines the contents of a memento.
- A caretaker requests a memento from an originator, holds it for a time, and passes it back to the originator, as the following interaction diagram illustrates
- Sometimes the caretaker won't pass the memento back to the originator, because the originator might never need to revert to an earlier state.
- Mementos are passive. Only the originator that created a memento will assign or retrieve its state.

6.9 Observer Design Pattern

Have you ever used RSS feeds? If so, you already know about *Observer* pattern. The observer pattern is a behavioral object design pattern. In the observer pattern, an object called the *subject* maintains a collection of objects called *observers*. When the subject changes, it notifies the observers.

Observers can be added or removed from the collection of observers in the subject. The changes in state of the *subject* can be passed to the observers so that the observers can change their own state to reflect this change.

Examples For Observer Design Pattern

The *Observer* pattern defines a link between objects so that when one object's state changes, all dependent objects are updated automatically (Producer/Consumer problem which we coded in *Java* is also a classic example). There is always an *Observer* (also called *Listeners*) and *Observable* (also called *Providers*) object around us. We are an *Observer*, TV is an *Observable* object.

Observer pattern is designed to help cope with one to many relationships between objects, allowing changes in an object to update many associated objects. This is a behavioral pattern.

UML Diagram For Observer Design Pattern

The *Subject* (also called *Listener*) has an interface that defines methods for adding and removing observers from the *Subject's* collection of observers. This interface also features a notification method. This method should be called when the state of the subject changes. This notifies the observers that the subject's state has changed.

The observers have an interface with a method to update the observer. This update method is called for each observer in the subject's notification method. Since this communication occurs via an interface, any concrete observer implementing the observer interface can be updated by the subject. This results in loose coupling between the subject and the observer classes.

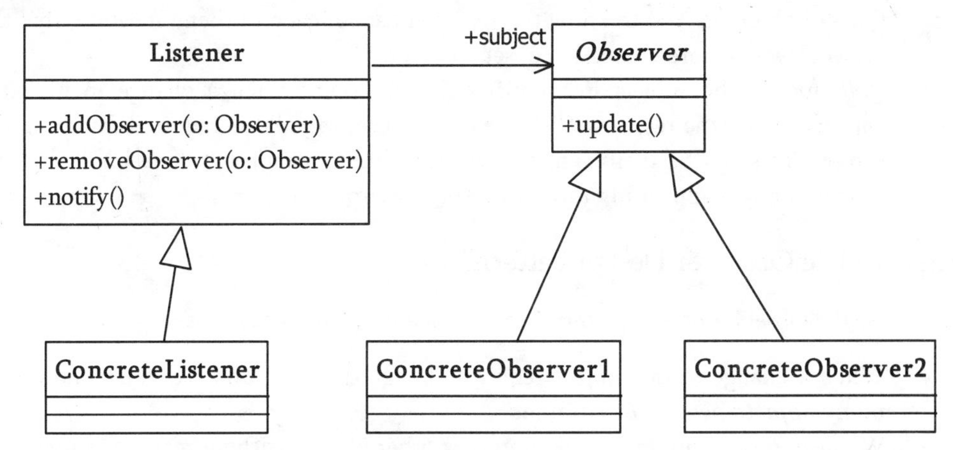

The participant's classes in *Observer* design pattern are:

- *Subject*: Interface or abstract class defining the operations for adding and removing observers to the client.
- *ConcreteSubject*: Concrete *Subject* class. It maintain the state of the object and when a change in the state occurs it notifies the added *Observers*.
- *Observer*: Interface or abstract class defining the operations to be used to notify this object.
- *ConcreteObserver*: Concrete Observer implementations.

Steps For Creating Observer Design Pattern

- Differentiate between the *core* functionality and the *optional* functionality.
- Represent the *core* functionality with a *subject* abstraction.
- Represent the *optional* functionality with an *observer* hierarchy.
- The *Subject* is coupled only to the *Observer* base class.
- The client configures the number and type of *Observers*.
- Observers *register* themselves with the *Subject*.
- The Subject *notifies* events to all registered Observers.
- The Subject may *update* information at the Observers *or* the Observers may *get* the information they need from the Subject.

Push and Pull Communication Methods

There are 2 methods of passing the data from the subject to the observer when the state is changed in the subject side:

- *Push model*: The subjects send information about the change to the observer whether it uses it or not. Because the subject needs to send the information to the observer this might be inefficient when a large amount of data needs to be sent and it is not used. Another approach would be to send only the information required by the observer. In this case the subject should be able to distinguish between different types of observers and to know the required data of each of them, meaning that the subject layer is more coupled to observer layer.

- *Pull model*: The subject just notifies the observers when a change in his state appears and it's the responsibility of each observer to pull the required data from the subject. This can be inefficient because the communication is done in 2 steps and problems might appear in *multithreading* environments.

When To Use Observer Design Pattern?

We can use the Observer design pattern in any of the following situations:

- When a change to one object requires changing others, and we don't know how *many objects* need to be *changed*.
- When an object should be able to *notify* other objects without making assumptions about who these objects are.
- When an abstraction has two aspects, one dependent on the other. Encapsulating these aspects in separate objects lets us vary and *reuse* them independently.

Observer Design Pattern Implementation

To implement *Observer* pattern, we need to define the interfaces for *Subject* and *Observer*. Now we'll look at an example of the observer pattern. We'll start by creating an interface for the subject called TemperatureSubject. This will declare three methods: *addObserver*(), *removeObserver*(), and *notify*().

```
public interface TemperatureSubject {
        public void addObserver(TemperatureObserver TemperatureObserver);
        public void removeObserver(TemperatureObserver TemperatureObserver);
        public void notify();
}
```

We'll also create an interface for the observers called *TemperatureObserver*. It features one method, a *update*() method.

```
public interface TemperatureObserver {
        public void update(int temperature);
}
```

The *TemperatureStation* class implements *TemperatureSubject*. It is our subject class. It maintains a set of *TemperatureObservers* which are added through *addObserver*() and removed through *removeObserver*(). When *TemperatureSubject's* state changes through *setTemperature*(), the *notify*() method gets called, which in turn contacts all the *TemperatureObservers* with the temperature through their *update*() methods.

```
import java.util.HashSet;
import java.util.Iterator;
import java.util.Set;

public class TemperatureStation implements TemperatureSubject {
	Set<TemperatureObserver> temperatureObservers;
	int temperature;

	public TemperatureStation(int temperature) {
		temperatureObservers = new HashSet<TemperatureObserver>();
		this.temperature = temperature;
	}

	public void addObserver(TemperatureObserver temperatureObserver) {
		temperatureObservers.add(temperatureObserver);
	}

	public void removeObserver(TemperatureObserver temperatureObserver) {
		temperatureObservers.remove(temperatureObserver);
	}

	public void notify() {
		Iterator<TemperatureObserver> it = temperatureObservers.iterator();
		while (it.hasNext()) {
			TemperatureObserver temperatureObserver = it.next();
			temperatureObserver.update(temperature);
		}
	}

	public void setTemperature(int newTemperature) {
		System.out.println("Setting temperature to " + newTemperature);
		temperature = newTemperature;
		notify();
	}
}
```

*TemperatureCustomer*1 is an observer which implements *TemperatureObserver*. Its *update*() method gets the current temperature from *TemperatureStation* and displays it.

```
public class TemperatureCustomer1 implements TemperatureObserver {
	public void update(int temperature) {
		System.out.println("Customer 1 found the temperature as:" + temperature);
	}
}
```

TemperatureCustomer2 performs similar functionality as *TemperatureCustomer1*.

```
public class TemperatureCustomer2 implements TemperatureObserver {
    public void update(int temperature) {
        System.out.println("Customer 2 found the temperature as:" + temperature);
    }
}
```

The *ObserverTest* class demonstrates the observer pattern. It creates a TemperatureStation and then a *TemperatureCustomer1* and a *TemperatureCustomer2*. The two customers are added as observers to the Temperature station. Then the *setTemperature*() method of the Temperature station is called. This changes the state of the Temperature station and the customers are notified of this temperature update. Next, the *TemperatureCustomer1* object is removed from the station's collection of observers. Then, the *setTemperature*() method is called again. This results in the notification of the TemperatureCustomer2 object.

```
public class ObserverTest {
    public static void main(String[] args) {
        TemperatureStation temperatureStation = new TemperatureStation(38);
        TemperatureCustomer1 tc1 = new TemperatureCustomer1();
        TemperatureCustomer2 tc2 = new TemperatureCustomer2();

        temperatureStation.addObserver(tc1);
        temperatureStation.addObserver(tc2);
        temperatureStation.setTemperature(34);
        temperatureStation.removeObserver(tc1);
        temperatureStation.setTemperature(35);
    }
}
```

Notes On Observer Design Pattern

- Also known as *Dependents*, *Publish-Subscribe* patterns.
- Define a *one – to – many* dependency between objects so that when one object changes state, all its dependents are notified and updated automatically.
- *Abstract* coupling between *Subject* and *Observer*. All a subject knows is that it has a list of observers, each conforming to the simple interface of the abstract Observer class. The subject doesn't know the concrete class of any observer.
- *Support* for *broadcast* communication: Unlike an ordinary request, the notification that a subject sends needn't specify its receiver. The notification is broadcast automatically to all interested objects that subscribed to it. The subject doesn't care how many interested objects exist; its only responsibility is to notify its observers. This gives you the freedom to add and remove observers at any time. It's up to the observer to handle or ignore a notification.

- *Unexpected updates*: Because observers have no knowledge of each other's presence, they can be blind to the ultimate cost of changing the subject. A seemingly innocuous operation on the subject may cause a cascade of updates to observers and their dependent objects. Moreover, dependency criteria that aren't well-defined or maintained usually lead to spurious updates, which can be hard to track down.

6.10 State Design Pattern

The state pattern is a behavioral object design pattern. The idea behind the state pattern is to change object behavior depending on its state. *State* pattern allows objects to behave differently depending on internal state (*Context*). The *Context* can have a number of internal states, whenever the *request*() method is called on the *Context*, the message is delegated to the *State* to handle.

The *State* interface defines a common interface for all concrete states, encapsulating all behavior associated with a particular state. The concrete state provides its own implementation for the request. When a Context changes state, what really happens is that we have a different *ConcreteState* associated with it.

Example For State Design Pattern

The control panel of a simple media player could be used as an example of the *State* design pattern. When the device is playing music, the *play* button could *pause* and *restart* the music. When the user is listening to the radio, the same button may search for the next radio station. To switch between the states of playback, radio tuning and standby mode, the user could press the *audio source* button.

UML Diagram For State Design Pattern

In the state pattern, we have a *Context* class, and this class has a *State* reference to a *Concrete State* instance. The *State* interface declares methods that represent the behaviours of a particular state. *Concrete States* implement these behaviors.

By changing a *Context's* Concrete State, we change its behavior. In essence, in the state pattern, a class (the *Context*) is supposed to behave like different classes depending on its state. The state pattern avoids the use of switch and if statements to change behaviour.

The UML class diagram above describes the state design pattern. The items in the diagram are described below:

- *Context*: The *Context* class is used by clients of the state design pattern. Clients do not access the state objects directly. The *Context* class holds a concrete state object that provides the behaviour according to its current state.

- *State*: This abstract class is the base class for all concrete state classes. State defines the interface that will be used by the *Context* object to access the changeable functionality. No state, in terms of fields or properties, is defined in the *State* class or its subclasses.
- *ConcreteState*: The concrete state classes provide the real functionality that will be used by the *Context* object. Each state class provides behaviour that is applicable to a single state of the Context object. They may also include instructions that cause the *Context* to change its state.

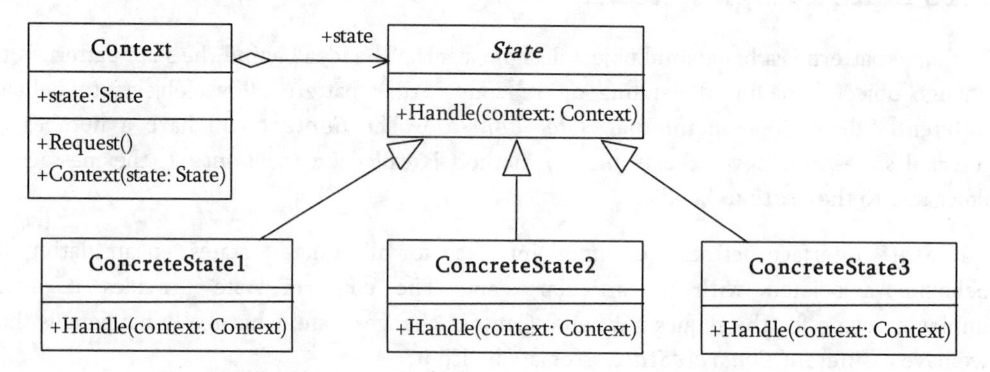

Steps For Creating State Design Pattern

- Identify an existing class, or create a new class, that will serve as the *State* from the client's perspective. That class is the *Context* class.
- Create a *State* class that replicates the methods of the state interface. Each method takes one additional parameter: an instance of the *Context* class.
- Create a *Concrete State* class for each state. These derived classes only override the methods they need to override.
- The *Context* class maintains a current *State* object.
- All client requests to the *Context* class are simply delegated to the current *State* object, and the *Context* object's this pointer is passed.
- The *State* methods change the *current* state in the *Context* object as appropriate.

State Design Pattern Implementation

This is all quite similar to the *Strategy* pattern, except the changes happen at runtime rather than the client deciding. *State* saves us from lots of conditional code in *Context*: by changing the *ConcreteState*object used, we can change the behavior of the context. Let us consider a real-time example for understanding the pattern (Music player). Similar to *Strategy* pattern here also we have *Context* and a *State* interface. First of all, we'll define the State interface. It declares a method, *pressPlay*().

```
public interface State {
      public void pressPlay(MusicPlayerContextInterface context);
```

```
}
```

The concrete implementations of the *State* interface are given below. The *StandbyState* class is a Concrete State that implements pressPlay() of *State*. This message indicates the standby mode of player cheerful (representing a *standby* state).

```
public class StandbyState implements State {
        public void pressPlay(MusicPlayerContextInterface context){
                context.setState(new PlayingState());
        }
}
```

The *PlayingState* class is a Concrete State that implements pressPlay() of *State*. This message indicates the *playing* mode of player cheerful (representing a *playing* state).

```
public class PlayingState implements State {
        public void pressPlay(MusicPlayerContextInterface context){
                context.setState(new StandbyState());
        }
}
```

In the below code, *MusicPlayerContext* class is the *Context* class. It contains a *MusicPlayerContextInterface* reference to a concrete state. In this example, we have *MusicPlayerContext* implement the *MusicPlayerContextInterface* reference, and we pass the calls to *MusicPlayerContext's requestPlay*() method on to the corresponding method on the *MusicPlayerContextInterface* reference.

As a result of this, a *MusicPlayerContext* object behaves differently depending on the state of *MusicPlayerContext* (ie, the current *MusicPlayerContextInterface* reference). A dependent abstract or interface *Context* class and its dependent concrete class can be given as:

```
//Context Interface
public interface MusicPlayerContextInterface{
      public State state;
      public void requestPlay();
      public void setState(State state);
      public State getState();
}

//Concrete Context
public class MusicPlayerContext implements MusicPlayerContextInterface {
        State state;
        public MusicPlayerContext(State state){
                this.state= state;
        }
```

```
        public void requestPlay(){
                state.pressPlay(this);
        }
        public void setState(State state){
                this.state = state;
        }
        public State getState(){
                return state;
        }
}
```

In the below code, the *ObserverTest* class demonstrates the state design pattern. First, it creates a *MusicPlayerContext* object with a *StandbyState* object and displays the results of *pressPlay*() when the player object is in the standby state. Next, we change the musicPlayer object's state with a *PlayingState* object and display the results of *pressPlay*(), and we see that in the playing state, the *musicPlayer* object's behavior is different.

```
//Sample Test Code
public class ObserverTest {
    public static void main(String[] args) {
        MusicPlayerContext musicPlayer =
                                    new MusicPlayerContext(new StandbyState());
        musicPlayer.requestPlay();
        musicPlayer.setState(new PlayingState());
        musicPlayer.requestPlay();
        return 0;
    }
}
```

This shows how the state pattern works at a simple level. Few advantages of *State* pattern are:

- State pattern provides a clear state representation of an object.
- It allows a clean way for an object to partially change its type at runtime.

6.11 Strategy Design Pattern

Strategy pattern is an example for behavioral pattern and is used when we want different algorithms needs to be applied on values (objects). That means, *Strategy* design pattern defines a set of algorithms and make them interchangeable. Strategy pattern is a design pattern where algorithms can be selected at *runtime*.

Strategy lets the algorithm vary independently from clients that use it. The strategy pattern is also known as the *Policy* pattern. We can apply *Strategy* pattern when we need different variants of an algorithm (each algorithm can be assumed as a separate class) and these related classes differ only in their behavior.

UML Diagram For Strategy Pattern

The participant's classes in this pattern are:

- *Strategy*: Defines an interface common to all supported algorithms. Context uses this interface to call the algorithm defined by a ConcreteStrategy.
- *ConcreteStrategy*: Each concrete strategy implements an algorithm.
- *Context*: Contains a reference to a strategy object. It may define an interface that lets strategy accessing its data. The Context objects contains a reference to the ConcreteStrategy that should be used. When an operation is required then the algorithm is run from the strategy object. The Context is not aware of the strategy implementation. If necessary, addition objects can be defined to pass data from context object to strategy. The context object receives requests from the client and delegates them to the strategy object. Usually the ConcreteStartegy is created by the client and passed to the context. From this point the clients interacts only with the context.

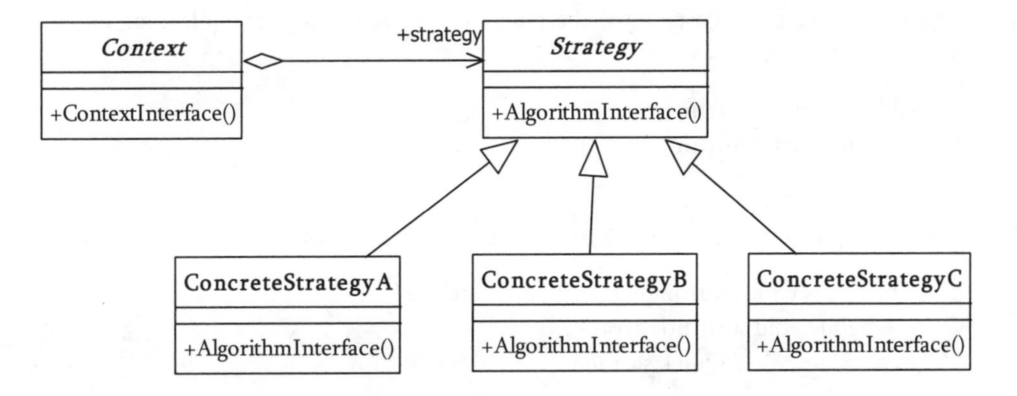

Examples For Strategy Design Pattern

A mode of transportation to an airport is an example of a Strategy. Several options exist such as driving one's own car, taking a taxi, an airport shuttle, or a city bus. Any of these modes of transportation will get a traveler to the airport, and they can be used interchangeably. The traveler must chose the Strategy based on trade-offs between cost, convenience, and time.

As an another example, assume we have a *vector or* an *array* container. To sort the items in that list, we can use bubble sort, quick sort, heap sort etc... But we can use only one algorithm at a time out of all the possible.

When To Use Strategy Design Pattern?

We can apply *Strategy* pattern when we need different variants of an algorithm (each algorithm can be assumed as a separate class) and these related classes differ only in their behavior. A Strategy defines a set of algorithms that can be used interchangeably.

Steps For Creating Strategy Design Pattern

1. Identify an algorithm (i.e. behaviour) that the client would prefer to.
2. Specify the signature (prototype) for that algorithm in an interface.
3. Provide the alternative implementation details in derived classes.
4. Clients of the algorithm couple themselves to the interface.

Strategy Pattern Implementation

Let us consider the above example (sorting *vector or* an *array* container elements) for understanding the pattern. To sort the items in that list, we can use bubble sort, quick sort, heap sort etc... But we can use only one algorithm at a time out of all the possible. As a first step we need to define the *Strategy* (algorithms) and *Context* (*vector or array* container) interfaces. Context pass data to *Strategy*.

Strategy has point to *Context* to get data from *Context*. Strategies can be used as template parameters (*Template* design pattern) if strategy can be selected at compile-time and does not change at run-time.

```
public interface SortInterface {
      public void sort(int[] array);
}
```

The concrete implementations of the SortInterface can be given as:

```
public class QuickSort implements SortInterface {
      public void sort(int[] array) {
                  //Quick sort logic
            }
}

public class BubbleSort implements SortInterface {
      public void sort(int[] array) {
                  //Bubble sort logic
      }
}
```

The dependent abstract *Context* class and its dependent concrete class can be given as:

```
public class Sorter {
```

```
        private SortInterface strategy;
        public void setSorter(SortInterface strategy) {
          this.strategy = strategy;
        }
        public SortInterface getSorter() {
          return this.strategy;
        }
        public abstract void doSort(int[] listToSort);
    }
    public class MySorter extends Sorter {
        public void doSort(int[] listToSort)
          getSorter().sort(listToSort);
          // other processing
        }
    }
```

Sample Client Code:

```
public class StrategyTest {
    public static void main(String[] args) {
        int[] listToBeSoted = {18, 26, 26, 12, 127, 47, 62, 82, 3, 236, 84, 5};
        MySorter mysorter = new MySorter();
        mysorter.setSorter(new BubbleSort());
        mysorter.doSort(listToBeSoted);
        mysorter.setSorter(new QuickSort());
        mysorter.doSort(listToBeSoted);
    }
}
```

Question: What is the difference between Strategy and Bridge design patterns?

Answer: Both of the patterns have the same UML diagram. But they differ in their intent since the strategy is related with the behavior and bridge is for structure.

Furthermore, the coupling between the context and strategies is tighter that the coupling between the abstraction and implementation in the bring pattern.

Question: What is the difference between State and Strategy patterns?

Answer: The difference between State and Strategy is in intent. In state design pattern, it is the object that is in control of deciding which algorithm to use (which depends on its current state), while in strategy; it is the client which is in control of what algorithm to use.

6.12 Template Method Design Pattern

The template method pattern is a behavioral class pattern. A template method defines the steps of an algorithm. One or more of the algorithm steps can be overridden by subclasses to allow different behaviors while ensuring that the overall algorithm is still followed.

A behavioral class pattern uses inheritance for distribution of behavior. In the template method pattern, a method (the *template method*) defines the steps of an algorithm. The implementation of these steps (ie, *methods*) can be deferred to subclasses. Thus, a particular algorithm is defined in the template method, but the exact steps of this algorithm can be defined in subclasses. The template method is implemented in an abstract class. The steps (methods) of the algorithm are declared in the abstract class, and the methods whose implementations are to be delegated to subclasses are declared abstract.

Examples For Template Method Design Pattern

The *Template Method* defines steps of an algorithm in an operation, and defers some steps to subclasses. *House* builders use the Template Method when developing a new subdivision. A typical subdivision consists of a limited number of floor plans with different variations available for each. Within a floor plan, the base, windows, plumbing work, and wiring works will be identical for each house. Variation can be introduced in the later stages of construction to produce different variety of models. For example, we can add extra front and back stairs to get a new model.

UML Diagram For Template Method Design Pattern

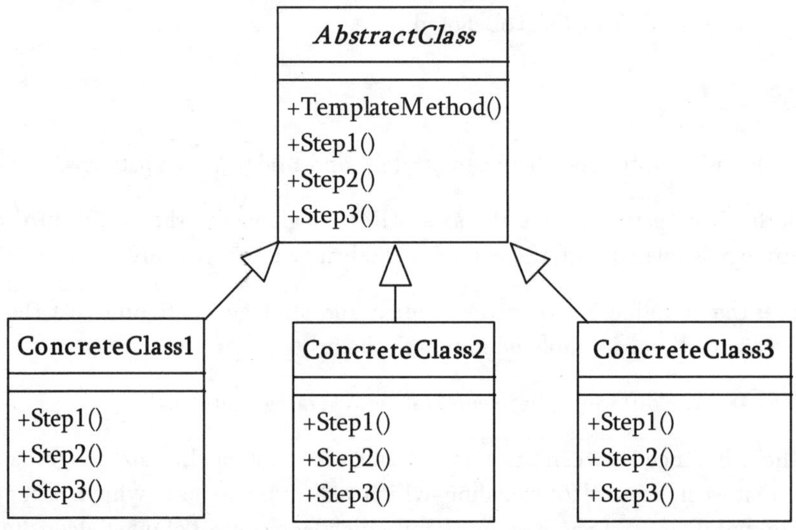

The UML class diagram above describes the template method design pattern. The items in the diagram are described below:

- *AbstractClass*: It defines abstract operations that concrete subclasses define to implement steps of an algorithm. It implements a template method which defines the steps of an algorithm. The template method calls primitive operations as well as operations defined in AbstractClass or those of other objects.
- *ConcreteClass*: They implement the primitive operations to carry out subclass-specific steps of the algorithm. When a concrete class is called the template method code will be executed from the base class while for each method used inside the template method will be called the implementation from the derived class.

Steps For Creating Template Method Design Pattern

- Understand the algorithm, and decide which steps are standard and which steps are peculiar to each of the current classes.
- Define a new abstract base class.
- Define the steps of the algorithm (now called the "template method").
- Define a method in the base class for each step that requires many different implementations. This method can have a default implementation – or – it can be defined as abstract.
- Invoke the method(s) from the template method.
- Each of the existing classes declares an "is-a" relationship to the new abstract base class.
- Remove from the existing classes all the implementation details that have been moved to the base class.
- The only details that will remain in the existing classes will be the implementation details specific to each derived class.

When To Use Template Method Design Pattern?

We can use the Template Method pattern in the following cases:

- When behavior of an algorithm can change and subclasses implement the behavior through overriding.
- When we want to avoid code duplication, implementing variations of the algorithm in subclasses.
- Template Method may not be an obvious choice in the beginning. The general indication that we should use the pattern is when we find that we have two almost identical classes working on some logic. At that stage, we should consider the power of the template method pattern to clean up our code.

Template Method Design Pattern Implementation

Let us consider an example for the template method pattern. Lunch is an abstract class with a template method called *prepareLunch*() that defines the steps involved in preparing a lunch. We declare the method as final so that it can't be overridden.

The algorithm defined by *prepareLunch*() consists of four steps: *prepareIngredients*(), *cooking*(), *eating*(), and *cleaning*(). The *eating*() method is implemented in abstract class and subclasses can override the implementation. The *prepareIngredients*(), *cooking*(), and *cleaning*() methods are are declared abstract so that subclasses need to implement them.

```
public abstract class Lunch {
    // template method
    public final void prepareLunch() {
    prepareIngredients();
        cooking();
        eating();
        cleaning();
    }
    public abstract void prepareIngredients();

    public abstract void cooking();

    public void eating() {
        System.out.println("I am eating. Please don't disturb me.");
    }

    public abstract void cleaning();
}
```

The McDonaldMeal class extends Lunch and implements Lunch's three abstract methods.

```
public class McDonaldMeal extends Lunch {
    public void prepareIngredients() {
        System.out.println("Getting chicken, onion, and French fries etc..");
    }

    public void cooking() {
        System.out.println("I am cooking McDonald Meal.");
    }

    public void cleaning() {
        System.out.println("Cleaning plates and throwing away the paper plates.");
    }
}
```

The KFCMeal class implements Lunch's three abstract methods and also overrides the *eating*() method.

```
public class KFCMeal extends Lunch {
    public void prepareIngredients() {
        System.out.println("Getting burger, cool drinks, and French fries etc..");
    }
```

```
        public void cooking() {
            System.out.println("I am cooking KFC Meal.");
        }

        public void eating() {
            System.out.println("The tacos are tasty.");
        }

        public void cleaning() {
            System.out.println("Cleaning the dishes.");
        }
    }
```

The *TemplateMethodTest* class creates a *McDonaldMeal* object and calls its template method *prepareLunch*() method. It creates a *KFCMeal* object and calls *prepareLunch*() on the *KFCMeal* object.

```
    public class TemplateMethodTest {
        public static void main(String[] args) {
            Lunch meal1 = new McDonaldMeal();
            meal1.prepareLunch();

            Lunch meal2 = new KFCMeal();
            meal2.prepareLunch();
        }
    }
```

6.13 Visitor Design Pattern

The visitor pattern is a behavioral object design pattern. The visitor pattern is used to simplify operations on groupings of related objects. These operations are performed by the *visitor* rather than by placing this code in the classes being visited. Since the operations are performed by the visitor rather than by the classes being visited, the operation code gets centralized in the visitor rather than being spread out across the grouping of objects. This gives better code maintainability. The visitor pattern also avoids the use of the *instanceof* operator in order to perform calculations on similar classes.

When To Use Visitor Pattern?

Visitor pattern is useful if we want to perform operations on a collection of objects of different types. One approach is to iterate through each element in the collection and then do something specific to each element, based on its class. If we don't know what type of objects are in the collection then that can get pretty tricky. If we just wanted to print out the elements in the collection, we could write a simple method like:

```
public void printCollection(Collection collection) {
  Iterator iterator = collection.iterator()
  while (iterator.hasNext())
    System.out.println(iterator.next().toString())
}
```

The above approach will not work if the objects are from different classes. I mean, what if, for example, we have a vector of hashtables? We must check the type of object returned from the collection:

```
public void printCollection(Collection collection) {
  Iterator iterator = collection.iterator()
  while (iterator.hasNext()) {
    Object o = iterator.next();
    if (o instanceof Collection)
      printCollection((Collection)o);
    else
      System.out.println(o.toString());
  }
}
```

Now, we have handled nested collections, but what about other objects that do not return the String that you need from them? What if we want to add extra string around String objects and add an *I* after Integer objects? The code gets still more complex:

```
public void printCollection(Collection collection) {
  Iterator iterator = collection.iterator()
  while (iterator.hasNext()) {
    Object o = iterator.next();
    if (o instanceof Collection)
      printCollection((Collection)o);
    else if (o instanceof String)
      System.out.println("This is a string and its value is "+ o.toString());
    else if (o instanceof Integer)
      System.out.println(o.toString() + "I");
    else
      System.out.println(o.toString());
  }
}
```

If we keep on adding if-else conditions, then the code will lose its maintainability. To solve this issue, Visitor pattern is used.

UML Diagram For Visitor Design Pattern

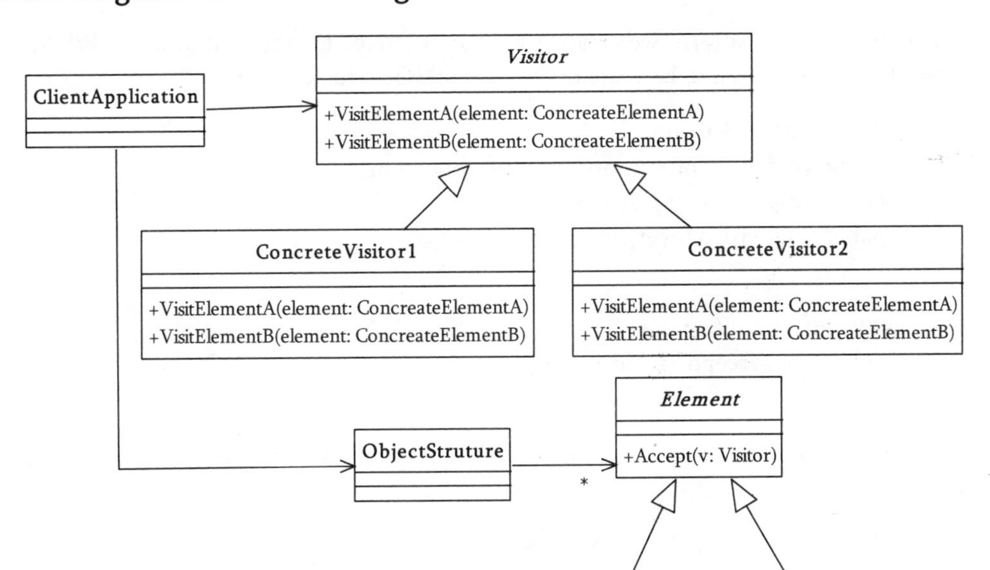

The participant's classes in this pattern are:

- *Visitor*: This is an interface or an abstract class used to declare the visit operations for all the types of visitable classes. Usually the name of the operation is the same and the operations are differentiated by the method signature: The input object type decides which of the method is called.
- *ConcreteVisitor*: For each type of visitor all the visit methods, declared in abstract visitor, must be implemented. Each Visitor will be responsible for different operations. When a new visitor is defined it has to be passed to the object structure.
- *Visitable*: is an abstraction which declares the accept operation. This is the entry point which enables an object to be "visited" by the visitor object. Each object from a collection should implement this abstraction in order to be able to be visited.
- *ConcreteVisitable*: Those classes implements the Visitable interface or class and defines the accept operation. The visitor object is passed to this object using the accept operation.
- *ObjectStructure*: This is a class containing all the objects that can be visited. It offers a mechanism to iterate through all the elements. This structure is not necessarily a collection. In can be a complex structure, such as a composite object.

Visitor Pattern Implementation

To implement Visitor pattern, we create a *Visitor* interface for the visitor, and a *Visitable* interface for the collection to be visited. The two interfaces look like this:

```
public interface Visitor{
  public void visitCollection(Collection collection);
  public void visitString(String string);
  public void visitInteger(Integer integer);
}

public interface Visitable{
  public void accept(Visitor visitor);
}
```

We then have concrete classes that implement the Visitor and Visitable interfaces. For a concrete String, you might have:

```
public class VisitableString implements Visitable{
  private String value;

  public VisitableString(String string) {
    value = string;
  }

  public void accept(Visitor visitor) {
    visitor.visitString(this);
  }
}
```

In the accept method, we call the correct visitor method for this type:

```
visitor.visitString(this)
```

That lets you implement a concrete Visitor as the following:

```
public class PrintVisitor implements Visitor{
  public void visitCollection(Collection collection) {
    Iterator iterator = collection.iterator()
    while (iterator.hasNext()) {
    Object o = iterator.next();
    if (o instanceof Visitable)
      ((Visitable)o).accept(this);
  }

  public void visitString(String string) {
    System.out.println("This is a string and its value is " + o.toString());
```

```
    }

    public void visitInteger(Integer integer) {
      System.out.println(integer.toString() + "I");
    }
  }
```

By then implementing a *VisitableInteger* class and a *VisitableCollection* class that each call the appropriate visitor methods, we get the same result as the messy if-else *printCollection* method but with a much cleaner approach.

In *visitCollection*(), we call Visitable.accept(this), which in turn calls the correct visitor method. That is called a *double-dispatch*; the *Visitor* calls a method in the *Visitable* class, which calls back into the *Visitor* class.

Problems With Visitor Design Pattern

With *Visitor* pattern, it is hard to add new concrete elements. Adding a *ConcreteElement* involves adding a new operation to the *Visitor* interface and a corresponding implementation in each concrete visitor implementation. Visitor pattern is best used in cases where the object structure is stable but the set of operations may change frequently.

Summary Of Visitor Design Pattern

The visitor simply provides methods for processing each respective data type and lets the data object determine which method to call. Since the data object intrinsically knows its own type, the determination of which method on the visitor algorithm to call is trivial.

Thus the overall processing of the data involves a dispatch through the data object and then a subsequent dispatch into the appropriate processing method of the visitor. This is called *double dispatching*.

One key advantage of using the Visitor Pattern is that adding new operations to perform upon our data structure is very easy. All we have to do is create a new visitor and define the operation there.

The problem with the visitor pattern is that because the each visitor is required to have a method to service every possible concrete data, the number and type of concrete classes cannot be easily altered once the visitor pattern is implemented.

Chapter-7

GLOSSARY AND TIPS

7.1 What Are Design Patterns?

A *design pattern* is a general repeatable solution to a commonly occurring problem in software design. A design pattern is not a *finished* design that can be transformed directly into code. It is a description for how to solve a problem that can be used in many different situations.

Since design patterns consist of proven reusable architectural concepts, they are reliable and they speed up software development process. In simple words, there are a lot of common problems which a lot of developers have faced over time.

These common problems ideally should have a common solution too. It is this solution when documented and used over and over becomes a design pattern.

We cannot always apply the same solution to different problems. Design patterns would study the different problems at hand and suggest different design patterns to be used.

However, the type of code to be written in that design pattern is solely the discretion of the Project Manager who is handling that project.

Design patterns should present a higher abstraction level though it might include details of the solution. However, these details are lower abstractions and are called *strategies*. There may be more than one way to apply these strategies in implementing the patterns.

7.2 How To Use Design Patterns?

To use design patterns in our application:

1. We need to understand the problem at hand. Break it down to fine grained problems. Each design pattern is meant to solve certain kinds of problems. This would narrow down our search for design patterns.
2. Read the problem statement again along with the solution which the design pattern will provide. This may instigate to change a few patterns that we are to use.
3. Now figure out the interrelations between different patterns. Also decide what all patterns will remain stable in the application and what all need to change.

7.3 Why Design Patterns?

Design patterns can speed up the development process by providing tested, proven development paradigms. Good software design requires considering issues that may not become visible until later in the implementation.

Reusing design patterns helps to prevent issues that can cause major problems, and it also improves code readability.

- Experienced designers reuse solutions that have worked in the past.
- Knowledge of the patterns that have worked in the past allows a designer to be more productive and the resulting designs to be more flexible and reusable.

7.4 What To Observe For A Design Pattern?

For each of the design pattern understand the following:

- What is the name of the pattern?
- What is the type of pattern? Whether it is a Structural, Creational or Behavioral pattern.
- What is the goal (also called *intent*) of the pattern?
- What are the other names for the pattern?
- When to use the pattern?
- What are the examples for the pattern?
- What is the UML diagram (aka *Structure*) for the pattern? A graphical representation of the pattern.
- Who are the participants in the pattern? A listing of the classes and objects used in the pattern and their roles in the design.
- How classes and objects used in the pattern interact with each other.
- A description of the results, side effects, and tradeoffs (Consequences) caused by using the pattern.
- How to implement the pattern?
- What are the related Patterns? Other patterns that have some relationship with the pattern; discussion of the differences between the pattern and similar patterns.

7.5 Using Patterns To Gain Experience

An important step in designing object-oriented system is discovering the objects. There are various techniques that help discovering the objects (for example, use cases and collaboration diagrams). Discovering the objects is the difficult step for inexperienced designers.

Lack of experience can lead to too many objects with too many interactions and therefore dependencies and that creates a system which is hard to maintain and impossible to reuse. This spoils the goal of object-oriented design.

Design patterns help overcome this problem because they teach the lessons distilled from experience by experts: patterns document expertise. Also, patterns not only describe how software is structured, but also tell how classes and objects interact, especially at run time. Taking these interactions and their into account leads to more flexible and reusable software.

7.6 How To Choose A Design Pattern?

In the previous chapters, we have discussed many design patterns. We can choose from them, but how do we identify which design pattern is appropriate for the given problem?

To know which design pattern to use and how to apply the pattern to a specific problem, it is important to understand these guidelines.

- We can't apply patterns without knowing about them. The first important step is studying the patterns. We can implement a pattern in many ways. The more you see different implementations of patterns, the more you will understand the intent of the pattern and how a single pattern can have varying implementations.
- Do you need to introduce the complexity of a design pattern? It's common for developers to try to use a pattern to solve every problem when they are studying patterns. You always need to weigh the upfront time needed to implement a pattern for the benefit that it's going to give. Try keeping it simple.
- Generalize your problem; identify the issues you're facing in a more abstract manner. Look at how the intent of each pattern and principle is written, and see if your problem fits with the problem that a particular pattern or principle is trying to solve. Remember that design patterns are high-level solutions; try to abstract your problem, and don't focus too hard on the details of your specific issue.
- Look at patterns of a similar nature and patterns in the same group. Just because you have used a pattern before doesn't mean it will always be the correct pattern choice when solving a problem.
- Encapsulate what varies. Look at what will likely change with your application. If you know that a special offer discount algorithm will change over time, look for a pattern that will help you change it without impacting the rest of your application.
- After chosing a design pattern, ensure that you use the language of your pattern along with the language of the domain when naming the participants in a solution.
- By using the patterns common vocabulary along with the language of your domain, you will immediately make your code more readable and understandable to other developers with patterns knowledge.

7.7 Can We Use Design Patterns Always?

Using design patterns properly gives reusable code, the consequences generally include some costs as well as benefits. Reusability is often obtained by introducing encapsulation, or indirection, which can decrease performance and increase complexity.

We should *not* try to *force* the code into a specific pattern, rather notice which patterns start to crystalise out of your code and help them along a bit. That means, writing a program that does *X* using pattern *Y* is *not* a *good idea*. It might work for hello world class programs (small programs) fit for demonstrating the code constructs for patterns, but not much more.

The main concern is that people often have a tendency to wrong design patterns. After learning a few, see the usefulness of them, and without realizing it turn those few patterns into a kind of golden hammer which they then apply to everything.

The key isn't necessarily to learn the patterns themselves. The key is to learn to identify the scenarios and problems which the patterns are meant to address. Then applying the pattern is simply a matter of using the right tool for the job. It's the job that must be identified and understood before the tool can be chosen.

The question is when did you start doing everything using patterns? Not all solutions fit neatly into an existing design pattern and adopting a pattern may mean that you muddy the cleanness of your solution.

You may find that rather than the design pattern solving your problem you generate a further problem by trying to force your solution to fit a design pattern.

We should not overuse the patterns in projects where they are really not necessary. The key is *try* to keep the code clean, modular and readable and make sure the classes aren't tightly coupled.

7.8 Categories Of Design Patterns

There are many types of design patterns. Lot of research is going to codify design patterns in particular domains, including use of existing design patterns as well as domain specific design patterns. Examples include:

- User interface design patterns
- Secure usability patterns
- Web design patterns
- Business model design patterns
- Information visualization design patterns
- Secure design patterns

This book deals with fundamental design patterns given by *GoF*. *GoF* gave 23 design patterns and they were categorized into to *three* types as given below.

- Creational design patterns
- Structural design patterns
- Behavioral design patterns

7.9 Creational Design Patterns

This design category is all about the class instantiation. Creational design patterns are design patterns that deal with object creation methods. These design patterns tries to create objects in a manner suitable to the situation.

If we do not follow creational patterns, the basic form of object creation may create design problems and adds complexity to the design. Creational design patterns solve this problem by controlling this object creation.

7.9.1 Categories Of Creational Design Patterns

Creational design patterns are sub-categorized into:

- Object-Creational patterns: Deals with Object creation and defer part of its object creation to another object. These patterns use delegation to get the job done.
- Class-Creational patterns: Deals with Class-instantiation and defer its object creation to subclasses. These patterns use inheritance effectively in the instantiation process.

Examples for creational design patterns (5 Design Patterns):

- *Abstract Factory* pattern: Provides an interface for creating related or dependent objects without specifying the objects' concrete classes.
- *Builder* pattern: Separates the construction of a complex object from its representation so that the same construction process can create different representation.
- *Factory Method* pattern: Allows a class to defer instantiation to subclasses.
- *Prototype* pattern: Specifies the kind of object to create using a prototypical instance, and creates new objects by cloning this prototype.
- *Singleton* pattern: Ensures that a class only has one instance, and provides a global point of access to it.

Object-Creational patterns	Class-Creational patterns
Abstract Factory Builder Prototype Singleton	Factory Method

7.10 Structural Design Patterns

Structural Patterns describe how objects and classes can be combined to form larger structures. In software engineering, structural design patterns are design patterns that help the design by identifying a simple way to realize relationships between entities.

Structural design patterns are used to organize our program into groups. This segregation will provide us clarity and gives us easier maintainability. Structural design patterns are used for structuring code and objects.

7.10.1 Categories Of Structural Design Patterns

Creational design patterns are sub-categorized into:

- Object-Structural patterns: Deals with how objects can be associated and composed to form larger, more complex structures.
- Class-Structural patterns: Deals with abstraction using inheritance and describe how it can be used to provide more useful program interface.

Examples for creational design patterns (7 Design Patterns):

- *Adapter* pattern: Allows us to provide a new interface for a class that already exists, allowing reuse of a class where our client requires a different interface.
- *Bridge* pattern: Allows us to decouple a class from it's interface. This allows the class and it's interface to be changed independently over time which can lead to more reuse and less future shock. It also allows us to dynamically switch between implementations at runtime allowing more runtime flexibility.
- *Composite* pattern: It allows the client to deal with complex and flexible tree structures. The trees can be built from various types of containers or leaf nodes, and it's depth or composition can be adjusted or determined at runtime.
- *Decorator* pattern: Allows us to dynamically modify an object at runtime by attaching new behaviors, or by modifying existing ones.
- *Facade* pattern: This pattern allows us to simplify the client by creating a simplified interface for a subsystem.
- *Flyweight* pattern: This pattern optimizes memory use when we need a design a class with which our client will need to create huge number runtime of objects.
- *Proxy* pattern: This pattern provides a surrogate object that controls access to some other object. The aim of this pattern is to simplify the client when it needs to use an object that has complications.

Object-Structural patterns	Class-Structural patterns
Bridge Composite Decorator Facade Flyweight Object Adapter Proxy	Class Adapter

7.11 Behavioral Design Patterns

Behavioral patterns *deals* with communication (*interaction*) between the objects. The interactions between the objects should be such that they are talking to each other and still are loosely coupled.

The *loose* coupling is the key for architectures. In this, the implementations and the client should be loosely coupled in order to avoid hard-coding and dependencies.

Behavioral design patterns deals with relationships among communications using different objects. They find common communication patterns and provide a well-known solution to implement this communication giving more flexibility.

7.11.1 Categories Of Behavioral Design Patterns

Behavioral patterns describe not just patterns of objects or classes but also the patterns of communication between them. Behavioral patterns are used to avoid hard-coding and dependencies. Behavioral design patterns are sub-categorized into:

- Object-Behavioral patterns: Behavioral object patterns use object composition rather than inheritance. Describes how a group of objects collaborate to perform some task that no single object can perform alone.
- Class-Behavioral patterns: Behavioral class patterns uses *inheritance* rather than inheritance to describe algorithms and flow of control.

Examples for creational design patterns (11 Design Patterns):

- *Chain* of *Responsibility* Pattern: A way of passing a request between a chain of objects.
- *Command* Pattern: The *Command* pattern is used when there is a need to issue requests to objects without knowing anything about the operation being requested or the receiver of the request.
- *Interpreter* Pattern: *Interpreter* provides way to include language elements in a program.
- *Iterator* Pattern: Iterators are used to access elements of an aggregate (collection) object sequentially without exposing its underlying representation.
- *Mediator* Pattern: Defines simplified communication between classes.
- *Momento* Pattern: Capture and restore an object's internal state.
- *Observer* Pattern: A way of notifying change to a number of classes.
- *State* Pattern: Changes an object's behavior when its state changes.
- *Strategy* Pattern: Encapsulates an algorithm inside a class.
- *Template Method* Pattern: Defer the exact steps of an algorithm to a subclass.
- *Visitor* Pattern: Defines a new operation to a class without change.

Object-Behavioral patterns	Class-Behavioral patterns
Chain of Responsibility	Interpreter

Command Iterator Mediator Memento Observer State Strategy Visitor	Template Method

7.12 What Are Antipatterns?

Though the use of patterns fulfills our objectives in the applications; there will be several cases where applications did not fulfill their goals. The architects of these applications too need to document these wrong decisions. This helps us in not repeating these mistakes in our future applications. Such documented mistakes are called *antipatterns*.

Thus antipatterns are negative solutions which cause more problems than what they address. For example, we might use entity beans which have fine-grained interfaces which can directly be accessed from the client side. This would result in considerable RMI and transaction management overhead. It results in poor performance and un-scalable applications.

7.13 Refactoring

Refactoring is a disciplined technique for restructuring an existing code, altering its internal structure without changing its external behavior. Learning different design patterns is not sufficient to becoming a good designer. We have to understand these patterns and use them where they have more benefits.

Using too many patterns (more than required) would be over-engineering and using less design patterns than required would be under-engineering. In both these scenarios we use refactoring. Refactoring is a change made to the internal structure of the software to make it easier to understand and cheaper to modify, without changing its observable behavior.

7.14 Design Patterns vs. Frameworks

Software frameworks can be confused with design patterns. They are closely related.

Design Patterns	Frameworks
These are recurring solutions to problems that arise during the life of a software application in a particular context.	A framework is a group of components that cooperate with each other to provide a reusable architecture for applications with a given domain.

The primary goal is to: • Help improve the quality of the software in terms of the software being reusable, maintainable, extensible, etc. • Reduce the development time	The primary goal is to: • Help improve the quality of the software in terms of the software being reusable, maintainable, extensible, etc. • Reduce the development time
Patterns are logical in nature.	Frameworks are more physical in nature, as they exist in the form of some software.
A design pattern does not exist in the form of a software component on its own. It needs to be implemented explicitly each time it is used.	Frameworks are not complete applications on their own. Complete applications can be built by inheriting the components directly.
Patterns provide a way to do *good* design and are used to help design frameworks.	Design patterns may be used in the design and implementation of a framework.

7.15 Tips

1. Provide consistent and intuitive class interface: Clients which uses the class only need to know how to use the class and should not be forced to know how the functionality if provided.
2. Provide common properties of classes in base class: Common properties of various classes should be identified and should be provided in a common base class (which may be an abstract, concrete or a pure interface class). Placing virtual methods in the base class interface is the basis of runtime polymorphism; it also avoids code duplication and unnecessary downcasts.
3. Do not expose implementation details in the public interface of the class: If the class interface exposes any implementation details of the class, it violates the rules of abstraction. Also, any changes to internal details of the class can affect the interface of the class, which is not desirable.
4. Consider providing helper classes while designing large classes.
5. Keep the data members private.
6. Provide lowest possible access to methods.
7. Try to keep *loose* coupling between classes: Classes should be either independent of other classes or they should use only the public interface of other classes. Strive for such loose coupling between the classes because such classes are easy to understand, use, maintain and modify.
8. While designing the classes beware of order of initialization as they are provided by the compiler or the implementation.
9. Avoid calling virtual functions in constructors (applicable to C++): Constructors do not support runtime polymorphism fully as the derived objects are still in

construction when base class constructor executes. So, avoid calling virtual functions from base class constructors, which might result bugs in the code.
10. Consider providing *factory* methods.
11. Make constructor *private* if there are *only* static members in the class: When there are only static members in the class, there is no need to instantiate it.
12. Avoid creating useless temporary objects.
13. Prefer virtual function over *RTTI* (RunTime Type Identification) [applicable to C++]: Extensive use of RTTI can potentially make the code difficult to manage. Whenever you find cascading *if – else* statements for matching particular types to take actions, consider redesigning it by using virtual functions.
14. Write unit test cases for classes.
15. Overload functions only if the functions semantically do the same thing.
16. Do not use inheritance when only values are different among classes.
17. Hierarchically partition the namespace.
18. Try eliminating all forms of code *duplication*.
19. Use *design patterns* whenever *appropriate*.
20. Know and make best use of the standard library (applicable to C++).
21. *Provide* catch *handlers* for specific exceptions before general exceptions.
22. Forget about inheritance when you're modeling objects. It is just one way of implementing common code. When you are modeling objects just pretend you're looking at each object through an interface that describes what it can be asked to do. Don't make decisions about inheritance relationships based on names.
23. Create loosely coupled classes: Often times when we give each object only one responsibility, the objects tightly couple together. This is a mistake, because it makes reuse harder later on.
24. Practice as many problems as possible. This gives more experience and control in designing the better objects.
25. *Don't* treat objects as place holders for data. Their objective is not to receive a message to do something.
26. Learn Test-Driven Development (*TDD*): It is fifficult to get object model right up front but if we do TDD we're putting in the groundwork to make sure our object model does what it needs to and making it safe to refactor when things change later.
27. Avoid *passing large* data objects as value parameters. If a method takes lot of parameters, the method might be in the wrong class. The best place for a method is right next to most of the fields it uses in the same class (or superclass).
28. Don't test an object to see what type it is and then take action based on that type – that's a code smell that the object should probably be doing the work. It's a hint that you should call the object and ask it to do the work.
29. Putting the methods and data in the *right* class's makes OO code run *faster*.
30. Put *documentation* for a class in the *header* file for the class (applicable to C++). Most users of a class never read the code for the class; the interface should be sufficient.

Chapter-8

DESIGN INTERVIEW QUESTIONS

8.1 Design Interview Questions

In this chapter, we will discuss few common interview questions. Along with them, we have presented few practice questions as well. Try designing classes for those problems so that you will get more confidence in object oriented designing.

For some design problems we have used $C++$ classes to explore $C++$ concepts. If you are not a $C++$ professional, feel free to download the $Java$ code online or try designing your own classes.

Problem-1 Can you explain about access specifiers in $Java$?

Solution: In $Java$, classes, variables, methods and constructors can have *access specifiers*. There are 4 types of access specifiers:

- *private*
- *protected*
- *public*
- No specifier or none

It is important to remember that constructors in $Java$ are treated differently than methods. Constructors are *not* considerd a class member. Class members are made of 2 things:

- Class's variables.
- Class's methods.

Access modifiers specify who can access them. Its effect is different when used on any of:

- Class
- Class variable
- Class method
- Class's constructor

Access Specifiers for Class Variables and Class Methods: Below is a table showing the effects of access specifiers for class members (i.e. class variable and class methods).

Yes = Can Access. No = No Access.

Specifier	Class	Subclass	Package	Other Packages
private	Yes	No	No	No
protected	Yes	Yes	Yes	No
public	Yes	Yes	Yes	Yes
No specifier	Yes	No	Yes	No

For example, if a variable is declared *protected*, then the same class can access it, its subclass can access it, and any class in the same package can also access it, but otherwise a class cannot access it.

If a class member doesn't have any access specifier (the *No specifier* row in above), its access level is sometimes known as *package*.

```
class Test {
   int x = 7;
}
public class Testing {
   public static void main(String[] args) {
      Test var = new Test ();
      System.out.println(var.x);
   }
}
```

The above code compiles and runs. But, if we add *private* in front of int *x*, then we will get a compiler error: "x has private access in Test". This is because when a member variable is *private*, it can *only* be accessed within that class.

Access Specifiers for Constructors: Constructors can have the same access specifiers used for variables and methods. Their meaning is same. For example, when a constructor has *private* declared, then, only the class itself can create an instance of it. Other class in the same package *cannot* create an instance of that class *nor* any subclass of that class. Nor any other class outside of this package.

```
class Test {
   public int x;
   private Test (int n) {
      x=n;
      System.out.println("Test Message!");
   }
}

public class Testing {
   public static void main(String[] args) {
      Test t = new Test (3);
```

```
        System.out.println(t.x);
    }
}
```

In the above code, it won't compile because Test's constructor is *private* but it is being created outside of itself. If we delete the *private* keyword in front of *Test*'s constructor, then it compiles.

Constructors in Same Class Can Have Different Access Specifiers: Remember that a class can have more than one constructor, each with different parameters. Each constructor can have different access specifier.

In the following example, the class *Test* has two constructors; one takes an *int* argument, the other takes a *double* argument. One is declared *private*, while the other with no access specifier (default package level access).

```
class Test {
    Test (int n) {
        System.out.println("Test Message-1");
    }
    private Test (double d) {
        System.out.println("Test Message-2");
    }
}

public class Testing {
    public static void main(String[] args) {
        Test t1 = new Test (3);
        // Test t2 = new Test (3.3);
    }
}
```

The fact that there can be constructors with different access specifiers means that in Java, the ability to create an object also depends on which constructor is called to create the object.

Access Specifiers for Classes: For classes, only the *public* access specifier can be used on classes. That is, in every java source code file, only one class in the file is public accessible and that class must have the same name as the file. For example, if the file is *ABC.java*, then there must be a class named *ABC* in it, and that is the class that's public. Optionally, the class can be declared with *public* keyword. By convention, class's names should start with capital letter. So, a class named *ABC* really should be *ABC*, with the file named *ABC.java*.

If we use any other access specifier on classes, or declare more than one class *public* in a file, the compiler will complain.

Problem-2 Given a database application, can you think of classes to generate unique sequence numbers?

Solution: We can use *Singleton* pattern to create a counter to provide unique sequential numbers. This can be used as *primary keys* in a database.

```
public class SequenceNumbers {
    private static SequenceNumber instance;
    private static int counter;
    private SequenceNumber(){
        counter = 0;                    // starting value
    }
    public static synchronized SequenceNumber getInstance(){
        if(instance == null){          // Lazy instantiation
            instance = new SequenceNumber();
        }
        return instance;
    }
    public synchronized int getNext(){
        return ++counter;
    }
}
```

Notes about this implementation:

- Synchronized methods are used to ensure that the class is thread-safe.
- This class cannot be subclassed because the constructor is private. This may or may not be a good thing depending on the resource being protected. To allow subclassing, the visibility of the constructor should be changed to protected.
- Object serialization can cause problems; if a Singleton is serialized and then de-serialized more than once, there will be multiple objects and not a singleton.

Problem-3 Simulate a supermarket (grocery store).

Solution: Before creating the objects let's understand the use-cases for simulating a grocery store. At very top-level, a customer walks into a grocery store, picks up a few items, pays for them, and leaves. To make the problem simple we will discard the corner cases (e.g., what if customer forgets to bring money after billing). The obvious objects of any grocery store are:

- A customer
- A store
- Grocery items of various sorts
- A cashier

One doubt that may arise here is: Do we need to subclass the grocery items (beauty, health, cook etc.)? The answer is no, because these items don't have different behaviors. There is no obvious reason for any of these to be a superclass (or subclass) of any of the others. Another doubt that may arise here is: Should we make a class Person and use it as a superclass of *Customer* and *Cashier*? To make it simple let us not do that. We can always do it later, if we find some data or actions that *Customer* and *Cashier* should both have.

Now, let us start creating classes. The grocery items should be in the *store*, and initially only the store needs to know about them, so we will let the *store* create those. The *Customer* and the *Cashier* both need to know about the *store* (but the *store* kind of just sits there). So, we probably should create the store first. This is because, when we create the *Cashier* and the *Customer*, we want to create them with knowledge of the *store*.

The store is the central idea of this program, so let's put a main method in the *store* to kick things off. Let us call our main class as *GroceryStore*. What does our main method need to do?

- Create a GroceryStore
- Create a Cashier for the store
- Create a Customer who knows about the store
- Tell the Customer to "shop"

```
class GroceryStore {
    public static void main(String args[]) {
        GroceryStore store = new GroceryStore();
        Cashier cashier = new Cashier(store);
        Customer customer = new Customer(store);
        customer.shop();
    }
}
```

With the above code, the customer only shops in this one store. This is adequate for our program, but it's very restrictive and it's trivial to fix. So, the Customer needs to shop: this includes selecting groceries and paying for them.

```
class Customer {
    public void shop(GroceryStore store) {
        selectGroceries(store); // because the store holds the groceries
        checkOut(???); // who or what do we pay?
}
```

Obviously, the *Customer* should pay the *Cashier*. But how does the *Customer* know about the *Cashier*? The Customer knows about (can reference) the GroceryStore and the Cashier knows about the *GroceryStore*. Neither the GroceryStore nor the Customer knows about the Cashier. To fix this, the *Customer* do not know about the *Cashier* as they don't know any clerks personally. Buy the GroceryStore know about the Cashier and the Cashier still needs to know about the GroceryStore. So, the customer class can be changed as:

```
class Customer {
    public void shop(GroceryStore store) {
        selectGroceries(store);
        checkOut(store);
}
```

At this point, we understand that the Customer knows about the GroceryStore, the GroceryStore knows about the Cashier and hence, the Customer can ask the GroceryStore about the Cashier.

```
class GroceryStore {
        GroceryStore() {...} // Constructor
        public static void main(String args[]) {...}
        public void hire(Clerk clerk) {...}
        public Clerk getClerk() {...}
}
class Customer {
        public void shop(GroceryStore store) {...}
        public void selectGroceries(GroceryStore  store) {...}
        checkOut(GroceryStore  store) {...}
}
```

There's just one Cashier, whom we hired like this:

```
GroceryStore store = new GroceryStore();
Cashier cashier = new Cashier();
store.hire(cashier);
```

So we need to write the hire method. Also, don't forget the store and Cashier need to know about each other.

```
class GroceryStore {
        Cashier myCashier;
        public void hire(Cashier cashier) {
                myCashier = Cashier;
                cashier.takePosition(this);
        }
}
class Cashier {
        GroceryStore myStore;
        public void takePosition(GroceryStore store) {
                myStore = store;
        }
}
```

The Customer call gets the Cashier from GroceryStore as:

```
class Store {
        Cashier myCashier;
        ...
        public Cashier getCashier() {
                return myCashier;
        }
        ...
}
```

Next, construct a Store containing an array of GroceryItems (along with how many of each).

```
public int KINDS_OF_ITEMS = 4;
public GroceryItem[ ] item = new GroceryItem[KINDS_OF_ITEMS];
public int[ ] itemCount = new int[KINDS_OF_ITEMS];

GroceryStore() {
        item[0] = new GroceryItem("milk", 2.12);
        item[1] = new GroceryItem("butter", 2.50);
        item[2] = new GroceryItem("eggs", 0.89);
        item[3] = new GroceryItem("bread", 1.59);
        for (int i = 0; i < KINDS_OF_ITEMS; i++) {
           itemCount[i] = 50;  // the store has lots of everything
        }
}
```

Customer selects the items as:

```
GroceryItem[ ] myShoppingBasket = new GroceryItem[20];
Random random = new Random();
public void selectGroceries(GroceryStore store) {
   int itemsInMyBasket = 0;
   for (int i = 0; i < store.KINDS_OF_ITEMS; i++) {
      for (int j = 0; j < 3; j++) {
         if (random.nextInt(2) == 1) {              // choose up to 3 of it
            myShoppingBasket[itemsInMyBasket] = store.item[i];
            store.itemCount[i] = store.itemCount[i] - 1;
            itemsInMyBasket = itemsInMyBasket + 1;
         }
      }
   }
}
```

The Customer can checkout as:

```
void checkOut(GroceryStore  store) {
    Cashier cashier = store.getCashier();
    double total = cashier.getBill(myShoppingBasket);
    myMoney = myMoney - total;
    cashier.pay(total);
}
```

The final code for our discussion is:

```
public class GroceryStore {
    Cashier myCashier;
    public int KINDS_OF_ITEMS = 4;
    public GroceryItem[ ] item = new GroceryItem[KINDS_OF_ITEMS];
    public int[ ] itemCount = new int[KINDS_OF_ITEMS];
    double money = 1000.00;

    GroceryStore() {
        item[0] = new GroceryItem("milk", 2.12);
        item[1] = new GroceryItem("butter", 2.50);
        item[2] = new GroceryItem("eggs", 0.89);
        item[3] = new GroceryItem("bread", 1.59);
        for (int i = 0; i < KINDS_OF_ITEMS; i++) {
            itemCount[i] = 50;  // the store has lots of everything
        }
    }

    public static void main(String args[]) {
        GroceryStore store = new GroceryStore();
        Cashier cashier = new Cashier();
        store.hire(cashier);
        Customer customer = new Customer();
        customer.shop(store);
    }

    public void hire(Cashier cashier) {
        myCashier = cashier;
        cashier.takePosition(this);        // "this" = this store
    }

    public Cashier getCashier() {
        return myCashier;
    }
}

public class Customer {
    GroceryItem[ ] myShoppingBasket = new GroceryItem[20];
```

```
    Random random = new Random();
    double myMoney = 100.00;

    public void shop(GroceryStore store) {
        selectGroceries(store); // because the store holds the groceries
        checkOut(store);
    }

    public void selectGroceries(GroceryStore store) {
        int itemsInMyBasket = 0;
        for (int i = 0; i < store.KINDS_OF_ITEMS; i++) { // for each kind of item
            for (int j = 0; j < 3; j++) {              // choose up to 3 of it
                if (random.nextInt(2) == 1) {
                    myShoppingBasket[itemsInMyBasket] = store.item[i];
                    store.itemCount[i] = store.itemCount[i] - 1;
                    itemsInMyBasket = itemsInMyBasket + 1;
                }
            }
        }
    }

    void checkOut(GroceryStore  store) {
        Cashier cashier = store.getCashier();
        double total = cashier.getBill(myShoppingBasket);
        myMoney = myMoney - total;
        cashier.pay(total);
    }
}

public class Cashier {
    GroceryStore myStore;

    public void takePosition(GroceryStore store) {
        myStore = store;
    }

    public double getBill(GroceryItem[] item) {
        double total = 0;
        int itemNumber = 0;
        while (item[itemNumber] != null) {
            total = total + item[itemNumber].price;
            System.out.println(item[itemNumber].name + " "
                                                + item[itemNumber].price);
            itemNumber = itemNumber + 1;
        }
        System.out.println("TOTAL     " + total);
```

```
            return total;
        }

        public void pay(double amount) {
            myStore.money = myStore.money + amount;
        }
    }

    public class GroceryItem {
        public String name;
        public double price;

        GroceryItem(String name, double price) {
            this.name = name;
            this.price = price;
        }
    }
```

In addition to above discussion, it is worth mentioning the other points for extensions:

- Providing interface for changing the prices of items.
- Providing discount coupons while checkouts.
- Categorizing the store employees and assigning roles and many more.

Problem-4 Consider a company which wants to process salary hikes of its employees during recession period. As a precautionary measure, instead of hiking all employee salaries it decided to hike only for the employees who met at least any two of the criteria. Can you design the classes and functions to help the company for processing the hike letters?

- Published at least two research papers.
- Got star of the year award.
- Completed at least 5 years of experience.

Solution: As the problem states, the two basic objects of the problem are: *Employee* and *Company*. For each employee, we need to maintain additional information such as number of papers published by employee, whether the employee got the award or not, and also the number of years he spend in current company. To maintain that information, we can define the interface of *Employee* as:

```
    public interface Employee{
        public int getName();            // returns name of employee
        public int getAge();             // returns age of employee
        public int getYearsOnJob();      // number of years on job
        public double getSalary();       // salary in dollars
        public int getID();              // unique employee ID number
        public beeloan gotAward();       // whether the employee got award or not
```

```
    public int getCountPublished(); //number of papers published by employee
}
```

One possible implementation for the employee would be:

```
public class EmployeeImpl implements Employee{
    private int myName;
    private int myAge;
    private int myYearsExp;
    private double mySalary;
    private int myID;
    private boolean gotAward;
    private int papersPublished;
    public EmployeeImpl(String name, int age, int yearsExp, double salary,
                        int id, boolean award, int papersCount){
        myName = name;
        myAge = age;
        myYearsExp = yearsExp;
        mySalary = salary;
        myID = id;
        gotAward = award;
        papersPublished = papersCount;
    }
    public String getName(){
        return myName;
    }
    public int getAge() {
        return myAge;
    }
    public int getYearsOnJob(){
        return myYearsExp;
    }
    public double getSalary(){
        return mySalary;
    }
    public int getID(){
        return myID;
    }
    public boolean gotAward(){
        return gotAward;
    }
```

```
        public int getCountPublished(){
                return papersPublished;
        }
    }
```

We are done with *Employee* class and let us start defining the *Company* class. For simplicity we can discard the unrelated functionality (for example, adding new employees, changing name of employee etc..). We can assume that the Company class is the main class for our problem (which means, Company class takes care of adding employees with the values defined). Once, it generates the employee list we can use that and process for salary hikes.

```
    public class Company{
        private final static int MIN_PUBLISH_COUNT  = 2;
        private final static int MIN_EXP = 5;
        private ArrayList myEmployees;
        private Employee[] empList = {
                new EmployeeImpl("James Bond", 25,3,12000,1, true, 3),
                new EmployeeImpl("Steve Jobs",35,6,13000,2,false, 4),
                new EmployeeImpl("Bill Gates",30,2,14000,true, 1),
                new EmployeeImpl("Jeff",23,1,9999,4, true, 5),
                new EmployeeImpl("Steve Gates",57,15,20000,5, true, 10)
        };
        private double myTotalSalary;

        //set myTotalSalary as total budget = sum of all salaries
        private void calcSalaries(){
                myTotalSalary = 0;
                Iterator it = myEmployees.iterator();
                while (it.hasNext()){
                    Employee e = (Employee) it.next();
                    myTotalSalary += e.getSalary();
                }
        }

        Company(){
                myEmployees = new ArrayList();
                myEmployees.addAll(Arrays.asList(empList));
                calcSalaries();
        }

        public double getBudget(){
                return myTotalSalary;   //returns total of all employee salaries
        }
```

```
    //prints information about all employees
    public void printAll(){
        System.out.println("Number of employees = " + myEmployees.size());
        for(int k=0; k < myEmployees.size(); k++){
           Employee e = (Employee) myEmployees.get(k);
           System.out.println(k + ".\t id = " + e.getID()+ "\t$"+e.getSalary());
        }
        System.out.println("total budget = "+getBudget());
    }
    private boolean employeeIsEligible(Employee emp){
      return (emp.getCountPublished() >= MIN_PUBLISH_COUNT
            && emp.gotAward()) ||
           (emp.getCountPublished() >= MIN_PUBLISH_COUNT
                        && emp.getYearsOnJob() >= MIN_EXP) ||
           (emp.getYearsOnJob() >= MIN_EXP && emp.gotAward());
    }
    public void processRetirements(){
        Iterator it = myEmployees.iterator();
        while (it.hasNext()){
           Employee e = (Employee) it.next();
           if (employeeIsEligible(e)){
                 System.out.println(e.getID() + " is eligible for salary hike\n");
           }
        }
    }
}
```

Problem-5 Design the library management system.

Solution: We all know how a library system works. The basic components of the library are: library items (like books, CDs, journals etc..), and a mechanism for giving books to users. The interface for LibraryItem is straightforward except for the decision to return a boolean for the method checkOut. To simplify our discussion, we can confine ourselves to only books. The book class can be defined as:

```
public class Book{
   private String theAuthor, theTitle, pageCount, year, edition;
   public Book(String author, String title, String pages,
                              String yearPublished, String bookEdition){
     theAuthor = author;
     theTitle = title;
     pageCount = pages;
     year = yearPublished;
```

```
        edition = bookEdition;
    }
    public String getAuthor(){
        return theAuthor;
    }
    public String getTitle(){
        return theTitle;
    }
    public String getPageCount(){
        return pageCount;
    }
    public String getYear(){
        return year;
    }
    public String getEdition(){
        return edition;
    }
}
public interface LibraryItem{
    public String getID(); // return id of this item
     //return true if checking out (no holder) possible
    //and assign a new holder otherwise (existing holder) return false
    public boolean checkOut(String holder);
    public String getHolder();//return current holder
    // We can add more functions based on requirement
}
```

Now, to create a library book we can simply implement the *LibraryItem* interface and extend the book class. It shouldn't duplicate state from the *Book* class (so no author/title, those are accessible via super.getXX methods), but a *LibraryBook* needs an ID and a holder, so those instance variables are required.

```
public class LibraryBook extends Book implements LibraryItem{
    private String theID;
    private String theHolder;
    public LibraryBook(String author, String title, String id,  int pageCount,
                                                        int year, int edition){
        super(author, title, pageCount, year, edition);
        theID = id;
    }
    public String getHolder(){
```

```
        return theHolder;
    }
    public boolean checkOut(String holder){
        if (theHolder == null){
            theHolder = holder;
            return true;
        }
        return false;
    }
    public String getID(){
        return theID;
    }
}
```

Now, let us define the library class which maintains the library items as a collection. The problem statement pretty much requires a mapping of IDs toLibraryItems to facilitate efficient implementation of the *checkOut* and *getHolder* methods. For this, we can use a hash map.

```
public class Library{
    private Map items;
    public Library(){
        items = new HashMap();
    }
    public void add(LibraryItem theItem){
        items.put(theItem.getID(), theItem);
    }
    public void checkout(String id, String holder){
        LibraryItem item = (LibraryItem) items.get(id);
        item.checkOut(holder); // ignore return value here
    }
    public String getHolder(String id){
        LibraryItem item = (LibraryItem) items.get(id);
        return item.getHolder(); // precondition: item in library
    }
}
```

Problem-6 Design a Cinema Management System.

Solution: Let us start our discussion by understanding the components of a typical Cinema Management System (CMS). As we know any cinema (movie that is being played) associated with a number of theaters and each theater contains a set of rows with a number of seats. Also, each seat will have a specification.

- *Seat specification*: Specifies the properties of a seat.
- *Seat*: A Seat keeps track of what type it is and whether or not it is reserved.
- *Row of seats*: Models a row of seats.
- *Seating chart*: Models a seating chart (set of rows of seats) for a theater.
- *Theater*: Models one theater, including its configuration of rows of seats.
- *Movie*: Models a movie. A movie screening may be the event at a Show.
- *CineGoer*: Models a cinema goer, a customer of the Cinema. Human customers will interact with the software system.
- *Show*: Models a show. For now, assume that the event at all shows is the screening of a movie, in one of the theaters of the Cinema, at a given time.
- *Reservation specification*: Specifies the properties of a reservation and mimics the SeatSpecification class.
- *Reservation*: Models a reservation by some movie-goer of some tickets for some show.
- *CinemaManagementSystem*: The Cinema class controls how many theatres it holds, and indexes those theatres.

Now, let us work on each of these components to make CMS complete. We can treat each of these as a separate class.

Seat specification: This class specifies the properties of a seat. For simplicity, we can implement this as a Hashmap <String, Object>. Also, as of this moment we need few methods to check what type a seat object is.

- *addFeature*: adds a specified feature to this seat featureLabel name of the feature e.g. aisle, front row, and featureValue value, typically true as input.
- *checkFeature*: returns the object of the given feature.
- *match*: returns true when this SeatSpecification has all the that givenSpec has, otherwise returns false. Assume that it takes givenSpec as input parameter and indicates the specification that this is being matched against.

```
public class SeatSpecification implements Serializable, Cloneable {
  private HashMap <String, Object> features;
  public SeatSpecification (){
    features = new HashMap <String, Object> ();
  }
  public void addFeature (String featureLabel, Object featureValue)
                              throws InvalidParameterException {
    if (featureValue == null)
      throw new InvalidParameterException ("feature value cannot be null");
    else  features.put (featureLabel, featureValue);
```

```
    }
    public Object checkFeature(String featureLabel) {
        return features.get (featureLabel);
    }
    public boolean match (SeatSpecification givenSpec) {
        String currFeature;
        if (givenSpec == null)
            return false;
        else {
            Iterator it = givenSpec.features.keySet().iterator();
            while (it.hasNext()) {
                currFeature = (String) it.next();
                if ( ! ( features.get(currFeature) .equals (
                        givenSpec.features.get(currFeature) ) ) )
                    return false;
            }
            return true;
        }
    }
    public SeatSpecification clone() {
        try {
            SeatSpecification c = (SeatSpecification) super.clone();
            c.features = new HashMap <String, Object> ();
            Iterator it = features.keySet().iterator();
            while(it.hasNext()){
                String currFeatureLabel = (String) it.next();
                Object currFeatureValue = features.get(currFeatureLabel);
                c.features.put (currFeatureLabel, currFeatureValue.clone());
            }
            return c;
        }
        catch (CloneNotSupportedException e) {
            return null;
        }
    }
}
```

Seat: A *seat* keeps track of what type it is and whether or not it is reserved. Every seat is associated with a SeatSpecification and a seat ID. Also, assume that we make a seat by combining a row id and seat# e.g. A1. Below are functions that can be added to *Seat* class.

- *setSeatFeature*: adds a specified feature to this seat (calls seat specification method)

- *match*: return true when this seat matches givenSpec, otherwise returns false (calls seat specification method)
- *isReserved*: return true if seat is reserved

```
public class Seat implements Serializable, Cloneable{
  private SeatSpecification spec;
  private String id;

  public Seat(String id) {
    this.id = id;
    spec = new SeatSpecification ();
  }
  public void setSeatFeature (String featureLabel, Object featureValue)
                throws InvalidParameterException {
    spec.addFeature (featureLabel,  featureValue);
  }

  public boolean match(SeatSpecification givenSpec)  {
    return spec.match(givenSpec);
  }

  public String getID() {
    return id;
  }

   public boolean isReserved(){
    return true;
  }
  public Seat clone() {
    Seat cloneSeat = new Seat(id);
    cloneSeat.clone();
    return cloneSeat;
  }
}
```

Row of seats: Models a row of seats. Assume that a collection of seats are maintained in a hash map (HashMap <String, Seat>). Below are functions that can be added to this class.

- *setSeatFeature*: adds a specified feature to a specified seat. It takes seatNum (desired seat number), featureLabel (name of the feature e.g. aisle, front row) and featureValue (value, typically true) as input.
- *addSeat*: adds a single seat to current row of seats.
- *removeSeat*: removes a specified seat from current row of seats.

```
public class RowOfSeats implements Serializable, Cloneable{
   private HashMap<String, Seat> seats;                    //collection of seats
```

```
private String rowId;
private int numOfSeats;
ArrayList<String> keys;
public RowOfSeats (String rowId, int numOfSeats)
    throws InvalidParameterException {
  seats = new HashMap();
  int i = 0; starts at 1
  Seat s;
  while (i < numOfSeats) {
    s = new Seat (Integer.toString(i));
    seats.put(s.getID(), s);
    i++;
  }
  keys = new ArrayList<String>();
  this.rowId = rowId;
  this.numOfSeats = numOfSeats;
}
public void setSeatFeature (String seatID, String featureLabel, Object featureValue)
            throws InvalidParameterException {
  if (seats.containsKey(seatID)) {
    Seat s = seats.get(seatID);
    s.setSeatFeature (featureLabel, featureValue);
  }
  else {
    throw new InvalidParameterException (" no seat " + seatID +
                    " in row " + rowId);
  }
}
public String getRowId() {
  return rowId;
}
public int getNumOfSeats() {
  return seats.size();
}
public void addSeat() {
  Seat s;
  numOfSeats += 1;
  s = new Seat (Integer.toString(numOfSeats));
  seats.put(s.getID(), s);
  keys.add(Integer.toString(numOfSeats));
}
```

```
    public void removeSeat(String seatID) throws InvalidParameterException {
      if (seats.containsKey(seatID)) {
        seats.remove(seatID);
      }
      else
      throw new InvalidParameterException("The specified Seat could not be found!");
    }
    public RowOfSeats clone() {
       RowOfSeats newRowOfSeats = (RowOfSeats) super.clone();
       Iterator it = seats.keySet().iterator();
       for(int i = 0; i <= keys.size(); i++) {
         String seatID = keys.get(i);
         while(it.hasNext()) {
           newRowOfSeats.put(seatID, seats.get(seatID).clone());
         }
       }
      return newRowOfSeats;
    }
  }
```

Seating chart: Models a seating chart for a theater and can be cloned by *Theater* class. Seating chart implements the following:

- Hash Map of Rows -> collection of rows with String keys
- *addRowToBack*: add a row from the chart
- *removeRow*: remove a row from the chart
- *setSeatFeature*: set a seat spec within a row
- *getNumberOfRows*: can return number of rows/ number of seats in a row

```
public class SeatingChart implements Cloneable, Serializable{
  HashMap <String, RowOfSeats> chart;
  ArrayList<String> keys;
  public SeatingChart() {
    chart = new HashMap <String, RowOfSeats>();
    keys = new ArrayList<String>();
  }
  public void addRowToBack(String rowId, int numOfSeats)
    throws InvalidParameterException {
      Iterator it = chart.keySet().iterator();
      while(it.hasNext()){
        if(chart.containsKey(rowId)){
          throw new InvalidParameterException ("The row id " + rowId +
```

```
                                                        "already exists.");
            }
        }
        RowOfSeats row = new RowOfSeats (rowId, numOfSeats);
        chart.put(rowId, row);
        keys.add(rowId);
}

public void removeRow(String rowId)
    throws InvalidParameterException {
    Iterator it = chart.keySet().iterator();
    while(it.hasNext()){
        if(chart.containsKey(rowId)){
            chart.remove(rowId);
            for(int i = 0; i <= keys.size(); i++){
                if(rowId.equals(keys.get(i))){
                    keys.remove(i);
                }
            }
        }
        else {
            throw new InvalidParameterException("that row id does not exist");
        }
    }
}

public void setSeatFeature (String rowId, String seatId, String featureLabel,
                                Object featureValue)
    throws InvalidParameterException {
    Iterator it = chart.keySet().iterator();
    while(it.hasNext()){
        if(chart.containsKey(rowId)){
        }
        else {
            throw new InvalidParameterException("that row id or seat id does not exist");
        }
    }
}

public int getNumberOfRows(){
    return chart.size();
}

public int getNumberOfSeatsInRow(String rowId) {
    RowOfSeats currentRow = chart.get(rowId);
```

```
        return currentRow.getNumOfSeats();
    }

    public SeatingChart clone() {
        try {
            SeatingChart c = (SeatingChart) super.clone();

            c.keys = new ArrayList<String> ();
            for (String s : keys)
                c.keys.add (s);

            c.chart = new HashMap <String, RowOfSeats> ();
            Iterator it = chart.keySet().iterator();
            while(it.hasNext()){
                String currRowId = (String) it.next();
                RowOfSeats currROS = chart.get(currRowId);
                c.chart.put (currRowId, (RowOfSeats) currROS.clone());
            }

            return c;
        }
        catch (CloneNotSupportedException e) {
            return null;
        }
    }
}
```

Theater: Models one theater, including its configuration of rows of seats. This class creates a new theatre by taking *theaterID* (the unique name), *startTime* (the hour of this theatre is allowed to begin showing events, in [0,23]), *setupTime* (the number of minutes that it takes to clean this theatre after an event), and *seatingChart* (the layout of rows for the given seating chart) as input. This class can also add a row of seats, adds a specified feature to a specified seat, and can set/get the clean-up time.

- *addRow*: adds a row of numOfSeats plain-vanilla seats to the back of this theater
- *setSeatFeature*: adds a specified feature to a specified seat
- *getBlankSeatingChart*: returns a SeatingChart with all seats unreserved
- *getCleanupTime*: returns the cleanup time needed for the theater (in minutes)
- *setCleanupTime*: sets the cleanup time for the theater (in minutes)

```
public class Theater implements Serializable, Cloneable{
    private SeatingChart seatingChart;
    private String theaterID;
    private int cleanupTime;

    public Theater(String theaterID, int cleanupTime, SeatingChart seatingChart) {
        this.theaterID = theaterID;
```

```
        this.cleanupTime = cleanupTime;
        this.seatingChart = seatingChart;
    }

    public void addRow (String rowId, int numOfSeats)
        throws InvalidParameterException {
        try{
            seatingChart.addRowToBack(rowId, numOfSeats);
        }
        catch(InvalidParameterException e){
            System.out.println("Invalid parameter passed to addRow");
        }
    }

    public void setSeatFeature (String rowId, String seatId, String featureLabel,
                                Object featureValue) throws InvalidParameterException {
        try {
            seatingChart.setSeatFeature(rowId, seatId, featureLabel, featureValue);
        }
        catch(InvalidParameterException e) {
            System.out.println("Invalid parameter passed to setSeatFeature");
        }
    }

    public SeatingChart getBlankSeatingChart() {
        SeatingChart newSeatingChart = seatingChart.clone();
        return newSeatingChart;
    }
    public String getID() {
        return theaterID;
    }

    public int getCleanupTime() {
        return cleanupTime;
    }

    public void setCleanupTime(int cleanupTime) {
        this.cleanupTime = cleanupTime;
    }

    public void setTheaterID(String theaterID){
        this.theaterID = theaterID;
    }

    public void setSeatingChart(SeatingChart seatingChart){
        this.seatingChart = seatingChart;
```

```
        }
    }
```

Movie: Models a movie. A movie screening may be the event at a *Show*. For now, the movie stores its title, director, actor(s), running time (in minutes), rating. It may need to store other attributes if required. This also provides a method for removing an actor from an ArrayList of actors. If the actor is in the ArrayList and is successfully removed then it returns true. If the actor is *not* in the ArrayList and is *not* removed it returns false. The GUI should display a message confirming that the actor was removed or tell them that the actor doesn't exist in this movie.

```
public class Movie implements Serializable{
    private String              title;
    private ArrayList<String>   actors;
    private String              director;
    private int                 runtime;
    private String              rating;
    private String              screenFormat;

    public Movie(String title, String director, int runtime,
            String rating, String screenFormat) {
        this.title = title;
        this.director = director;
        this.runtime = runtime;
        this.rating = rating;
        this.screenFormat = screenFormat;
        actors = new ArrayList<String>();
    }

    public String getTitle() {
        return title;
    }

    public String getDirector() {
        return director;
    }

    public String getRating() {
        return rating;
    }

    public int getRuntime() {
        return runtime;
    }

    public String getScreenFormat() {
        return screenFormat;
```

```
    }
    public void setTitle(String title) {
        this.title = title;
    }
    public void setDirector(String director) {
        this.director = director;
    }
    public void setRating(String rating) {
        this.rating = rating;
    }
    public void setRuntime(int runtime) {
        this.runtime = runtime;
    }
    public void setScreenFormat(String screenFormat) {
        this.screenFormat = screenFormat;
    }
    public void addActor(String actor) {
        actors.add(actor);
    }
    public boolean removeActor(String actor) {
        int i=0;
        boolean removed = false;
        for(String actor1 : actors){
            if(actor.equals(actors.get(i))){
                actors.remove(i);
                removed = true;
                break;
            }
        }
       return removed;
    }
    public ArrayList<String> getActors() {
        return actors;
    }
}
```

CineGoer: Models a cinema goer, a customer of the Cinema. Human customers will interact with the software system. This class manages the user profiles and uses phone number as a default password for the user. Also, it provides a method for changing the password of the user.

```
public class CineGoer{
    private String firstName;
    private String lastName;
    private String phoneNumber;         // default password to log into their account
    private int seatNumber;             // The Number of the seat that they reserved
    private String movieGoingToSee;     // The Movie they are going to see
    private String password;            // The password used to access the account
    private String username;
    private String address;
    private String town;
    private String state;
    private String zipcode;

    public CineGoer(String firstName, String lastName, String phoneNumber,
                    String address, String town, String state, String zipcode){
        this.firstName = firstName;
        this.lastName = lastName;
        this.phoneNumber = phoneNumber;
        this.address = address;
        this.town = town;
        this.state = state;
        if(zipcode.length() == 5){
            this.zipcode = zipcode;
        }
        else
            this.zipcode = "00000";
    }
    public String getFirstName() {
        return firstName;
    }
    public String getLastName() {
        return lastName;
    }
    public String getPhoneNumber() {
        return phoneNumber;
    }
    public String getAddress(){
        return address;
    }
```

```
        public String getTown() {
            return town;
        }

        public String getState() {
            return state;
        }

        public String getZipcode() {
            return zipcode;
        }

        public int getSeatNumber(){
            return seatNumber;
        }

        public String getMovieGoingToSee() {
            return movieGoingToSee;
        }
        public void setMovieGoingToSee(String newMovie) {
            movieGoingToSee = newMovie;
        }

        public void getSeatNumber(int newSeatNumber) {
            seatNumber = newSeatNumber;
        }

        public boolean setPassword(String newPassword) {
            boolean accepted = false;
            if(newPassword.length() >= 6 && newPassword.length() <= 16) {
                password = newPassword;
                accepted = true;
            }
            return accepted;
        }

        public String getPassword() {
            return password;
        }
    }
```

Show: Models a show. For now, we can assume that the event at all shows is the screening of a movie, in one of the theaters of the Cinema, at a given time.

```
    public class Show {
        Movie m;        //needs the movie for the movie class
```

```
        Theater t;          // needs the theater id from theater class
        int startTime;  // the time the actual movie begins to show
        public Show (Theater t, Movie m, int startTime) {
            this.m = m;
            this.t = t;
            if(startTime > 9 && startTime < 22)
                this.startTime = startTime;

        }
        public void setReservation(Reservation r) {
        }
        public int getMovieTime() {
            return startTime;
        }
        public Movie getMovieTitle() {
            return m;
        }
    }
```

Reservation specification: Specifies the properties of a reservation and mimics the SeatSpecification class. Below are the functions of this class:

- *isValidMovie*: Checks to see if the movie is showing in the theater.
- *isValidTime*: Checks to see if the time listed is available for a movie showing.
- *isValidDate*: Checks to see if the date listed is available for a movie showing.
- *isValidRow*: Checks to see if the row is available.
- *isAvailableSeat*: Checks to see if the seat is available.

```
public class ReservationSpecification implements Serializable {
    private HashMap <String, Object> features;
    public ReservationSpecification (){
        features = new HashMap <String, Object> ();
    }
    public boolean IsValidMovie(Show m){
        return(true);
    }
    public boolean IsValidTime(){
        return(true);
    }
    public boolean IsValidDate(){
        return(true);
```

```
    }
    public boolean isValidRow(RowOfSeats r){
        return(true);
    }
    public boolean isAvailableSeat(Seat s){
        return(true);
    }
}
```

Reservation: Models a reservation by some movie-goer of some tickets for some show. Each reservation is associated with a reservation spec. This class provides a method for adding a seat to reservation.

- *addReservedSeat*: adds the given Seat to this reservation.
- *getShow*: getShow retrieves the current show the moviegoer reserved.

```
public class Reservation{
    private ArrayList<Seat> seat;
    MovieGoer moviegoer;
    Show show;
    ReservationSpecification resSpec;
    Movie movie;
    public Reservation(MovieGoer moviegoer, Show show,
                            ReservationSpecification resSpec, Movie movie) {
        this.moviegoer = moviegoer;
        this.show = show;
        this.resSpec = resSpec;
        this.movie = movie;
    }
    public void addReservedSeat (Seat s) {
        seat.add(s);
    }
    public ArrayList<Seat> getListOfSeats() {
        return seat;
    }
    public MovieGoer getMovieGoer() {
        return moviegoer;
    }
    public Show getShow() {
        return show;
    }
```

```
    public Movie getMovie(){
        return movie;
    }
    public String toString(){
        String result;
        result = "Reservation for: " + moviegoer.getFirstName() + " " +
                 moviegoer.getLastName() +  ". " + "Reserved Movie: " + movie.getTitle() +
                 ". " + "Movie Time: " + show.getMovieTime() + ". " + " Movie Duration: "
             + movie.getRuntime() + "mins" + ". " + "Seat #: " + moviegoer.getSeatNumber();
        return result;
    }
    public void PrintReservation(){
       System.out.println("Reservation for: " + moviegoer.getFirstName() + " " +
            moviegoer.getLastName() +  ". " + "Reserved Movie: " + movie.getTitle() + ". " +
                 "Movie Time: " + show.getMovieTime() + ". " + " Movie Duration: " +
            movie.getRuntime() + "mins" + ". " + "Seat #: " + moviegoer.getSeatNumber());
    }
}
```

CinemaManagementSystem: The Cinema class controls how many theatres it holds, and indexs those theatres. This class provides methods for adding a theater.

- *newTheatre*: creates a new theatre and adds it to the collection of theatres
- *saveToFile*: saves current configuration of this cinema
- *open*: restores the configuration of this cinema from the user file
- *addRow*: adds a row of numOfSeats seats to the back of an existing theatre
- *setSeatFeature*: adds a specified feature to a specified seat
- *makeReservation*: this will make a reservation for a CineGoer
- *addMovieGoer*: this will add a movie goer
- *addShow*: this will make a new show
- *createSeatingChart*: creates a seating chart for a theater
- *newMovie*: creates a new movie

```
public class CinemaManagementSystem implements Serializable{
   private HashMap<String, Theater> theaters;           //collection of theatres
   private static final int MIN_CLEAN_UP_TIME = 10; // in minutes
   private static final int EARLIEST_START_TIME = 9; // 9 am, every day private
   Theater th;
   public CinemaManagementSystem () {
      theaters = new HashMap();
   }
```

```
public void saveToFile(String fileName){
   String fn = "cinema.ser"; // filename used to store this

      try{
         ObjectOutputStream outFile = new ObjectOutputStream (
                                             new FileOutputStream(fileName));
         outFile.writeObject(this);
         outFile.close();
      }
      catch(IOException ex){
         ex.printStackTrace();
      }
}
public void open(String fileName) {
   String fn = "cinema.ser";
      try{
         ObjectInputStream inFile = new ObjectInputStream(
                                             new FileInputStream(fileName));
         inFile.readObject();
         inFile.close();
      }
      catch(IOException ex){
         ex.printStackTrace();
      }
      catch(ClassNotFoundException ex){
         ex.printStackTrace();
      }
}
public Theater newTheatre(String theaterID,int cleanUpTime,
                                             SeatingChart seatingChart)
   throws InvalidParameterException {
      Iterator it = theaters.keySet().iterator();
      // check whether theaterId is unique
      while(it.hasNext()){
         if(theaters.containsKey(theaterID)){
            throw new InvalidParameterException ("The theater id " + theaterID
                                                   +"already exists.");
         }
      }
      Theater t1 = new Theater(theaterID, cleanUpTime, seatingChart);
      theaters.put(theaterID, t1);
```

```
        return t1;
    }

    public void changeTheater(Theater th1)
      throws InvalidParameterException{
    }

    public void addRow (Theater th, String rowId, int numOfSeats)
      throws InvalidParameterException {
        Iterator it = theaters.keySet().iterator();
        while(it.hasNext()){
          if(theaters.containsKey(th.getID())){
            th.addRow(rowId, numOfSeats);
          }
            else{
            throw new InvalidParameterException("There is no Theater with that ID");
          }
        }
    }

    public void setSeatFeature (String theaterId, String rowId, int seatNum, String
                featureLabel, Object featureValue) throws InvalidParameterException {
    }

    public Reservation makeReservation(MovieGoer moviegoer, Show show,
                ReservationSpecification resSpec)  throws InvalidParameterException{
        return null;
    }
    public void addMovieGoer(MovieGoer name) { }
    public void addShow(Show s){ }
    public SeatingChart createSeatingChart(SeatingChart sc){
      return sc;
    }
    public Movie newMovie(Movie m){
      return m;
    }
    public void listTheaters() {
      Iterator it = theaters.keySet().iterator();

      while(it.hasNext()){
        System.out.println("Theater ID: " + it.next() + "\n");
      }
    }
```

```
    public void seatingChart(Theater th1)
      throws InvalidParameterException{
      //prints out a seating chart for a theater
    }
}
```

Apart from the above classes we need few more classes which provides the GUI (Graphical User Interface) for the users and admins. For example, we can use an *Admin* view class to access methods in the Cinema Management System to provide necessary interactions for all required functionalities.

- Create Theaters in a Cinema
- Create RowOfSeats in a Theater
- Make changes to all of the above
- Save File
- Open File

Similarly, we can use *CineGoerView* class to provide GUI for the customer and it will provide the following functionality:

- Create a new movie goer, create a new reservation, view movie times
- Modify a movie goer, modify a reservation
- Delete a movie goer, delete a reservation

Problem-7 Design a cache mechanism which uses LRU (Least Recently Used) in *Java*.

Solution: The processing costs for selecting a value from a database-table are fairly high compared to the costs having the value already in memory. So, it seems preferable to use some smart caching-mechanism that keeps often used values in your application instead of retrieving these values from resources somewhere *outside*.

A critical factor when using caches in Java is the size of the cache; when the cache grows too big, the Java Garbage Collector has to cleanup more often (which consumes time) or our application even crashes with a *out of memory* error. One way to control the memory-consumption of caches is to by implementing a caching-strategy like e.g. LRU. Instead of reinventing the wheel, Java provides an easy way to implement a LRU cache.: the *LinkedHashMap*. *LinkedHashMap* class allows us to implement both an LRU and FIFO queues almost without coding. Instantiating *LinkedHashMap* with the third parameter passed as true in this constructor:

```
public LinkedHashMap(int initialCapacity, float loadFactor, boolean accessOrder)
```

causes the map to become an LRU map. That's because the map is ordered by access-order. But passing the third parameter as false makes it a FIFO, because the map is ordered by insertion order. So if you want to use it as an LRU, do the following:

```
HashMap  map = new LinkedHashMap(0, 0.75F, true);
```

One such possible implementation could be given as:

```
import java.util.LinkedHashMap;
import java.util.Map.Entry;
public class LRUCache extends LinkedHashMap {
        private static final long serialVersionUID = 1L;
        private final int capacity;
        private long accessCount = 0;
        private long hitCount = 0;

        public LRUCache(int capacity) {
                super(capacity + 1, 1.1f, true);
                this.capacity = capacity;
        }

        public Object get(Object key) {                    @Override
                accessCount++;
                if (super.containsKey(key)) {
                        hitCount++;
                }
                Object value = super.get(key);
                return value;
        }

        public boolean containsKey(Object key) {           @Override
                accessCount++;
                if (super.containsKey(key)) {
                        hitCount++;
                        return true;
                }else{
                        return false;
                }
        }

        protected boolean removeEldestEntry(Entry eldest) {
                return size() > capacity;
        }

        public long getAccessCount() {
                return accessCount;
        }

        public long getHitCount() {
                return hitCount;
```

```
        }
    }
```

What if the interviewer does not allow us to use LinkedHashMap? An LRU cache solution needs at least two main operations add and search:

1. add(key, value): Adds a key-value pair into the cache. If the cache has reached its capacity then remove the least recently used entry and add the given entry. If the cache is not full then check if the given key-value pair is already in the cache. If it is, then the entry needs to be updated such that it becomes the most recently used entry. In the default case just add entry into the cache and make it the most recently used entry.
2. search(key): Search cache for an entry with the given key. If an entry exist, then make it the most recently used entry and return its value otherwise return null.

Now on to the exciting part of how it works internally. The cache works with two data structures, a HashMap and doubly linked list. HashMap facilitates a constant time look up for a given key. Its value is a *CacheEntry* object that internally stores the key and value (yes, key is stored twice but we'll get to that). CacheEntry objects also have pointers to previous and next cache entries which forms a doubly linked list. The cache has access to head and tail dummy nodes of the doubly linked list to easily add entries in front and remove from the end.

In the below implementation we are storing the key twice: once in a HashMap (for constant-time lookups) and another time in CacheEntry object. Reason for storing the key in a CacheEntry object is being able to remove the eldest entry from the list and subsequently from the map to keep them consistent with each other. Following is the code.

```
class CacheEntry {
        private CacheEntry prev, next;
        private String key, value;

        CacheEntry(String key, String value) {
                this.key = key;
                this.value = value;
        }
        public String getKey() {
                return key;
        }
        public String getValue() {
                return value;
        }

        public void setValue(String value) {
                this.value = value;
```

```
		}
		public CacheEntry getPrev() {
			return prev;
		}
		public void setPrev(CacheEntry prev) {
			this.prev = prev;
		}
		public CacheEntry getNext() {
			return next;
		}
		public void setNext(CacheEntry next) {
			this.next = next;
		}
	}

	class LRUCache {
		private Map<String, CacheEntry> map;
		private CacheEntry head, tail;
		private int maxSize;
		// maxSize specify maximum size of the cache
		public LRUCache(int maxSize) {
			if(maxSize < 1) {
			  throw new IllegalArgumentException("Cache maxSize
							has to be at least 1");
			}
			this.map = new HashMap<String, CacheEntry>();
			head = new CacheEntry("head", NULL);
			tail = new CacheEntry("tail", NULL);
			head.setNext(tail);
			tail.setPrev(head);
			this.maxSize = maxSize;
		}
		public void add(String key, String value) {
			CacheEntry entry = map.get(key);
			if(entry == NULL) {
				// the key is not stored
				entry = new CacheEntry(key, value);
				if(map.size() == maxSize) {
					// max number of elements in cache reached,
					// delete the eldest entry
					CacheEntry deleteEntry = tail.getPrev();
					// remove from the map
					map.remove(deleteEntry.getKey());
```

```
                        // remove from the queue
                        remove(deleteEntry);
                }
                // add entry to the queue
                addFront(entry);
                //add to the map
                map.put(entry.getKey(), entry);
        } else {
                // update the value in case it is different
                entry.setValue(value);
                // access the entry
                accessed(entry);
        }
}

public String search(String key) {
        CacheEntry entry = map.get(key);
        if(entry == NULL) {
                return NULL;
        }
        // update the access
        accessed(entry);
        return entry.getValue();
}

public void accessed(CacheEntry entry) {
        if (entry.getPrev() != head) {
                // remove from its current location in queue
                remove(entry);
                addFront(entry);
        }
}

private void remove(CacheEntry entry) {
        if (entry == head || entry == tail) {
                return;         // error
        }
        entry.getPrev().setNext(entry.getNext());
        if (entry.getNext() != NULL) {
                entry.getNext().setPrev(entry.getPrev());
        }
}

private void addFront(CacheEntry entry) {
        // add the new entry in queue at head
```

```
                    CacheEntry nextEntry = head.getNext();
                    head.setNext(entry);
                    entry.setPrev(head);
                    entry.setNext(nextEntry);
                    if (nextEntry != NULL) {
                          nextEntry.setPrev(entry);
                    }
          }
          // prints the content of the cache
          public void print() {
                    CacheEntry entry = head.getNext();
                    while(entry != tail) {
                          System.out.println("{" + entry.getKey() + ":"
                                                           + entry.getValue() + "}");
                          entry = entry.getNext();
                    }
                    System.out.println();
          }
}
```

Problem-8 Design a simple chat server.

Solution: Chat application can be described as a connection-oriented service, because a user establishes a connection and maintains that connection, sends and receives text for the duration of the session.

This is different from *Web* protocol. In *Web*, the browser asks for a page, and the server sends it; the connection is then closed. But in, *chat* application client need to maintain the connection for the *session*. As a first step, let us understand the basic elements required for designing a chat server. They were:

- Server class (*Listener* class) which can be started as a standalone application.
- Mechanism for *accepting* the connections.
- Mechanism for *reading* and *writing* data on *server* side.
- *Client* class which can be started as a standalone application.
- A thread class which creates separate *thread* for each client.
- Mechanism for *reading* and *writing* data on *client* side.
- *Closing* the chat connections.

Server class (*Listener* class): For simplicity assume that our server will be a stand-alone program. That means, a single Java process running on its own machine. The first thing we have to do is to get ready to receive incoming connections. To do this, we must listen on a port.

Port: A port can be thought of as an address within a single computer. Remember that often a single machine might serve as a Web server, a chat server, an FTP server, and several other kinds of servers at the same time. Because of this, a connection to a server needs to specify not only the address of the machine itself, but also the particular service within the machine.

This internal address is a port and is represented by a single integer between 1 and 65535. Many standard services have a dedicated port number. For example, telnet uses port 23, FTP uses ports 20 and 21, and Web servers, by default, use port 80. Since our chat system is not famous (yet), we're going to have to use one of the port numbers allocated for general use.

We'll use the port number 9999. This means that our server is going to listen for connections on port 9999. Our clients, when connecting to our server machine, will specify that they want to connect to port 9999 on our server machine. This way, our clients and our server will be able to talk.

Sockets: Our communications between client and server will pass through a Java object called a Socket. The most important thing to know about a Socket object is that it contains two Streams. One is for reading data coming in, and the other is for writing data out. That is to say, a Socket has an InputStream and an OutputStream.

Now, let us write the *Server* class code snippet for accepting the connections from clients.

```
public class Server{
   public Server( int port ) throws IOException {
      // All we have to do is listen
      listen( port );
   }

   // Usage: java Server >port<
   static public void main( String args[] ) throws Exception {
      // Get the port # from the command line
      int port = Integer.parseInt( args[0] );
      // Create a Server object, which will begin accepting connections.
      new Server( port );
   }
}
```

Accepting the connections: Our program will be serving many clients. The socket class provides a solution: it serializes the incoming connections. That is, it makes them seem as if they are coming in one at a time.

```
private void listen( int port ) throws IOException {
   // Creating the Server Socket
   ss = new ServerSocket( port );
   System.out.println( "Server is listening on "+ ss );
```

```
    // accepting connections forever
    while (true) {
        // Accept the next incoming connection
        Socket s = ss.accept();
        System.out.println( "Accepted connection from " + s );
        // Create a output stream for writing data
        DataOutputStream dout = new DataOutputStream( s.getOutputStream() );
        // Save this stream so we don't need to make it again
        outputStreams.put( s, dout );
        // Create a new thread for this connection
        new ServerThread( this, s );
    }
}
```

The *accept*() routine is the main function and it is called, it returns a new Socket object that represents a new connection that has come in. After we've dealt with this connection, we call *accept*() and get the next one. This way, no matter *how fast* connections are coming, we get the connections one at a time. The last line of this listing creates a thread to deal with the new connection. This thread is an object called a *ServerThread*.

Server Thread: In Java programs, any class can be made into a thread by implementing the Runnable interface or we can simply create a subclass from the class java.lang.Thread.

The Socket object is essential, because the whole purpose of this thread is to use a socket to communicate with the other side. The Server object will come in handy later on.

```
public class ServerThread extends Thread{
    // Constructor.
    public ServerThread( Server server, Socket socket ) {
        this.server = server;
        this.socket = socket;
        // Start the thread
        start();
    }
}
```

Note that this constructor code is still being run in the main, server thread. The last line, where *start*() is called, is the point at which the new thread comes into being. This thread executes the *run*() method of this object.

How to send/receive data? Every client/server system has a communications protocol, which is nothing more than the format you use to send the data back and forth. The Java language has useful classes called DataInputStream and DataOutputStream. So our protocol will be:

- When a user types something into their chat window, their message will be sent as a string through a DataOutputStream.
- When the server receives a message, through a DataInputStream, it will send this same message to all users, again as a string through a DataOutputStream.
- The users will use a DataInputStream to receive the message.

Removing dead connections: If the thread class realizes that the connection has closed, must ask the Server to remove that connection so that we can be done with it.

```
// The connection is closed for one reason or another,
// so have the server dealing with it
server.removeConnection( socket );
```

It is important to inform the main Server object each time a connection has closed, so that the server can remove the connection from any internal lists, and also so that the server doesn't waste time sending messages to clients that are no longer connected.

Client class: Our client has a graphical user interface (GUI), because it must interact neatly with the user. The server could get by with just a command-line interface, because once it starts running, the user (or administrator) doesn't really need to do anything. But the whole point of the client side is user interaction.

```
public Client( String host, int port ) {
    // Set up the screen
    setLayout( new BorderLayout() );
    add( "North", tf );
    add( "Center", ta );
    // We want to receive messages when someone types a line and hits return,
    //using an anonymous class as a callback
    tf.addActionListener( new ActionListener() {
        public void actionPerformed( ActionEvent e ) {
            processMessage( e.getActionCommand() );
        }
    });
    // ...
```

We won't go into too much detail about this, except to say that our chat window contains a text entry field, for typing new messages, and a text display window, for showing messages from other users. Each time the user types something into the input field, the string is passed to the method *processMessage*().

Connecting to server: The next thing the constructor does is initiate a connection to the server, as follows:

```
    // Connect to the server
```

```
        try {
            // Initiate the connection
            socket = new Socket( host, port );
            System.out.println( "connected to "+socket );
            din = new DataInputStream( socket.getInputStream() );
            dout = new DataOutputStream( socket.getOutputStream() );
            // Start a background thread for receiving messages
            new Thread( this ).start();
        } catch( IOException ie ) {
                System.out.println( ie );
        }
    }
```

Note that we've created a separate thread to process incoming messages.

User input: An applet runs as a component embedded in a larger GUI framework. In this implementation, code generally runs in response to an input event received in one of the GUI windows of the program. The applet processes the event, doing what it needs to do, and then it returns, waiting for the system to send another event along. In this case, the user might type something in the input field. This triggers a call to the anonymous inner class we created in the constructor. This anonymous inner class, in turn, calls *processMessage*(), which is a method we have created.

This method is passed the string that the user typed. What this method then does is simple: it writes the string to the server, and then clears out the text input field so that the user can type something else.

```
        // Gets called when the user types something
        private void processMessage( String message ) {
            try {
                // Send it to the server
                dout.writeUTF( message );
                // Clear out text input field
                tf.setText( "" );
        } catch( IOException ie ) {
                System.out.println( ie );
        }
```

Complete Code:

Server.java

```
    public class Server{
        // The Server Socket for accepting connections
        private ServerSocket ss;
```

```
// A mapping from sockets to DataOutputStreams.
private Hashtable outputStreams = new Hashtable();
public Server( int port ) throws IOException {
    // Listening
    listen( port );
}
private void listen( int port ) throws IOException {
    // Creating the ServerSocket
    ss = new ServerSocket( port );
    System.out.println( "Listening on "+ss );
    while (true) {
        // Accept the connection
        Socket s = ss.accept();
        System.out.println( "Connection from "+s );
        // Create a DataOutputStream for writing data
        DataOutputStream dout = new DataOutputStream( s.getOutputStream());
        // Save this stream so we don't need to make it again
        voutputStreams.put( s, dout );
        // Create a new thread for this connection
        new ServerThread( this, s );
    }
}
// Get an enumeration of all the OutputStreams, one for each client
Enumeration getOutputStreams() {
    return outputStreams.elements();
}
// Send a message to all clients
void sendToAll( String message ) {
    // We synchronize on this because another thread
    // might be calling removeConnection()
    synchronized( outputStreams ) {
        // For each client ...
        for (Enumeration e = getOutputStreams(); e.hasMoreElements(); ) {
            DataOutputStream dout = (DataOutputStream)e.nextElement();
            try {
                dout.writeUTF( message );
            } catch( IOException ie ) {
                    System.out.println( ie );
            }
        }
    }
}
```

```
    // Remove a connection thread that has discovered dead.
    void removeConnection( Socket s ) {
      synchronized( outputStreams ) {
        System.out.println( "Removing connection to "+s );
        // Remove it from our hashtable/list
        outputStreams.remove( s );
        // Closing the socket
        try {
           s.close();
        } catch( IOException ie ) {
          System.out.println( "Error closing "+s );
          ie.printStackTrace();
        }
      }
    }
    // Usage: java Server <port>
    static public void main( String args[] ) throws Exception {
      // Get the port # from the command line
      int port = Integer.parseInt( args[0] );
      // Create a Server object
      new Server( port );
    }
  }
```

ServerThread.java

```
  public class ServerThread extends Thread{
    private Server server;
    private Socket socket;
    public ServerThread( Server server, Socket socket ) {
      this.server = server;
      this.socket = socket;
      start();   // Start the thread
    }
    // This runs in a separate thread when start() is called in the constructor.
    public void run() {
      try {// The client is using a DataOutputStream to write to us
        DataInputStream din = new DataInputStream( socket.getInputStream() );
        while (true) {
          // ... read the next message ...
          String message = din.readUTF();
          System.out.println( "Sending "+message );
          // ... and have the server send it to all clients
```

```
                server.sendToAll( message );
            }
        } catch( EOFException ie ) {
            // This doesn't need an error message
        } catch( IOException ie ) {
            ie.printStackTrace();
        } finally {
            server.removeConnection( socket );
        }
    }
}
```

Client.java

```
public class Client extends Panel implements Runnable{
    // Components for the visual display of the chat windows
    private TextField tf = new TextField();
    private TextArea ta = new TextArea();
    // The socket connecting us to the server
    private Socket socket;
    private DataOutputStream dout;
    private DataInputStream din;
    public Client( String host, int port ) {
        // Set up the screen
        setLayout( new BorderLayout() );
        add( "North", tf );
        add( "Center", ta );
        // We want to receive messages when someone types a line and hits return,
        // using an anonymous class as a callback
        tf.addActionListener( new ActionListener() {
                        public void actionPerformed( ActionEvent e ) {
                                    processMessage( e.getActionCommand() ); } } );
        // Connect to the server
        try {
            // Initiate the connection
            socket = new Socket( host, port );
            System.out.println( "connected to "+socket );
            din = new DataInputStream( socket.getInputStream() );
            dout = new DataOutputStream( socket.getOutputStream() );
            // Start a background thread for receiving messages
            new Thread( this ).start();
        } catch( IOException ie ) {
                    System.out.println( ie );
```

```
        }
    }
    // Gets called when the user types something
    private void processMessage( String message ) {
        try {
            dout.writeUTF( message );     // Send it to the server
            tf.setText( "" );             // Clear out text input field
        } catch( IOException ie ) {
                System.out.println( ie );
        }
    }
    // Background thread runs this: show messages from other window
    public void run() {
        try {
            while (true) {                        // Receive messages one-by-one, forever
                String message = din.readUTF();           // Get the next message
                // Print it to text window
                ta.append( message+"\n" );
            }
        } catch( IOException ie ) {
                    System.out.println( ie );
        }
    }
}
```

ClientApplet.java

```
public class ClientApplet extends Applet{
    public void init() {
    String host = getParameter( "host" );
    int port = Integer.parseInt( getParameter( "port" ) );
    setLayout( new BorderLayout() );
    add( "Center", new Client( host, port ) );
    }
}
```

Limitations of above implementation:

- The chat system we've created has only one chat room. Remember that every message that came into the server was sent out to every single client. This is not satisfactory in the real world, not only because real-world users want separate chat rooms, but because it's a terrible waste of bandwidth.

- In some Java implementations, it's not a good idea to create a thread for each client, because having a lot of threads -- even if they are all asleep -- can bog down the system.
- The comments inside the code for Server.java mention that some thread synchronization is used to prevent problems related to properly maintaining the list of active connections. This is just the kind of synchronization that can really impact performance. If synchronization turns out to be a bottleneck, there are a couple of things you can try:
    - Change removeConnection() to simply make a note of which connection should be removed, perhaps in another list. Then, do the actual removing inside sendToAll(), during or after traversal.
    - Use more than one thread to do the writing in sendToAll().

Problem-9 Which design pattern suits better for an application that prints out the data for visiting (business) cards of all the employees of a large organization?

Solution: A typical business card can be assumed to have the following layout:

<Employee Name>
<Employee Designation>
<Company Name>
<Office Location>
<City><State><County><Zip Code>

From the business card data layout, it can be observed that:

- The *name* and *title* are unique for every employee.
- The company *name* remains the same for all employees and every employee working under a divisional *office* is given the same divisional office address.

One of the simplest strategies for designing this example application is to create a *BusinessCard* class representing a business card as in figure. The *display*() method can be implemented to display the business card data.

BusinessCard
-empName: String -designation: String -company: String -address: String -city: String -state: String -zipCode: String
+display()

Usually, there will be thousands of employees in a large organization (say, IBM) and hence the application may need to create thousands of *BusinessCard* objects. As discussed earlier, the address part of the *BusinessCard* class remains constant for all employees working under a given divisional office.

Hence, using the class representation shown above could lead to duplicate data being created and maintained as part of every new *BusinessCard* instance created. Using the *Flyweight* pattern, the need for storing the duplicate data can be eliminated.

Problem-10 Dice-It is a simple two-person dice game with many possible strategies at varying levels of complexity.

Summary of the game: The game is played by two players using a single pair of dice. The game consists of a series of rounds. During each round, each player take one turn. During their turn, a player rolls a pair of dice and attempt to get the highest possible turn score among the range of value 2 to 12. He or she may continue to roll the dice as along as no score matches their score on the first roll of the turn.

If no such match occurs, the player decides when to stop their turn, and the highest score on that turn is added to the player's total score. If a roll matches the first roll of that turn, the player's turn ends, the turn score for that round is 0, and therefore the player's total score does not change. The winner is the player with the highest score at the end of the game.

By considering the above description, design classes for $Dice - It$.

Solution: From the game description, we can draw the following rules.

1. A game of $Dice - It$ involves two players. The player with the highest total score after given number of rounds is the winner.
2. During a round, each player takes a turn. At the beginning of the game, each player rolls a dice, with the higher roll going first each round. A player's total score is the sum of their turn scores.
3. At the beginning of their turn, a player rolls two sixsided dice and remembers the sum, called their first roll.
4. After their first roll, a player must decide whether to stop or continue.
5. If a player decides to stop, then their turn ends and their score for that turn is their maximum roll during that turn; if the player decides to continue, they roll the dice again.
6. If, in re-rolling the dice, a player re-rolls their first roll, then their turn ends and their score for that turn is zero; otherwise, they must decide (return to rule 5).

For this problem, the following are the trivial objects:

- The Dice-It game
- The player who goes first each roll

- The player who goes second each roll
- Two dice

The dice are simple to model in Java, these dice can be modeled using *Java's* predefined *Random* class. The following *Die* class models a 6-sided die. It constructs a new *Die* object that uses the specified random-number generator. It will have a roll method which returns the result of rolling a die. The value returned is a pseudorandom integer between 1 and 6.

```
public class Die{
    Random generator;
    public Die(Random r) {
        generator = r;
    }
    public int roll(){
        /* The value returned by nextInt(6) will be a pseudorandom integer value
         * between 0 and 5, inclusive. Map this to a value between 1 to 6. */
        return generator.nextInt(6) + 1;
    }
}
```

Since each player roll pair of dice, we can create a Dice with two Die class objects inside it as shown below. It returns the result of rolling a pair of dice. The value returned is a pseudorandom integer between 2 and 12.

```
public class Dice{
    private Die die1;
    private Die die2;
    public Dice(){
        Random r = new Random();
        die1 = new Die(r);
        die2 = new Die(r);
    }
    public int roll(){
        return die1.roll() + die2.roll();
    }
}
```

Each player has public methods to construct itself, return its name, retrieve its score, and take a turn. In addition to these public methods, we have found it useful to add three private utility methods: one to update its local store using the opponent's last roll, one to raise its total score by a given amount, and one to decide whether or not to stop rolling.

Player1 class models one player in the game of Dice-It. It maintains the following data:

- *name*: The player's name.

- *dice*: The Dice object shared by both players.
- *currentRoll*: The value obtained by the most recent roll of the dice.
- *firstRoll*: The value obtained the first time that the dice are rolled during a turn. During the turn, if the player rolls this value a second time, the turn ends and the turn score for is 0
- *turnScore*: The score obtained during the current turn.
- *totalScore*: he player's cumulative score; i.e., the sum of the turn scores for all of the rounds played so far.
- opponentsTurnScore: The most recent turnScore obtained by the other player. This value may be useful when formulating the strategy that determines when to stop rolling the dice.
- *takeTurn*(): Takes one turn for current player. It takes otherTurnScore as parameter (The most recent turn score obtained by the other player. This value may be useful when formulating the strategy that determines when to rolling the dice) and returns the score obtained by this player during the turn.
- *stopRolling*(): This method encapsulates the strategy used by this player to determine when to stop rolling the dice during each turn.

```
public class Player1{
  private String name;
  private Dice dice;
  private int currentRoll;
  private int firstRoll;
  private int turnScore;
  private int totalScore;
  private int opponentsTurnScore;

  /*Creates a new player using the specified dice. The dice object shared by all players.*/
  public Player1(Dice d, String name){
    dice = d;
    this.name = name;
    totalScore = 0;
  }

  /*Resets this player's total score to 0. */
  public void resetTotalScore(){
    totalScore = 0;
  }
  public int score(){
    return totalScore;
  }
  public String name(){
    return this.name;
```

```
    }
    public int takeTurn(int otherTurnScore){
        System.out.println("\t\tFirst roll: " + firstRoll);
        System.out.println("\t\tStopping with turn score = " + turnScore
                                                    + ", total score = " + totalScore);
        System.out.println("\t\tNext  roll: " + currentRoll);
        System.out.println("\t\tOops! Rolled a match!" + "\t\tStopping with turn score = "
                                        + turnScore + ", total score = " + totalScore);
    }
    private boolean stopRolling(){ }
  }

  //Player2 models one player in the game of Dice-It.
   public class Player2{
    private String name;
    private Dice dice;
    private int currentRoll;
    private int firstRoll;
    private int turnScore;
    private int totalScore;
    private int opponentsTurnScore;
    public Player2(Dice d, String name){
        dice = d;
        this.name = name;
        totalScore = 0;
    }
    public void resetTotalScore(){
        totalScore = 0;
    }
    public int score(){
        return totalScore;
    }
    public String name(){
        return this.name;
    }
    public int takeTurn(int otherTurnScore){
        System.out.println("\t\tFirst roll: " + firstRoll);
        System.out.println("\t\tStopping with turn score = " + turnScore
                                                    + ", total score = " + totalScore);
        System.out.println("\t\tNext  roll: " + currentRoll);
        System.out.println("\t\tOops! Rolled a match!" + "\t\tStopping with turn score = "
                                        + turnScore + ", total score = " + totalScore);
    }
```

```
    private boolean stopRolling(){
    }
  }
```

Now using the above class objects let us design the Dice-It class.

```
public class DiceItGame{
  private int numberOfRounds;

  //The player who takes the first turn in each round.
  private Player1 player1;

  //The player who takes the second turn in each round.
  private Player2 player2;

  /*Constructs a new Dice-It game with the specified number of rounds.
   * rounds: The number of rounds in a game.
   * player1Name: Name of player who takes the first turn in each round.
   * player2Name: Name of player who takes the second turn in each round.*/
  public DiceItGame(int rounds, String player1Name, String player2Name){
    numberOfRounds = rounds;

    Dice dice = new Dice();

    // Both players share the same dice.
    player1 = new Player1(dice, player1Name);
    player2 = new Player2(dice, player2Name);
  }

  public void playGame(){
    player1.resetTotalScore();
    player2.resetTotalScore();

    int turnScore = 0;

    for (int round = 1; round <= numberOfRounds; round++) {
      System.out.println("Round " + round + ":");
      // The first player takes a turn.
      System.out.println("\t" + player1.name() + ":");
      turnScore = player1.takeTurn(turnScore);

      // The second player takes a turn.
      System.out.println("\t" + player2.name() + ":");
      turnScore = player2.takeTurn(turnScore);

      // Summarize the results of this round.
     System.out.println("After round " + round + "\n" +
                player1.name() + "'s score: " + player1.score() + "\n" +
                player2.name() + "'s score: " + player2.score());
```

```
            System.out.println();
        }

        // Display the winner of the game.
        if (player1.score() > player2.score()) {
            System.out.println(player1.name() + " wins the game.");
        } else if (player1.score() < player2.score()) {
            System.out.println(player2.name() + " wins the game.");
        } else {
            System.out.println("We have a tie.");
        }
    }
}
```

Problem-11 Consider an application which does the following:

- Accepts customer details (account, address and credit/debit card details)
- Validates the input data
- Saves the input data to appropriate data files

For this application, can you come-up with classes where we can use Facade design pattern?

Solution: To use façade design pattern, there should be some tight coupling between the classes. Let us say that there are three classes — *CustAccount*, *CustAddress* and *CustCreditCard* available in the application, each with its own methods for validating and saving the respective data.

CustAccount.java

CustAccount
-firstName: String -lastName: String
+isValid(): boolean +save(): boolean +getFirstName(): String +getLastName(): String

```
public class CustAccount {
    String firstName;
    String lastName;
    final String ACCOUNT_FILE = "CustAccountData.txt";
    public CustAccount(String fname, String lname) {
        firstName = fname;
        lastName = lname;
```

```
    }
    public boolean isValid() {
        //Let's go with simpler validation here to keep the example simpler.
        ...
    }
    public boolean save() {
        FileUtil futil = new FileUtil();
        String dataLine = getLastName() + "," + getFirstName();
        return futil.writeToFile(ACCOUNT_FILE, dataLine, true, true);
    }
    public String getFirstName() {
        return firstName;
    }
    public String getLastName() {
        return lastName;
    }
}
```

CustAddress.java

CustAddress
-address: String -city: String -state: String
+isValid(): boolean +save(): boolean +getAddress(): String +getCity(): String +getState(): String

```
public class CustAddress {
    String address;
    String city;
    String state;
    final String ADDRESS_FILE = "CustAddress.txt";
    public CustAddress(String add, String cty, String st) {
        address = add;
        city = cty;
        state = st;
    }
    public boolean isValid() {
        /* Validation algorithm could be complex in real-world        applications.
```

```
            Let's go with simpler validation here to keep the example simpler. */
        if (getState().trim().length() < 2)
            return false;
        return true;
    }
    public boolean save() {
        FileUtil futil = new FileUtil();
        String dataLine = getAddress() + "," + getCity() + "," + getState();
        return futil.writeToFile(ADDRESS_FILE, dataLine, true, true);
    }
    public String getAddress() {
        return address;
    }
    public String getCity() {
        return city;
    }
    public String getState() {
        return state;
    }
}
```

CustCreditCard.java

CustCreditCard
-cardType: String -cardNumber: String -cardExpDate: String
+isValid(): boolean +save(): boolean +getCardType(): String +getCardNumber(): String +getCardExpDate(): String

```
public class CustCreditCard {
    String cardType;
    String cardNumber;
    String cardExpDate;
    final String CC_FILE = "CustCC.txt";
    public CustCreditCard(String ccType, String ccNumber, String ccExpDate) {
        cardType = ccType;
        cardNumber = ccNumber;
        cardExpDate = ccExpDate;
```

```
        }
        public boolean isValid() {
            /* Let's go with simpler validation here to keep the example simpler. */
            if (getCardType().equals(AccountManager.VISA)) {
                return (getCardNumber().trim().length() == 16);
            }
            if (getCardType().equals(AccountManager.DISCOVER)) {
                return (getCardNumber().trim().length() == 15);
            }
            if (getCardType().equals(AccountManager.MASTER)) {
                return (getCardNumber().trim().length() == 16);
            }
            return false;
        }
        public boolean save() {
            FileUtil futil = new FileUtil();
            String dataLine = getCardType() + ,"" + getCardNumber()
                                                  + "," + getCardExpDate();
            return futil.writeToFile(CC_FILE, dataLine, true, true);
        }
        public String getCardType() {
            return cardType;
        }
        public String getCardNumber() {
            return cardNumber;
        }
        public String getCardExpDate() {
            return cardExpDate;
        }
    }
```

Now, let us build a client AccountManager that displays the user interface to a user to input the customer data. In order to validate and save the input data, the client AccountManager would:

- Create CustAccount, CustAddress and CustCreditCard objects.
- Validate the input data using these objects.
- Save the input data using these objects.

```
public class AccountManager extends JFrame {
    public static final String newline = "\n";
    public static final String VALIDATE_SAVE = "Validate & Save";
    ...
    public AccountManager() {
```

```
        super(" Facade Pattern - Example ");
        cmbCardType = new JComboBox();
        cmbCardType.addItem(AccountManager.VISA);
        cmbCardType.addItem(AccountManager.MASTER);
        cmbCardType.addItem(AccountManager.DISCOVER);
        ...
        //Create buttons
        JButton validateSaveButton = new JButton(AccountManager.VALIDATE_SAVE);
        ...
    }
    public String getFirstName() {
        return txtFirstName.getText();
    }
    ...
}
```

Applying the *Facade* pattern in this case can give a better design as it promotes low coupling between the client and the subsystem components (*CustAccount*, *CustAddress* and *CustCreditCard* classes in this case).

CustomerFacade
-address: String -city: String -state: String -cardType: String -cardNumber: String -cardExpDate: String -fname: String -lname: String
+setAddress(inAddress: String): void +setCity(inCity: String): void +setState(inState: String): void +setFName(inFName: String): void +setLName(inLName: String): void +setCardType(inCardType: String): void +setCardNumber(inCardNumber: String): void +setCardExpDate(inCardExpDate: String): void +saveCustomerData(): boolean

Applying the *Facade* pattern, let us define a Facade class *CustomerFacade* that offers a higher level, simplified interface to the subsystem consisting of customer data processing classes (*CustAccount*, *CustAddress* and *CustCreditCard*).

```
public class CustomerFacade {
    private String address;
    private String city;
    private String state;
    private String cardType;
    private String cardNumber;
    private String cardExpDate;
    private String fname;
    private String lname;
    public void setAddress(String inAddress) {
        address = inAddress;
    }
    public void setCity(String inCity) {
        city = inCity;
    }
    public void setState(String inState) {
        state = inState;
    }
    public void setFName(String inFName) {
        fname = inFName;
    }
    public void setLName(String inLName) {
        lname = inLName;
    }
    public void setCardType(String inCardType) {
        cardType = inCardType;
    }
    public void setCardNumber(String inCardNumber) {
        cardNumber = inCardNumber;
    }
    public void setCardExpDate(String inCardExpDate) {
        cardExpDate = inCardExpDate;
    }
    public boolean saveCustomerData() {
        CustAddress objAddress;
        CustAccount objAccount;
        CustCreditCard objCreditCard;
        //client is transparent from the following set of subsystem related operations.
        boolean validData = true;
        String errorMessage = "";
        objAccount = new CustAccount(fname, lname);
        if (objAccount.isValid() == false) {
```

```
            validData = false;
            errorMessage = "Invalid FirstName/LastName";
        }
        objAddress = new CustAddress(address, city, state);
        if (objAddress.isValid() == false) {
            validData = false;
            errorMessage = "Invalid Address/City/State";
        }
        objCreditCard = new CustCreditCard(cardType, cardNumber, cardExpDate);
        if (objCreditCard.isValid() == false) {
            validData = false;
            errorMessage = "Invalid CreditCard Info";
        }
        if (!validData) {
            System.out.println(errorMessage);
            return false;
        }
        if (objAddress.save() && objAccount.save() && objCreditCard.save()) {
            return true;
        } else {
            return false;
        }
    }
}
```

The *CustomerFacade* class offers a higher level business service in the form of the saveCustomerData method. Instead of interacting with each of the subsystem components directly, the client *AccountManager* can make use of the simplified interface offered by the *CustomerFacade* object to validate and save the input customer data.

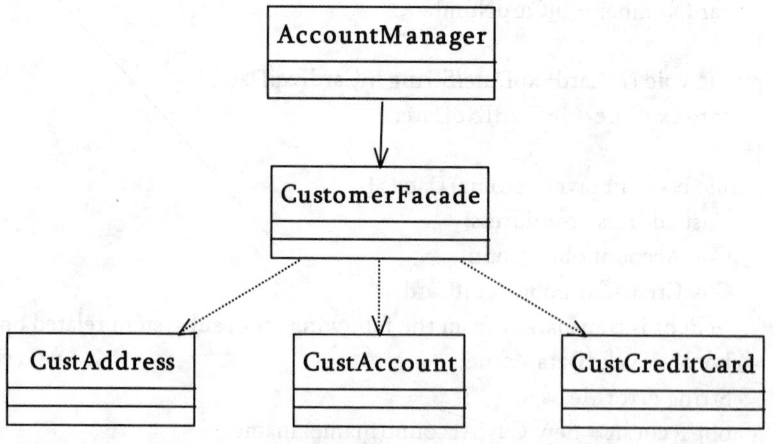

In the revised design, to validate and save the input customer data, the client needs to:

- Create or obtain an instance of the façade CustomerFacade class
- Send the data to be validated and saved to the CustomerFacade instance
- Invoke the saveCustomerData method on the CustomerFacade instance

The *CustomerFacade* handles the details of creating necessary subsystem objects and calling appropriate methods on those objects to validate and save the customer data. The client is no longer required to directly access any of the subsystem (*CustAccount*, *CustAddress* and *CustCreditCard*) objects.

Problem-12 Can you design an online reading system similar to *Amazon Kindle* or *Barne's Nook*?

Solution: Any typical book reader (say, *Amazon Kindle* or *Barne's Nook*) will contain the following options:

- User Profiles
- User Manager: adding/deleting users
- Adding/Removing a book
- Searching for a book
- Reading a book
- Going to specific page of a book and many more

As a first step of design, we can define an interface which captures all the information to be maintained for each of the users (*UserInfoInterface*).

```
public interface UserInfoInterface {
        public void setFirstName(String firstName);
        public void setLastName(String lastName);
        public void setEMail(String eMail);
        public void setAge(String age);
        public void setPhone(String phone);
        public void setSex(String sex);
        public String getFirstName(String firstName);
        public String getLastName(String lastName);
        public String getEMail(String eMail);
        public String getAge(String age);
        public String getPhone(String phone);
        public String getSex(String sex);
}
```

A sample concrete class for *UserInfoInterface* can be given as (*UserInfo*):

```
public class UserInfo implements UserInfoInterface{
        private String firstName;
        private String lastName
```

```
private String eMail
private String age;
private String phone;
private String sex;

UserInfo(String firstName, String lastName, String eMail,
                        String age, String phone, String sex){
        this.firstName = firstName;
        this.lastName = lastName;
        this.eMail = eMail;
        this.age = age;
        this.phone = phone;
        this.sex = sex;
}

public void setFirstName(String firstName) {
        this.firstName = firstName;
}

public void setLastName(String lastName) {
        this.firstName = firstName;
}

public void setEMail(String eMail) {
        this.firstName = firstName;
}

public void setAge(String age) {
        this.firstName = firstName;
}

public void setPhone(String phone) {
        this.firstName = firstName;
}

public void setSex(String sex) {
        this.firstName = firstName;
}

public String getFirstName(String firstName) {
        return firstName;
}

public String getLastName(String lastName) {
        return lastName;
}
```

```
        public String getEMail(String eMail) {
                return eMail;
        }

        public String getAge(String age) {
                return age;
        }

        public String getPhone(String phone) {
                return phone;
        }

        public String getSex(String sex) {
                return sex;
        }
}
```

The below class (*UserManager*) takes care of managing the list of all users. It maintains an arraylist of all users and provides *functionality* like: searching for an user, adding new users, deleting existing users, getting user information of a given user etc...

```
public class UserManager {
  private ArrayList<UserInfo> mUsers = new ArrayList<UserInfo>();

  UserManager() {}
  public List<UserInfo> getUsers() {
    synchronized (mUsers) {
      ArrayList<UserInfo> users = new ArrayList<UserInfo>(mUsers.size());
      for (int i = 0; i < mUsers.size(); i++) {
        users.add(mUsers.valueAt(i));
      }
      return users;
    }
  }

  public UserInfo getUser(int userId) {
    synchronized (mUsers) {
      UserInfo info = mUsers.get(userId);
      return info;
    }
  }

  public boolean exists(int userId) {
    synchronized (mUsers) {
      return (mUsers.get(userId) != null);
```

```
        }
    }

    public void updateUserName(int userId, String name) {
        synchronized (mUsers) {
            UserInfo info = mUsers.get(userId);
            if (name != null && !name.equals(info.name)) {
                info.name = name;
            }
        }
    }

    public static void addUser(String firstName, String lastName,
                            String eMail, String age, String phone, String sex) {
        mUsers.add(new UserInfo(firstName, lastName, eMail, age, phone, sex));
    }

    public boolean removeUser(int id) {
        synchronized (mUsers) {
            return mUsers.remove(id);
        }
    }
}
```

With above steps we are done with user profiles and their maintenance. Now, let us define the interface for a book (*BookInterface*).

```
public interface BookInterface {
        public void addBookMark(int pageNumber);
        public List<Integer> getBookmarks();
        public String getPage(int pageNumber);
}
```

A sample concrete class for *BookInterface* can be given as (*ConcreteBook*):

```
public class ConcreteBook  implements BookInterface{
        private final String authorName;
        private final String bookTitle;
        private final int numberOfPages;
        private final List<String> content;
        private final List<Integer> chapterIndex;
        private List<Integer> bookmarks;

        public ConcreteBook(String authorName, String bookTitle, int
          numberOfPages, ArrayList<String> content, List<Integer> chapterIndex) {
```

```
                this.authorName = authorName;
                this.bookTitle = bookTitle;
                this.numberOfPages = numberOfPages;
                this.content = content;
                this.chapterIndex = chapterIndex;
        }

        public void addBookMark(int pageNumber) {
                bookmarks.add(pageNumber);
        }

        public List<Integer> getBookmarks() {
                return bookmarks;
        }

        public String getPage(int pageNumber) {
                return content.get(pageNumber);
        }
}
```

Finally, we can define the interface for reader (*ReaderInterface*) and its concrete classes (*MyReader*).

```
public interface ReaderInterface {
        public void openBook(String authorName, String bookTitle);
        private boolean finished();
        public void addBookMark();
        public void displayAllBookMark();
        public void nextPage();
        public void previousPage();
        public void goToPage(int pageNumber);
}

public class MyReader implements ReaderInterface{
        private Map<String, Map<String, ConcreteBook>> bookMap;
        private ConcreteBook currentBook;
        private int currentPage;

        public void openBook(String authorName, String bookTitle) {
              currentBook = bookMap.get(authorName).get(bookTitle);
              List<Integer> bookmarks = currentBook.getBookmarks();
              if (bookmarks.isEmpty())
                    bookmarks.add(0);
              currentPage = bookmarks.get(bookmarks.size() - 1);
              System.out.println(currentBook.getPage(currentPage));
```

```
    }

    private boolean finished() {
        return currentPage == currentBook.numberOfPages - 1;
    }

    public void addBookMark() {
        if (!currentBook.getBookmarks().contains(currentPage))
            currentBook.addBookMark(currentPage);
    }

    public void displayAllBookMark() {
        System.out.println(currentBook.getBookmarks());
    }

    public void nextPage() {
        List<Integer> bookmarks = currentBook.getBookmarks();
        bookmarks.remove(currentPage);
        currentPage = finished() ? currentPage : currentPage + 1;
        bookmarks.add(currentPage);
        System.out.println(currentBook.getPage(currentPage));
    }

    public void previousPage() {
        List<Integer> bookmarks = currentBook.getBookmarks();
        bookmarks.remove(currentPage);
        currentPage = currentPage == 0 ?  currentPage : currentPage - 1;
        bookmarks.add(currentPage);
        System.out.println(currentBook.getPage(currentPage));
    }

    public void goToPage(int pageNumber) {
        if (pageNumber < 0 || pageNumber >= currentBook.numberOfPages)
            return;
        List<Integer> bookmarks = currentBook.getBookmarks();
        bookmarks.remove(currentPage);
        currentPage = pageNumber;
        bookmarks.add(currentPage);
        System.out.println(currentBook.getPage(currentPage));
    }
}
```

With all the above classes it is very straight forward to write a sample test class.

Problem-13 Design a simple address book which stores the contacts.

Solution: The basic functionality of any phonebook are adding a contact, searching for a contact, editing a contact, deleting a contact, viewing contact details and so on. Let us assume that *Contact* struct holds information for one contact entry and contacts with *no* first name will be recognised as deleted.

```
struct Contact{
        char firstName[20];        /*First Name*/
        char lastName[30];         /*Last Name*/
        char areaCode[6];          /*Area Code*/
        char phoneNumber[10];  /*Telephone Number*/
        char email[60];            /*E-Mail*/
        char webaddr[60];          /*website*/
        char address[60];          /*Home Address*/
};
```

Now, let us define the class to support the above functionality.

```
class PhoneBook{
        Contact contact;
  public:
        //ensures that the first name is not empty.
        bool CreateMe(){ //ensures that the first name is not empty.
                if(contact.first[0]=='\\')
                        return true;
                else return false;
        };
        void EditContact();
        void DeleteContact();
        void PrintContact(bool showall);
        bool SearchContact(char SearchThis[60]);
};
```

SearchContact() prompts the user to enter a string and locates the entry matching that string in *phonebook*. If a matching entry is found, it returns true else returns false. To make the search operation efficient, we can match the given data with any of the details of contact (with preference given to name, area code, phone number, mail, website and home address).

```
bool PhoneBook::SearchContact(char searchThis[60]){
        if(!strcmp(contact.first, searchThis)){
                return true;
        }
        else if(!strcmp(contact.last, searchThis)){
                return true;
        }
```

```
        else if(!strcmp(contact.areacode, searchThis)){
                return true;
        }
        else if(!strcmp(contact.number, searchThis)){
                return true;
        }
        else if(!strcmp(contact.email, searchThis)){
                return true;
        }
        else if(!strcmp(contact.webaddr, searchThis)){
                return true;
        }
        else if(!strcmp(contact.address, searchThis)){
                return true;
        }
        else {
                return false;
        }
}
```

To edit the contact we can simply read the data from user and see whether we have any such contact in phonebook or not. If so, we can edit the contact by taking new values from user. *EditContact*() prompts the user to the details for that name.

If *phonebook* contains an entry mathcing the entered string, the details for that entry is changed to the new data. If no entry matching the entered string is found, *phonebook* is unchanged.

```
void PhoneBook::EditContact(){
        cout << endl << "First Name: "; cin >> contact.firstName;
        cout << endl << "Last Name: "; cin >> contact.lastName;
        cout << endl << "Area Code: "; cin >> contact.areaCode;
        cout << endl << "Phone Number: "; cin >> contact.phoneNumber;
        cout << endl << "E-mail: "; cin >> contact.email;
        cout << endl << "WebAddress: "; cin >> contact.webaddr;
        cout << endl << "HomeAddress: "; cin >> contact.address;
        cout << "OK." << endl;
}
```

DeleteContact() makes the first name of contact empty and it indicates the non-existence of contact in phonebook.

```
void PhoneBook::DeleteContact{
        contact.first[0]='\\';
```

```
}
```

PrintContact() prints the current contact first name and last name. If we pass true as argument to it, it prints all details of the contact as shown below.

```
void PhoneBook::PrintContact(bool showall){
        cout << endl << "First Name: " << contact.first
                << endl << "Last Name: " << contact.last;
        if(showall){
                cout << endl << "Area Code: " << contact.areacode
                    << endl << "Phone Number: " << contact.number
                    << endl << "E-mail: " << contact.email
                    << endl << "WebAddress: " << contact.webaddr
                    << endl << "HomeAddress: " << contact.address
                    << endl << "---" << endl <<  "OK." << endl;
        }
}
```

clearscreen() clears the screen and put the header.

```
inline void clearscreen(){
        system("CLS"); /* Clear the screen */
        cout << "Simple PhoneBook " << endl
            << "--------------------------------" << endl << endl;
}
```

Now, let us put all the above discussion together and write sample code to test the functionality. For simplicity, let us assume that user selects a menu option and based on his/her selection we call the corresponding functions as show below.

```
#define MAX_CONTACTS 100
int main(){
        /*Definitions and preparations*/
        PhoneBook book[MAX_CONTACTS];
        char menuOption='0';
        int i;
        char buff[60];
        bool found;
        for(int j=0; j<MAX_CONTACTS; j++)
                book[j].Delete();

        clearscreen();
        while(PhoneBook != '6'){
                found=false;
                i=0;
```

```
cout << "1. Create New Contact" << endl;
cout << "2. Edit Contact's data" << endl;
cout << "3. Delete a Contact" << endl;
cout << "4. Search a Contact" << endl;
cout << "5. Save All Data" << endl;
cout << "6. Terminate program" << endl;

cout << endl << "Selection: ";
cin >> menuOption;
switch(menuOption){
        case '1':
                do{
                        if(book[i].CreateMe()){
                                book[i].Edit();
                                found = true;
                        }
                        i++;
                }while(i < MAX_CONTACTS && !found);
                break;
        case '2':
                cout << "Please, give me a name or sth..." << endl;
                cin >> buff;
                if(book[i].SearchContact(buff) && !book[i].CreateMe()){
                        cout << endl << "EDITING: ";
                        book[i].Print(false);
                        book[i].Edit();
                }
                else{
                        i++;
                }
                break;
        case '3':
                cout << "Please, give me a name or sth..." << endl;
                cin >> buff;
                if(book[i].SearchContact(buff) && !book[i].CreateMe()){
                        cout << endl << "DELETING: ";
                        book[i].Print(true);
                        cout << endl << "Are you sure? (y/n)";
                        cin >> buff[0];
                        if(buff[0]=='y') book[i].Delete();
                }
                else{
```

```
                    i++;
                }
                break;
            case '4':
                cout << endl << "Search: " << endl;
                cin >> buff;
                if(book[i].SearchContact(buff) && !book[i].CreateMe()){
                    book[i].Print(true);
                    cout << endl;
                }
                else{
                    i++;
                }
                break;
                cout << endl << "Type a number to continue ";
                cin >> i;
            case '5':
                /*SAVE Data*/
                break;
        }
    }
    cout << endl << endl << "END. " << endl;
    system("PAUSE");
    return 0;
}
```

Before ending the discussion, we can further note down a list of additional functionality that can be added to above list.

- *ImportPhoneBook*() reads contacts from the text file.
- *ExportPhoneBook*() writes contacts from the text file.
- *MatchContacts*() matches multiple contacts with regular expressions.
- *SortContacts*() sorts contacts based on given parameter.

Problem-14 *Grading a class*: Assume that we are given a file of student's data and the objective of this problem is to write a report of student grades in a class. Assume that each line of the students data file consists of a name, a mark for the midterm, a mark for the final, and marks for assignments.

The number of assignments is not fixed; students do as many as they want to. The name is a single name with no embedded blanks. A line of the output file is similar to a line of the input file, but the first number is the total mark, computed as 25% of the midterm mark plus 55% of the final mark plus the median of the assignments. The output is written twice, once sorted by name, and once sorted by total mark.

Sample Input:

Gates 47 83 9 8 4 7 6 9 8
Jobs 36 88 8 6 7 4 9 7 8 7
...

Sample Output:

Sorted by student name:

Jobs 67.5 36 88 8 6 7 4 9 7 8 7
Gates 67.2 47 83 9 8 4 7 6 9 8
...

Sorted by student marks:

Gates 67.2 47 83 9 8 4 7 6 9 8
Jobs 67.5 36 88 8 6 7 4 9 7 8 7
...

Solution: Goal of the design is to use an object to store a student record and to put as much problem-specific information as possible into the corresponding class. Below code shows the action items of the problem. The first paragraph takes a file name and tries to open the file.

The second paragraph declares the principal data object of the program, a vector of *Students*. From this paragraph, we can tell that the *Student* class must provide a reading capability (>>) and a method process to compute the final mark. The last part of the program opens an output file and writes the data to it twice, first sorted by name and then sorted by total marks. From this, we understand that the *Student* class must provide two sorting functions, *sortByNames* and *sortByMarks*.

```
int main(){
        string inputFileName;
        cout << "Please enter file name: ";
        cin >> inputFileName;
        ifstream ifs(inputFileName.c_str());

        if (!ifs){
           cerr << "Failed to open " << inputFileName << endl;
           return 1;
        }
        vector<Student> classData;
        Student stud;
        while (ifs >> stud){
           stud.process();
           classData.push_back(stud);
        }
        ofstream ofs("StudentGrades.txt");
        sort(classData.begin(), classData.end(), sortByNames);
        ofs << "Sorted by name:\n";
        showClass(ofs, classData);
        sort(classData.begin(), classData.end(), sortByMarks);
        ofs << "\nSorted by marks:\n";
        showClass(ofs, classData);
```

```
}
```

The function *showClass* is straightforward and uses an iterator to traverse the vector of marks data.

```
void showClass(ostream & os, const vector<Student> & classData){
    for ( vector<Student>::const_iterator it = classData.begin(); it != classData.end(); ++it )
        os << *it << endl;
}
```

Below code shows the declaration for class *Student*.

```
class Student{
        friend ostream & operator<<(ostream & os, const Student & stud);
        friend istream & operator>>(istream & is, Student & stud);
        friend bool sortByNames(const Student & left, const Student & right);
        friend bool sortByMarks(const Student & left, const Student & right);
        public:
            void process();
            string getName();
            void getName(string newName);
        private:
            static string::size_type maxNameLen;
            string name;
            int midterm;
            int final;
            vector<int> assignments;
            double total;
};
```

There is a public method, *process*, which performs any necessary computation on the data read from the marks file. The private data includes the information that is read from the marks file (*name*, *midterm*, *final*, and *assignments*) and computed information, *total*.

For formatting the output, we need to know the length of the longest name. This is an attribute of the class, not the object, and so it is declared as a static data member. We need methods for input (>>) and output (<<); these are declared as *friends*.

We need comparison functions that will be used for sorting: *sortByNames* orders by students names, and *sortByMarks* orders by students total marks. There is an important design choice here. The four friend functions cannot be member functions, because of the way they are called.

The next step is to complete the implementation of class *Student* by providing definitions for functions and initial values for static variables. The static data member can be initialized like this:

```
int Student::maxNameLen = 0;
```

The public function *process* calculates the total mark. Calculating the total mark requires finding the median of the assignments. The median is meaningless for an empty vector, and the median function requires a non-empty vector as its argument. Thus process, calls median only if the student has done at least one assignment.

```
void Student::process(){
    if (maxNameLen < name.size())
        maxNameLen = name.size();
    total = 0.25 * midterm + 0.55 * final;
    if (assignments.size() > 0)
        total += median(assignments);
}
```

The *median* calculation is performed by the function shown below. The main design issue for this function is how to pass the vector of scores. Since we have to sort the vector in order to find the median, we cannot pass it by constant reference. If we pass it by reference, the caller will get back a sorted vector. Although this does not matter much for this program, a function should not in general change the data it is given unless the caller needs the changed value. Consequently, we choose to pass the vector by value, incurring the cost of copying it.

```
// Requires: scores.size() > 0.
double median(vector<int> scores) {
    typedef vector<int>::size_type szt;
    szt size = scores.size();
    assert(size > 0);
    sort(scores.begin(), scores.end());
    szt mid = size / 2;
    return size % 2 == 0 ? 0.5 * (scores[mid] + scores[mid+1]) : scores[mid];
}
```

Below code shows the comparison functions that we need for sorting. The parameter lists of these functions are determined by the requirements of the sort algorithm: there must be two parameters of the same type, both passed by constant reference. Since we have declared these functions as friends of Student, they have access to Student's private data members. The type of name is string and the type of total is double; both of these types provide the comparison operator <.

After sorting, the records will be arranged in increasing order for the keys and names will be alphabetical. Records sorted by marks will go from lowest mark to highest mark. To reverse this order, putting the students with highest marks at the "top" of the class, all we have to do is change < to >.

```
bool sortByNames(const Student & left, const Student & right){
```

```
    return left.name < right.name;
}
bool sortByMarks(const Student & left, const Student & right){
    return left.total < right.total;
}
```

The compiler has to perform a number of steps to determine that these functions are called by the statements

```
sort(classData.begin(), classData.end(), sortByNames);
sort(classData.begin(), classData.end(), sortByMarks);
```

Finally, below functions shows the extractor and inserter for class Student.

```
istream & operator>>(istream & ifs, Student & stud){
    if (ifs >> stud.name){
        ifs >> stud.midterm >> stud.final;
        int mark;
        stud.assignments.clear();
        while (ifs >> mark)
            stud.assignments.push_back(mark);
        ifs.clear();
    }
    return ifs;
}
ostream & operator<<(ostream & os, const Student & stud){
    os << left << setw(static_cast<streamsize>(Student::maxNameLen)) <<
        stud.name << right << fixed << setprecision(1) << setw(6) << stud.total <<
        setw(3) << stud.midterm << setw(3) << stud.final;
    for ( vector<int>::const_iterator it = stud.assignments.begin();
                                        it != stud.assignments.end(); ++it )
        os << setw(3) << *it;
    return os;
}
```

The extractor (input function, >>) is a bit tricky, because we rely on the failure management of input streams. The key problem is this: since students complete different numbers of assignments, how do we know when we have read all the assignments? The method we use depends on what follows the last assignment: it is either the name of the next student or the end of the file. If we attempt to read assignments as numbers, either of these will cause reading to fail. Consequently, we can use the following code to read the assignments:

```
while (ifs >> mark)
```

```
stud.assignments.push_back(mark);
```

However, we must not leave the stream in a bad state, because this would prevent anything else being read. Therefore, when the loop terminates, we call *clear*()to reset the state of the input stream.

```
ifs.clear();
```

We assume that, if a student name can be read successfully, the rest of the record is also readable. If the name is not read successfully, the function immediately returns the input stream in a bad state, telling the user that we have encountered end of file. What happens if there is a format error in the input? Some markers, although they are asked to provide integer marks only, include fractions. Suppose that the input file contains this line:

```
Ram 45 76 9 9 8.5 9 9 8 8 9
```

The corresponding output file contains these lines:

```
Ram 63.6 45 76 9 9 8
.5 15.2 9 9 8 8 9
```

We see that *Ram* has lost all his assignment marks after 8.5 and we have a new student named ".5". It is clear that, if this was a production program, we would have to do more input validation.

There are many ways of solving this problem. If we are not given input file then we can ask the users to give input as shown below.

```
// This method is use to register one student
void RegisterStudent(){
   string name;
   double English, Maths, CompSc; //we can add other subjects as required
   cout << "\nPlease register the student\n";
   cout << "\nEnter the student's information\n";
   cout << "English Subject Marks: "; cin >> English;
   cout << "Mathematics Subject Marks: "; cin >> Maths;
   cout << "Comp Science Subject Marks: "; cin >> CompSc;
   //...
}
```

Problem-15 Design an elevator system at a shopping complex using Java threads to support multithreading.

Solution: Let us understand the scenarios which need to be considered while designing an elevator system. Shoppers arrive in the building at random times. During the time a shopper is in the building he may request elevator service from the floor where he is currently located. The request always specifies a direction, *up* or *down*. Shoppers on the lowest floor may only request up service; those on the top floor may only request down service; all others may request either service.

On entering an elevator a shopper selects a destination floor. The elevator then closes its doors and moves to that destination floor, possibly stopping on intermediate floors to deliver other shoppers who may have selected intermediate floors. When an elevator arrives at a destination floor it stops, opens its doors, and discharges any shoppers who have selected that floor.

Having stopped, opened its doors and unloaded its passengers, the elevator then admits any shoppers who may be waiting for service in the direction the elevator may be currently moving, subject to the restriction that the elevator may not exceed its capacity to carry passengers. Shoppers who do not succeed in boarding the elevator because it is full must make a fresh request to obtain service at the floor on which they are waiting.

For our implementation, we can assume that the elevator moves passengers from floor to floor in simulation. The basic objects of the system are: *Elevator*, *Person*, *Building* and the *Simulator* which controls the elevators. *Elevator* class keeps track of current state of it (whether it is moving up or down), its capacity, service time required at each floor and time required to move to next floor, current number of passengers on elevator, number of passengers getting off at each floor while moving etc... Operations on Elevator object are synchronized to make the system thread safe.

```
public class Elevator extends Thread {
        private final String name;            // name of elevator
        private final int capacity;           // number of people that will fit
        private int currentFloor;             // where elevator is now
        private boolean goingUp = true;
        private Building thisBuilding;        // Building containing elevator
        private long floorServiceTime;        // How long takes at each floor
        private long travelTime;              // How long it takes between floors
        private int numPassengers;            // number of passengers on elevator
        private Vector[] passengers;          // Names of passengers getting off at each floor
        private int numberFloors;             // number of floors in building
        private boolean running = true;       // whether elevators are running

        public Elevator(string name, int numberOfFloors, int startingFloor,
                        int capacity, Building office,
                        long floorServiceTime, long travelTime) {
                name = name;
                numberFloors = numberOfFloors;
                currentFloor = startingFloor;
                thisBuilding = office;
                floorServiceTime = floorServiceTime;
```

```
            travelTime = travelTime;
            numPassengers = 0;
            capacity = capacity;
    }
    public void stopElevator() {
            running = false;
    }

    public synchronized int getCurrentFloor() {
            return currentFloor;
    }
    // run elevator up and down in building, picking up and depositing passengers.
    public void run() {
            System.out.println(toString() + " starting");
            while (running) {
              System.out.println(toString()+" now on floor "+ currentFloor
                                    + " at time "+ System.currentTimeMillis());
                    // Should elevator change direction
                    if (currentFloor == numberFloors-1){
                            goingUp = false;
                    } else if (currentFloor == 0) {
                            goingUp = true;
                    }
                    // tell passengers so they can exit or load
                    notifyPassengers();
                    thisBuilding.tellAt();
                    try{    // wait for passengers to leave and new ones to load
                            sleep(floorServiceTime);
                    } catch (InterruptedException exc) {
                            System.out.println(toString() + " sleep interrupted");
                    }
                    System.out.println(toString() + " now leaving floor "
                            + currentFloor + " at time " +  System.currentTimeMillis());

                    // Go to next floor
                    if (goingUp) {
                            currentFloor++;
                    } else {
                            currentFloor--;
                    }
                    try{    // wait for elevator to arrive at next floor
                            sleep(travelTime);
                    } catch (InterruptedException exc) {
```

```
                        System.out.println(toString() + " sleep interrupted");
                }
            }
        }

        //If elevator on currFloor and there is room for new passenger
        //      then return destFloor, otherwise return currFloor.
        public synchronized int takeElevator(int destFloor, int currFloor, Person waiter) {
            if (currentFloor == currFloor && numPassengers < capacity) {
                numPassengers++;
                System.out.println(waiter + " getting on " + toString() +  " on floor "
                        + currFloor + " at time "+ System.currentTimeMillis());
                while (currentFloor != destFloor){
                    try{     // wait is in loop in case someone else sneaks in
                      wait();
                    } catch (InterruptedException ie){
                      System.out.println(toString() +
                                  " interrupted: "+ ie.toString());
                    }
                }
                numPassengers--;
                return destFloor;
            } else {
                return currFloor;
            }
        }
        //Woke up all passengers who may be waiting for elevator
        private synchronized void notifyPassengers(){
            notifyAll();
        }

        public String toString(){
            return name;     // post: return name of elevator
        }
        public boolean isGoingUp(){
            return goingUp;
        }
}
```

Each building is associated with a number of floors and can have multiple elevators. This class takes care of starting/stopping the elevators. Whenever a passenger adds a request, it finds the elevator which reaches the passenger floor first and updates the status of elevators.

```
public class Building {
        public final int NUM_FLOORS;          // number of floors in building
        public final int NUM_ELEVATORS; // number of elevators in building
        private Elevator[] lift;              // array of elevators

        public Building(int numFloors, int numElevators, int elevatorCapacity,
                        int serviceFloor, int travelTime) {
                NUM_FLOORS = numFloors;
                NUM_ELEVATORS = numElevators;
                lift = new Elevator[numElevators];
                for (int liftNum = 0; liftNum < numElevators; liftNum++) {
                        lift[liftNum] = new Elevator("lift "+liftNum, NUM_FLOORS,
                                        liftNum % numFloors, elevatorCapacity,
                                        this, serviceFloor, travelTime);
                }
        }

        // Start all of the elevators running
        public void startElevators(){
                for (int liftNum = 0; liftNum < NUM_ELEVATORS; liftNum++) {
                        lift[liftNum].start();
                }
        }

        // Stop all of the elevators from running
        public void stopElevators(){
                for (int liftNum = 0; liftNum < NUM_ELEVATORS; liftNum++) {
                        lift[liftNum].stopElevator();
                }
        }

        //Notified all of those waiting that an elevator has arrived at currentFloor
        public synchronized void tellAt() {
                notifyAll();
        }

        // Returns the first elevator to reach the current floor going in right direction.
        // Wait if necessary for one to arrive.
        public synchronized Elevator callElevator(int personFloor, boolean goingUp){
                while (true) {
                        for (int liftNum = 0; liftNum < NUM_ELEVATORS; liftNum++) {
                                if(lift[liftNum].getCurrentFloor() == personFloor &&
                                                lift[liftNum].isGoingUp() == goingUp) {
                                        return lift[liftNum];
                                }
```

```
                }
                try {
                        wait();
                } catch (InterruptedException e) {
                        e.printStackTrace();
                }
            }
    }
    public synchronized void waitForElevatorToCome() {
            try{
                    wait();
            } catch  (InterruptedException e) {
                    e.printStackTrace();
            }
    }
}
```

Now, let us concentrate on passenger class. The shopper maintains the information about his state. To link the shopper and building, we can pass the building information to shopper (*Person* class) constructor.

```
public class Person extends Thread {
  private static final int WAITING = 0;
  private static final int SHOPPING = 1;
  private static final int ON_ELEVATOR = 2;
  private static final int DONE = 3;
  private int status = WAITING;            // what person is doing
  private final int[] itinerary;           // floors that shopper must visit
  private final String name;               // name of shopper
  private final int busyTime;              // how long it takes to shop on one floor
  private final Building building;         // where shopping takes place
  private int itemNumber;                  // index of floor in itinerary shopping in now
  private int currentFloor;                // floor shopping in now

  public Person(String name, int[] itinerary, int busyTime,
                                        int startingFloor, Building building) {
    super("Person " + name);
    this.name = name;
    this.itinerary = itinerary;
    this.busyTime = busyTime;
    this.itemNumber = 0;
    this.currentFloor = startingFloor;
    this.building = building;
```

```
    // sanity checking that parameters are OK
    for (int i = 0; i < itinerary.length; i++)
        checkFloor(itinerary[i], building);
    checkFloor(currentFloor, building);
    if (busyTime < 0)
            busyTime = 0;
}

// if floor not legal floor in building office then throw exception
private void checkFloor(int floor, Building office) {
    if (floor < 0 || floor >= office.NUM_FLOORS)
    throw new RuntimeException("Illegal floor " + floor);
}

// Have shopper move through store using elevators to get to new floors.
public void run() {
    while (itemNumber < itinerary.length) {
        int dest = itinerary[itemNumber];
        // If I'm on elevator, check to see if on the floor I want to be on to get off
        if (dest == currentFloor && status == ON_ELEVATOR) {
            System.out.println(name+" exiting elevator on floor "
                                    + dest + " at time " + System.currentTimeMillis());
            shopOnFloor();
            System.out.println(name+" done shopping on floor "
                                    + dest + " at time " + System.currentTimeMillis());
            itemNumber++;
        }
        // take the next elevator to my floor
        else {
            System.out.println( name + " waiting on " + currentFloor
                            + " for floor " + dest + " at time "+ System.currentTimeMillis());

            // wait for an elevator
            Elevator elevatorHere = building.callElevator(currentFloor, dest > currentFloor);

            // found one --- try to get on
            System.out.println(name + " tries to get on " + elevatorHere + " to floor "
                                    + dest + " at time " + System.currentTimeMillis());
            status = ON_ELEVATOR;
            currentFloor = elevatorHere.takeElevator(dest, currentFloor, this);

            if (currentFloor != dest) { // no room for me
                status = WAITING;
                System.out.println("oops! " + name + " didn't make it onto elevator to " + dest);
```

```
                building.waitForElevatorToCome();
            }
        }
    }
    System.out.println(name + " is done shopping");
  }

  // printed message about starting shopping and then shop for busyTimeSecs.
  private void shopOnFloor() {
    System.out.println(name + " arrived at floor " + currentFloor
                                                   + " at time " + System.currentTimeMillis());
    status = SHOPPING;
    try {
      Thread.sleep(busyTime);
    } catch (InterruptedException e) {
      System.exit(1); // just die
    }
    status = WAITING;
  }

  public String toString() {
    return name;
  }
}
```

Finally, the *Simulator* class creates necessary objects for running the elevator. It gives sample inputs to all the classes defined earlier as given below.

```
public class Simulator {
        // how long it takes to get to next floor
        private static final int TRAVEL_TIME = 1000;
        // how long elevator stays on a floor
        private static final int FLOOR_TIME = 500;
        // time shopper is shopping on a floor
        private static final int BUSY_TIME = 3000;
        // number of elevators in building
        private static final int NUM_ELEVATORS = 2;
        // number of people that each elevator can hold
        private static final int ELEVATOR_CAPACITY = 2;
        // number of floors in building
        private static final int NUM_FLOORS = 3;

        // Report all events of simulations, including length of  simulation.
        public static void main(String args[]) throws InterruptedException {
```

```
        // Create building
        Building shop= new Building(NUM_FLOORS, NUM_ELEVATORS,
                        ELEVATOR_CAPACITY,  FLOOR_TIME, TRAVEL_TIME);

        // create itineraries for shoppers
        int[] p1Itinerary = { 1, 2, 0 };
        int[] p2Itinerary = { 2, 1, 0 };

        // Creating shoppers
        Person Steve = new Person("Steve", p1Itinerary, BUSY_TIME, 0, shop);
        Person Jeff = new Person("Jeff", p2Itinerary, BUSY_TIME, 0, shop);
        Person Bill = new Person("Bill", p1Itinerary, BUSY_TIME, 0, shop);
        Person Einstene = new Person("Einstene", p2Itinerary, BUSY_TIME, 0, shop);

        shop.startElevators();                  // start all threads running
        Steve.start();
        Jeff.start();
        Bill.start();
        Einstene.start();

        // Keeps track of when we started
        long startTime = System.currentTimeMillis();

        Steve.join();   // Don't continue until all threads complete
        Jeff.join();
        Bill.join();
        Einstene.join();
        shop.stopElevators();

        // Report time that simulation ran
        long elapsedTime = System.currentTimeMillis() - startTime;
        System.out.println("Total simulation time: " + elapsedTime + " ms");
    }
}
```

Problem-16 What is the difference between architectural and design patterns?

Solution: *Architectural* patterns are concerned with *strategic* aspects of a system. They have a global impact on the whole implementation of a system. *Design* patterns are concerned with *technical* aspects of an implementation. They have a local impact on specific parts of the implementation of a system. Architectural patterns are on a higher level of abstraction than Design patterns.

There are *many* other *types* of patterns (like UI patterns which deals with presentation of UI) depending on domain. If you are appearing for architect position, I would request you refer those resources to fill the domain gap.

Problem-17 Explain MVC Pattern.

Solution: Model–View–Controller (*MVC*) is an architectural pattern.

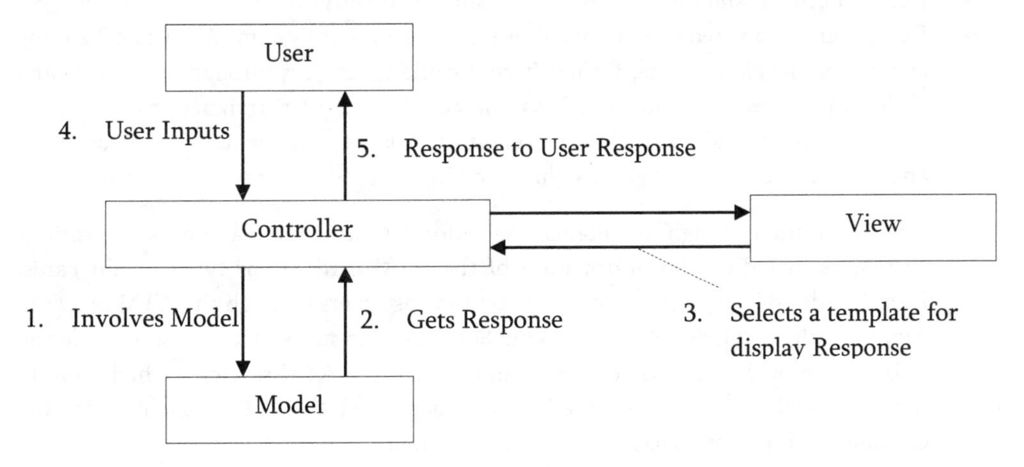

In MVC Design Pattern, the application is divided into three components known as *Model*, *View* and *Controller*. The pattern aims at separating out the inputs to the application (*Controller*), the business processing logic (*Model*) and the output format logic (*View*).

- Controller associates the user input to a Model and a View
- Model fetches the data to be presented from persistent storage
- View deals with how the fetched data is presented to the user

Controller can be considered as a middle man between user and processing (*Model*) and formatting (*View*) logic. It is an entry point for all the user requests or inputs to the application. The controller accepts the user inputs, parses them and decides which type of *Model* and *View* should be invoked. Accordingly, it invokes the chosen *Model* and then the chosen *View* to provide to the user what it requested.

Model represents the business processing logic of the application. This component would be an encapsulated version of the application logic. *Model* is also responsible for working with the databases and performing operations like *Insertion*, *Update* and *Deletion*. Every model is meant to provide a certain kind of data to the controller, when invoked. Further, a single model can return different variants of the same kind of data based on which method of the *Model* gets called. What exactly gets returned to the controller, could be controlled by passing arguments to a given method of the model.

View, also known as *presentation* layer, is responsible for displaying the results obtained by the controller from the model component in a way that user wants them to see or a pre-determined format. The format in which the data can be visible to users can be of any *type* like HTML or XML. It is responsibility of the controller to choose a view to display data to the user. Type of view could be chosen based on the model chosen, user configuration etc.

8.2 Sample Design Questions For Practice

- Design a *billing* and *auctioning* system similar to *ebay*.
- Design an Automated Teller Machine (ATM) Banking System: ATM is a banking application developed to perform different banking services through the Automated Teller Machines. The all functions include the regular transactions like cash deposits, cash withdrawals, balance enquiry, balance statements, savings account, and current account; change PIN Number, Credit card Withdrawals and so on.

  The application design maintains the information of the accounts of various customers including the information of the ATM cards, their types Credit cards, Debit Cards and the transactions done by the customers through the ATM machine centers with co-relation of the Banking Services. The stored details also include the information of the various centers in and around the ATM services, which help in the relational maintenance of every transaction in the ATM Machine by the customers with their concerned branch operations.
- Design a *flight take − off* control system.
- Design a *Net Banking System*: The main objective is to be automated the various functions and activities of the bank through Internet. The solution will facilitate to the bank employees and the account holders with the different modules. This solution is very much necessary for the private sector banks and the corporate sector. The banking industry will take a new shape and explore like never before. Using the solution the bankers and account holders can generate various kinds of reports.
- Design question answer system similar to *StackOverFlow* and *CareerMonk*.com.
- Design the *hospital* management system.
- Design a*Resource Planner*: Resource Planner is an online tool to manage projects currently running with the company as well as future projects. This tool tracks the employees working for the existing projects and details of new projects like no. of employees required, location, etc. This tool is very useful in estimating revenue, etc. which helps higher management to know the status of the various projects and work force.
- Design a system similar to *CricInfo.com* [score boards].
- Design an online *ticket reservation* system.
- Design a *Bug Tracking System*: Bug Tracking System (BTS) is an automated system that can be useful to employees and the managers in any functional organization. Bug Tracking System gives the facility to define the tasks in the organization and also allows the managers to track the bugs spent by the employee for that particular task. A report generation facility is supported in BTS that allows the managers to analyze which are those skills by employee are utilized and those which are not utilized. This tool can help managers for Bug estimation per project or application. This tool helps employees to document their Bugs and analyze them.
- Design a *traffic control system*.

- Design a *Placement Automation System*: The importance of placement system is increasing day by day. Thousands of applicants are depending on placement cell and the applicants are facing so many problems. This project should attempt to minimize the problems of an applicant to find a correct job. Placement Automation System is useful for institutions, where student's information is required. This student information is used for campus placements. System should also maintain the information related to companies.
- Design a system for *car service*.
- Design a *Virtual White Board*: The Virtual White Board is used as the Virtual Class Room Where the server acts as students. This project will establish a Teacher-Student communication. Being a web based project the people may be located anywhere across the world and still can communicate. The server acts as the teacher and clients as students. The students can clear their doubts through chatting. The teacher can send the files, pictures, sounds and videos.
- Design a *Student Record System*: The system maintains records of students, the courses and modules on which they are registered and the outcome of their studies. The application is distributed application because the data is stored centrally by the university but accessed by academic staff and administrators across the university. Students also access the system to view their results. The real system would be service oriented and would expose some of its functionality as a set of services which could be consumed by other applications.
- Design a *Resorts Management*: The system aims at the maintenance and management of the different accommodations that are available in the different parts of the world. It mainly takes care of the resort management at the core area of the database. The system provides the information regarding the different resorts that are available and their status specific to availability. The database also manages the atomic information regarding the different units that are available under one resort and the architectural details of the Unit facilities that are available. Each unit is well furnished and is well designed for the basic flexibility of the tourists who are expected to stay.
- Design an *Online Recruitment System*: Online Recruitment System is an online website in which jobseekers can register themselves online and apply for job and attend the exam. Online Recruitment System provides online help to the users all over the world. Candidates can upload their CV's and apply for jobs suited to them. Such sites also make it possible for recruiters and companies to post their staffing requirements and view profiles of interested candidates.

Chapter-9

MISCELLANEOUS CONCEPTS

9.1 Java Interview Questions

Question: What is the difference between an *Interface* and an *Abstract* class?

Answer: An abstract class can have instance methods that implement a default behavior. An Interface can only declare constants and instance methods, but cannot implement default behavior and all methods are implicitly abstract. A class may be declared abstract even if it has no abstract methods. This prevents it from being instantiated.

```
public abstract class TestClass {
  // declare fields
  // declare non-abstract methods
  abstract void draw();
}
```

An interface has *all* public members and no implementation. An abstract class is a class which may have the usual flavors of class members (private, protected, etc.), but has some abstract methods.

```
public interface TestInterface {
        public double function1();
        public int function2();
}
```

Question: What is the purpose of garbage collection in Java, and when is it used?

Answer: The purpose of garbage collection is to identify and discard objects that are no longer needed by a program (goes out of scope) so that their resources can be reused. A Java object is subject to garbage collection when it becomes unreachable to the program in which it is used.

Question: What are pass by reference and pass by value?

Answer: Pass By Reference means the passing the address itself rather than passing the value. Pass by Value means passing a copy of the value to be passed.

Question: What is *HashMap* and *Map*?

Answer: Map is an *Interface* and Hashmap is class that *implements* that.

Question: Difference between HashMap and HashTable?

Answer: The *HashMap* class is roughly equivalent to Hashtable, except that it is unsynchronized and permits NULLs. (HashMap allows NULL values as key and value whereas Hashtable doesn't allow). HashMap does not guarantee that the order of the map will remain constant over time. HashMap is unsynchronized and Hashtable is synchronized.

Question: Difference between Vector and ArrayList?

Answer: Vector is *synchronized* whereas ArrayList is not.

Question: Difference between Swing and Awt?

Answer: AWT are heavy-weight components. Swings are light-weight components. Hence swing works faster than AWT.

Question: What is the difference between a *constructor* and a *method*?

Answer: A constructor is a member function of a class that is used to create objects of that class. It has the same name as the class itself, has no return type, and is invoked using the new operator. A method is an ordinary member function of a class. It has its own name, a return type (which may be void), and is invoked using the . operator.

Question: What is an Iterator?

Answer: Java collection classes provide traversal of their contents via a java.util.Iterator interface. This interface allows us to walk through a collection of objects, operating on each object in turn.

Note that when using Iterators they contain a snapshot of the collection at the time the Iterator was obtained; generally it is not advisable to modify the collection while traversing an Iterator.

Question: What is *final*?

Answer: A *final class* can't be extended (i.e., can't be subclassed). A *final method* can't be overridden when its class is inherited. We can't change value of a *final* variable (is a constant).

Question: What is *static* in java?

Answer: *Static* means one per class, not one for each object no matter how many instances of a class might exist. This means that we can use them without creating an instance of a class. Static methods are implicitly *final*, because overriding is done based on the type of the object, and static methods are attached to a class, not an object.

A *static* method in a superclass can be shadowed by another static method in a subclass, as long as the original method was not declared *final*.

However, we can't *override* a static method with a nonstatic method. In other words, we can't change a static method into an instance method in a subclass.

Question: What is Overriding?

Answer: When a class defines a method using the same name, return type, and arguments as a method in its superclass, the method in the class overrides the method in the superclass.

When the method is invoked for an object of the class, it is the new definition of the method that is called, and not the method definition from superclass. Methods may be overridden to be more public, not more private.

Question: What if the main method is declared as *private*?

Answer: The program compiles properly but at runtime it will give "Main method not public." message.

Question: What if the static modifier is removed from the signature of the main method?

Answer: Program compiles. But at runtime throws an error "NoSuchMethodError".

Question: What if we write *static public void* instead of *public static void*?

Answer: Program compiles and runs properly.

Question: What if we do not provide the *String* array as the argument to the method?

Answer: Program compiles but throws a runtime error "NoSuchMethodError".

Question: What is the first argument of the String array in *main* method?

Answer: The String array is empty. It does not have any element. This is unlike C/C++ where the first element by default is the program name.

Question: If we do not provide any arguments on the command line, then the String array of *Main* method will be empty or null?

Answer: It is empty. But not null.

Question: How can one prove that the array is not *null* but empty using one line of code?

Answer: Print args.length. It will print 0. That means it is empty. But if it would have been null then it would have thrown a NullPointerException on attempting to print args.length.

Question: What environment variables do we need to set on my machine in order to be able to run *Java* programs?

Answer: CLASSPATH and PATH are the two variables.

Question: Can an application have multiple classes having main method?

Answer: Yes it is possible. While starting the application we mention the class name to be run. The JVM will look for the Main method only in the class whose name we have mentioned. Hence there is not conflict amongst the multiple classes having main method.

Question: Can we have multiple main methods in the same class?

Answer: No the program fails to compile. The compiler says that the main method is already defined in the class.

Question: Do we need to import java.lang package any time? Why?

Answer: No. It is by default loaded internally by the JVM.

Question: Can we import same package/class twice? Will the JVM load the package twice at runtime?

Answer: One can import the same package or same class multiple times. Neither compiler nor JVM complains about it. And the JVM will internally load the class only once no matter how many times you import the same class.

Question: What are *Checked* and *UnChecked* Exception?

Answer: A checked exception is some subclass of Exception (or Exception itself), excluding class RuntimeException and its subclasses. Making an exception checked forces client programmers to deal with the possibility that the exception will be thrown. e.g., IOException thrown by java.io.FileInputStream's read() method·

Unchecked exceptions are *RuntimeException* and any of its subclasses. Class Error and its subclasses also are unchecked. With an unchecked exception, however, the compiler doesn't force client programmers either to catch the exception or declare it in a throws clause.

In fact, client programmers may not even know that the exception could be thrown. e.g., *StringIndexOutOfBoundsException* thrown by String's *charAt*() method· Checked exceptions must be caught at compile time. Runtime exceptions do not need to be. Errors often cannot be.

Question: What are different types of *inner* classes?

Answer: Nested top-level classes, Member classes, Local classes and Anonymous classes.

Nested top – level classes- If you declare a class within a class and specify the static modifier, the compiler treats the class just like any other top-level class. Any class outside the declaring class accesses the nested class with the declaring class name acting similarly to a package. e.g., outer.inner. Top-level inner classes implicitly have access only to static variables. There can also be inner interfaces. All of these are of the nested top-level variety.

Member classes: Member inner classes are just like other member methods and member variables and access to the member class is restricted, just like methods and variables. This means a public member class acts similarly to a nested top-level class. The primary difference between member classes and nested top-level classes is that member classes have access to the specific instance of the enclosing class.

Local classes: Local classes are like local variables, specific to a block of code. Their visibility is only within the block of their declaration. In order for the class to be useful beyond the declaration block, it would need to implement a more publicly available interface. Because local classes are not members, the modifiers public, protected, private, and static are not usable.

Anonymous classes: Anonymous inner classes extend local inner classes one level further. As anonymous classes have no name, you cannot provide a constructor.

Question: Are the imports checked for validity at compile time? e.g. will the code containing an import such as java.lang.ABCD compile?

Answer: Yes the imports are checked for the semantic validity at compile time. The code containing above line of import will not compile. It will throw an error saying, cannot resolve symbol : class ABCD location: package io import java.io.ABCD;

Question: Does importing a package imports the sub packages as well? e.g. Does importing com.MyTest.* also import com.MyTest.UnitTests.*?

Answer: No you will have to import the sub packages explicitly. Importing com.MyTest.* will import classes in the package MyTest only. It will not import any class in any of its subpackage.

Question: What is the difference between declaring a variable and defining a variable?

Answer: In declaration we just mention the type of the variable and its name. We do not initialize it. But defining means declaration + initialization. e.g. String s; is just a declaration while String s = new String ("abcd"); Or String s = "abcd"; are both definitions.

Question: What is the default value of an object reference declared as an instance variable?

Answer: null unless we define it explicitly.

Question: Can a top level class be private or protected?

Answer: No. A top level class cannot be private or protected. It can have either *public* or no modifier. If it does not have a modifier it is supposed to have a default access. If a top level class is declared as private the compiler will complain that the "modifier private is not allowed here".

This means that a top level class cannot be private. Same is the case with protected.

Question: What type of parameter passing does Java support?

Answer: In Java the arguments are always passed by value .

Question: Primitive data types are passed by reference or pass by value?

Answer: Primitive data types are passed by value.

Question: Objects are passed by value or by reference?

Answer: *Java* only supports pass by value. With objects, the object reference itself is passed by value and so both the original reference and parameter copy both refer to the same object.

Question: What is serialization?

Answer: Serialization is a mechanism by which you can save the state of an object by converting it to a byte stream.

Question: How do we serialize an object to a file?

Answer: The class whose instances are to be serialized should implement an interface Serializable. Then you pass the instance to the ObjectOutputStream which is connected to a fileoutputstream. This will save the object to a file.

Question: Which methods of Serializable interface should we implement?

Answer: The serializable interface is an empty interface, it does not contain any methods. So we do not implement any methods.

Question: How can we customize the serialization process? i.e. how can one have a control over the serialization process?

Answer: Yes it is possible to have control over serialization process. The class should implement Externalizable interface. This interface contains two methods namely readExternal and writeExternal. You should implement these methods and write the logic for customizing the serialization process.

Question: What is the common usage of serialization?

Answer: Whenever an object is to be sent over the network, objects need to be serialized. Moreover if the state of an object is to be saved, objects need to be serialized.

Question: What is Externalizable interface?

Answer: Externalizable is an interface which contains two methods readExternal and writeExternal. These methods give you a control over the serialization mechanism. Thus if your class implements this interface, you can customize the serialization process by implementing these methods.

Question: When you serialize an object, what happens to the object references included in the object?

Answer: The serialization mechanism generates an object graph for serialization. Thus it determines whether the included object references are serializable or not. This is a recursive process. Thus when an object is serialized, all the included objects are also serialized along with the original object.

Question: What one should take care of while serializing the object?

Answer: One should make sure that all the included objects are also serializable. If any of the objects is not serializable then it throws a NotSerializableException.

Question: What happens to the static fields of a class during serialization?

Answer: There are three exceptions in which serialization does not necessarily read and write to the stream. These are

1. Serialization ignores static fields, because they are not part of any particular state.
2. Base class fields are only handled if the base class itself is serializable.
3. Transient fields.

Question: Does Java provide any construct to find out the size of an object?

Answer: No there is not *sizeof* operator in *Java*. So there is not direct way to determine the size of an object directly in *Java*.

Question: Give a simplest way to find out the time a method takes for execution without using any profiling tool?

Answer: Read the system time just before the method is invoked and immediately after method returns. Take the time difference, which will give you the time taken by a method for execution. To put it in code:

```
long start = System.currentTimeMillis ();
method ();
long end = System.currentTimeMillis ();
System.out.println ("Time taken for execution is " + (end - start));
```

Remember that if the time taken for execution is too small, it might show that it is taking zero milliseconds for execution. Try it on a method which is big enough, in the sense the one which is doing considerable amount of processing.

Question: Why is Java not a pure Object Oriented Programming Language?

Answer: Java is a OOP language but not a pure Object Oriented Programming Language. Many languages are Object Oriented. There are few qualities that need to be satisfied for a programming language to be Object Oriented. They are:

- Encapsulation/Data Hiding
- Inheritance
- Polymorphism
- Abstraction

Java supports all the above qualities and is not a pure OOP language because it supports primitive data types such as int, byte, long... etc., to be used, which are not objects.

An example for pure OOP language is *Smalltalk*, where there are no primitive types, and boolean, int and methods are all objects.

Question: What are wrapper classes?

Answer: Java is an object-oriented language and as said everything in java is an object. But what about the primitives? They are sort of left out in the world of objects, that is, they cannot participate in the object activities, such as being returned from a method as an object, and being added to a Collection of objects, etc.. As a solution to this problem, Java allows us to include the primitives in the family of objects by using what are called wrapper classes.

There is a wrapper class for every primitive date type in Java. This class encapsulates a single value for the primitive data type. For instance the wrapper class for int is Integer, for float is Float, and so on. Remember that the primitive name is simply the lowercase name of the wrapper except for char, which maps to Character, and int, which maps to Integer.

The wrapper classes in the Java API serve two primary purposes:

- To provide a mechanism to "wrap" primitive values in an object so that the primitives can be included in activities reserved for objects, like as being added to Collections, or returned from a method with an object return value.
- To provide an assortment of utility functions for primitives. Most of these functions are related to various conversions: converting primitives to and from String objects, and converting primitives and String objects to and from different bases (or radix), such as binary, octal, and hexadecimal.

Question: Why do we need wrapper classes?

Answer: It is sometimes easier to deal with primitives as objects. Moreover most of the collection classes store objects and not primitive data types. And also the wrapper classes provide many utility methods also. Because of these reasons we need wrapper classes.

And since we create instances of these classes we can store them in any of the collection classes and pass them around as a collection. Also we can pass them around as method parameters where a method expects an object.

Question: What are checked exceptions?

Answer: Checked exceptions are those which the Java compiler forces you to catch. e.g. IOException are checked Exceptions.

Question: What are runtime exceptions?

Answer: Runtime exceptions are those exceptions that are thrown at runtime because of either wrong input data or because of wrong business logic etc. These are not checked by the compiler at compile time.

Question: What is the difference between error and an exception?

Answer: An error is an irrecoverable condition occurring at runtime. Such as OutOfMemory error. These JVM errors and you cannot repair them at runtime. While exceptions are conditions that occur because of bad input etc. e.g. *FileNotFoundException* will be thrown if the specified file does not exist Or a *NullPointerException* will take place if you try using a null reference. In most of the cases it is possible to recover from an exception (probably by giving user a feedback for entering proper values etc.).

Question: How to create custom exceptions?

Answer: Your class should extend class Exception, or some more specific type thereof.

Question: If we want an object of class to be thrown as an exception object, what should we do?

Answer: The class should extend from Exception class. Or you can extend your class from some more precise exception type also.

Question: If class already extends from some other class what should we do if we want an instance of my class to be thrown as an exception object?

Answer: One cannot do anything in this scenario. Because *Java* does not allow multiple inheritance and does not provide any exception interface as well.

Question: How does an exception permeate through the code?

Answer: An unhandled exception moves up the method stack in search of a matching. When an exception is thrown from a code which is wrapped in a try block followed by one or more catch blocks, a search is made for matching catch block. If a matching type is found then that block will be invoked. If a matching type is not found then the exception moves up the method stack and reaches the caller method.

Same procedure is repeated if the caller method is included in a try catch block. This process continues until a catch block handling the appropriate type of exception is found. If it does not find such a block then finally the program terminates.

Question: What are the different ways to handle exceptions?

Answer: There are two ways to handle exceptions,

1. By wrapping the desired code in a try block followed by a catch block to catch the exceptions. and
2. List the desired exceptions in the throws clause of the method and let the caller of the method handle those exceptions.

Question: What is the basic difference between the 2 approaches to exception handling.

1. try catch block and
2. specifying the candidate exceptions in the throws clause?

When should you use which approach?

Answer: In the first approach as a programmer of the method, we deal with the exception. This is fine if we are in a position to decide should be done in case of an exception. Whereas if it is not the responsibility of the method to deal with its own exceptions, then do not use this approach. In this case use the second approach.

In the second approach we are forcing the caller of the method to catch the exceptions that the method is likely to throw. This is often the approach library creator's use. They list the exception in the throws clause and we must catch them. We will find the same approach throughout the java libraries.

Question: Is it necessary that each try block must be followed by a catch block?

Answer: It is not necessary that each try block must be followed by a catch block. It should be followed by either a *catch* block OR a *finally* block.

Question: If we write return at the end of the try block, will the finally block still execute?

Answer: *Yes* even if we write return as the last statement in the try block and no exception occurs, the finally block will execute. The finally block will execute and then the control return.

Question: If we write System.exit (0); at the end of the try block, will the finally block still execute?

Answer: No in this case the *finally* block will not execute because when we say System.exit (0); the control immediately goes out of the program, and thus finally never executes.

Question: Does garbage collection *guarantee* that a program will not run out of memory?

Answer: Garbage collection *does not* guarantee that a program will not run out of memory. It is possible for programs to use up memory resources faster than they are garbage collected. It is also possible for programs to create objects that are not subject to garbage collection

Question: When a *thread* is created and started, what is its *initial* state?

Answer: A thread will be in *ready* state after it has been created and started.

Question: What is the purpose of finalization (*finalize*() method)?

Answer: The purpose of finalization is to give an unreachable object the opportunity to perform any cleanup processing before the object is garbage collected.

Question: Can an unreachable object become reachable again?

Answer: An unreachable object may become reachable again. This can happen when the object's *finalize*() method is invoked and the object performs an operation which causes it to become accessible to reachable objects.

Question: What is the use of *Locale* class?

Answer: The *Locale* class is used to tailor program output to the conventions of a particular geographic, political, or cultural region.

Question: What is the difference between a *while* statement and a *do* statement?

Answer: A while statement checks at the beginning of a loop to see whether the next loop iteration should occur. A do statement checks at the end of a loop to see whether the next iteration of a loop should occur. The do statement will always execute the body of a loop at least once.

Question: What is the difference between *static* and *non – static* variables?

Answer: A static variable is associated with the class as a whole rather than with specific instances of a class. Non-static variables take on unique values with each object instance.

Question: How are *this*() and *super*() used with constructors?

Answer: this() is used to invoke a constructor of the same class. super() is used to invoke a superclass constructor.

Question: What is daemon thread and which method is used to create the daemon thread?

Answer: Daemon thread is a low priority thread which runs intermittently in the back ground doing the garbage collection operation for the java runtime system. *setDaemon* method is used to create a daemon thread.

Question: What are the steps in the JDBC connection?

Answer: While making a JDBC connection we go through the following steps :

1. Register the database driver by using :
   Class.forName(\" driver class for that specific database\");
2. Now create a database connection using :
   Connection con = DriverManager.getConnection(url,username,password);
3. Now Create a query using :
   Statement stmt = Connection.Statement(\"select * from TABLE NAME\");
4. Execute the query.
   stmt.exceuteUpdate();

Question: How does a *try* statement determine which catch clause should be used to handle an exception?

Answer: When an exception is thrown within the body of a try statement, the catch clauses of try statement are examined in the order in which they appear. The first catch clause that is capable of handling the exception is executed. The remaining catch clauses are ignored.

Question: Describe synchronization in respect to *multithreading*.

Answer: With respect to multithreading, synchronization is the capability to control the access of multiple threads to *shared* resources.

Without synchonization, it is possible for one *thread* to modify a *shared* variable while another thread is in the process of using or updating same shared variable. This usually leads to *major* errors.

Question: Explain different way of using thread?

Answer: The thread could be implemented by using *runnable* interface *or* by inheriting from the *Thread* class. The former is more advantageous, when we are going for multiple inheritance.

Question: What method must be implemented by all threads?

Answer: All tasks must implement the *run*() method, whether they are a subclass of *Thread* or implement the *Runnable* interface.

Question: What are *synchronized* methods and *synchronized* statements?

Answer: Synchronized methods are methods that are used to control access to an object. A thread only executes a synchronized method after it has acquired the lock for the method object or class.

Synchronized statements are similar to synchronized methods. A synchronized statement can only be executed after a thread has acquired the lock for the object or class referenced in the synchronized statement.

Question: What is Externalizable?

Answer: Externalizable is an *interface* that extends *Serializable* interface and sends data into Streams in *Compressed* format. It has two methods:

- writeExternal(ObjectOuput out)
- readExternal(ObjectInput in)

Question: What modifiers are allowed for methods in an *interface*?

Answer: Only *public* and abstract modifiers are allowed for methods in interfaces.

Question: What are few alternatives to inheritance?

Answer: Delegation is an alternative to inheritance. Delegation means that we include an instance of another class as an instance variable, and forward messages to the instance. It is often safer than inheritance because it forces us to think about each message we forward, because the instance is of a known class, rather than a new class, and because it doesn't force us to accept all the methods of the super class: we can provide only the methods that really make sense.

On the downside, it makes us write more code, and it is harder to re-use (because it is not a subclass).

Question: What does it mean that a *method* or *field* is *static*?

Answer: Static variables and methods are instantiated only once per class. In other words they are class variables, not instance variables. If you change the value of a static variable in a particular object, the value of that variable changes for all instances of that class. Static methods can be referenced with the name of the class rather than the name of a particular object of the class (though that works too).

That is how library methods like *System.out.println*() work (it is a static method defined in java.lang.System class).

Question: What is the *catch rule* for method declarations?

Answer: If a checked exception may be thrown within the body of a method, the method must either catch the exception or declare it in its throws clause.

Question: Is empty *.java* file a valid source file?

Answer: Yes, an empty .java file is a perfectly valid source file.

Question: Can a *.java* file contain more than one java classes?

Answer: *Yes*, a .java file contain more than one java classes, provided at the most one of them is a public class.

Question: Is *String* a primitive data type in *Java*?

Answer: It is *not* a primitive data type in Java. But it is one of the most extensively used object. Strings in *Java* are instances of *String* class defined in java.lang package.

Question: Is *main* a keyword in *Java*?

Answer: No, *main* is not a keyword in *Java*.

Question: Is *next* a keyword in *Java*?

Answer: No, *next* is not a keyword.

Question: Is *delete* a keyword in *Java*?

Answer: No, *delete* is not a keyword in *Java*. *Java* does not make use of explicit destructors the way $C++$ does.

Question: Is *exit* a keyword in *Java*?

Answer: It is not a keyword in Java. To *exit* a program use *exit* method in *System* object.

Question: What happens if we don't initialize an instance variable of any of the primitive types in Java?

Answer: Java initializes it to a default value for that primitive type. For example, an *int* will be initialized to 0, a *boolean* will be initialized to *false*.

Question: What will be the initial value of an object reference which is defined as an instance variable?

Answer: The object references are all initialized to *null* in Java. However in order to do anything useful with these references, we must set them to a valid object, else we will get *NullPointerExceptions* everywhere we try to use such default initialized references.

Question: What are the *different* scopes for Java variables?

Answer: The scope of a *Java* variable is determined by the context in which the variable is declared. Thus a java variable can have one of the three scopes at any given point in time.

1. *Instance*:- These are typical object level variables, they are initialized to default values at the time of creation of object, and remain accessible as long as the object accessible.
2. *Local*:- These are the variables that are defined within a method. They remain accessible only during the course of method execution. When the method finishes execution, these variables fall out of scope.
3. *Static*:- These are the class level variables. They are initialized when the class is loaded in JVM for the first time and remain there as long as the class remains loaded. They are not tied to any particular object instance.

Question: What is the default value of the local variables?

Answer: The local variables are not initialized to any default value, neither primitives nor object references. If we try to use these variables without initializing them explicitly, the java compiler will not compile the code. It will complain about the local variable not being initialized.

Question: How many objects are created in the following piece of code?

```
SomeClass c1, c2, c3;
c1 = new SomeClass ();
c3 = new SomeClass ();
```

Answer: Only 2 objects are created, c1 and c3. The reference c2 is only declared and not initialized.

Question: Can a public class *SomeClass* be defined in a source file named *OurClass*.java?

Answer: No the source file name, if it contains a public class, must be the same as the public class name itself with a .java extension.

Question: Can *main* method be declared *final*?

Answer: Yes, the main method can be declared final, in addition to being public static.

Question: What will be the output of *System.out.println* ("2" + 7);?

Answer: It will print 27.

Question: What will be the default values of all the elements of an array defined as an instance variable?

Answer: If the array is an array of primitive types, then all the elements of the array will be initialized to the default value corresponding to that primitive type. e.g. All the elements of an array of int will be initialized to 0, while that of boolean type will be initialized to false. Whereas if the array is an array of references (of any type), all the elements will be initialized to null.

References

[1] Erich Gamma, Richard Helm, Ralph Johnson, and John Vlissides. Design Patterns: Elements of Reusable Object-Oriented Software. Addison-Wesley Professional Computing Series. Addison-Wesley Publishing Company, New York, NY, 1995.

[2] Patterns in Java: A Catalog of Reusable Design Patterns Illustrated with UML by Mark Grand (Wiley, 1998).

[3] Core J2EE Patterns: Best Practices and Design Strategies by Deepak Alur, John Crupi, and Dan Malks (Prentice Hall, 2001).

[4] UML Distilled: Applying the Standard Object Modeling Language by Martin Fowler with Kendall Scott (Addison-Wesley, 2000).

[5] The Unified Modeling Language User Guide by Grady Booch, Ivar Jacobson, and James Rumbaugh (Addison-Wesley, 1998).

[6] The OO design process: Getting started by Allen Holub.

[7] The object primer: Using object-oriented techniques to develop software by Scott W. Ambler.

[8] A UML workbook (Part 1, Part 2, and Part 3) by Granville Miller.

[9] Use your singletons wisely: Know when to use singletons, and when to leave them behind by J. B. Rainsberger.

[10] Developing Java solutions using Design Patterns by Kelby Zordrager.

[11] Implementing the Singleton Pattern in Java by Rod Waldhoff.

[12] When is a singleton not a singleton? by Joshua Fox.

[13] Java Papers (Design Papers) by Joe.

[14] Xahelee Information on Java.

[15] The Timeless Way of Building, by Christopher Alexander.

[16] Design Patterns Explained: A New Perspective on Object-Oriented Design (2nd Edition), by Alan Shalloway and James Trott.

[17] Emergent Design: The Evolutionary Nature of Professional Software Development, by Scott Bain.

[18] Head First Design Patterns, by Elisabeth and Eric Freeman.

[19] Lee Ackerman and Celso Gonzalez. Patterns-Based Engineering: Successfully Delivering Solutions via Patterns. Addison-Wesley, Boston, 2010.

[20] Walter Zimmer. Relationships between design patterns. In Coplien and Schmidt [CS95], pages 345-364.

[21] Peter Coad, David North, and Mark Maryfield. Object Models: Strategies, Patterns, and Application. Yourdon Press, New Jersey, NJ, 2nd edition, 1997.